Only the prism's obstruction shows aright
The secret of a sunbeam, breaks its light
Into the jewelled bow from blankest white;
   So may a glory from defect arise.

"Deaf and Dumb: A Group by Woolner"
Robert Browning, 1862

HISTORY AND THE PRISM OF ART
BROWNING'S POETIC EXPERIMENTS

MARY ELLIS GIBSON

OHIO STATE UNIVERSITY PRESS
COLUMBUS

Copyright © 1987 by the Ohio State University Press
All Rights Reserved.

Library of Congress Cataloging-in-Publication Data

Gibson, Mary Ellis, 1952–
  History and the prism of art.

  Bibliography: p.
  Includes index.
  1. Browning, Robert, 1812–1889—Knowledge—History.
2. Browning, Robert, 1812–1889—Technique. 3. Historical
poetry, English. 4. Literature, Experimental—History and
criticism. I. Title.
PR4242.H5G5   1987   821'.8   86-21849
ISBN 0-8142-0418-X

For Charles and for Emily

CONTENTS

- *ix*   Acknowledgments
- *1*   1. Introduction: Browning and His Readers
- *24*   2. Contextualism and Historical Poetry
- *55*   3. Poetic Personae and the Interpretation of History
- *110*   4. Simultaneity in Browning's Longer Poems
- *160*   5. Historical Perspective and Irony in Some Dramatic Monologues
- *215*   6. The Ambiguous Present and the Language of Poetry
- *262*   7. Conclusion
- *279*   Abbreviations
- *281*   Notes
- *319*   Bibliography
- *335*   Index

ACKNOWLEDGMENTS

THE HAPPIEST OBLIGATION OF A SCHOLAR IS TO THANK THOSE who have taught, debated with, and encouraged her. This book owes its beginning to a long winter in Chicago when I was first encouraged to come to terms with Browning's understanding of history. For those promptings and later suggestions and thoughtful reading, I am indebted to Norman Maclean, Elizabeth Helsinger, James Chandler, and Stuart Tave. Robert von Hallberg and William Harmon read early chapters with care and forebearance. I am indebted for encouragement and discussion to Judith Page, Nancy Guttierez, Richard Alan Schwartz, Barbara Hanrahan, and Charles Orzech and to my colleagues Walter Beale and Chris Anderson. For meticulous and stimulating comments on the manuscript and its revisions I am especially grateful to Lawrence Poston.

I am also pleased to acknowledge the support of the University of North Carolina at Greensboro Excellence Foundation, which provided a summer stipend. Completion of a first draft was supported by a grant from the American Council of Learned Societies. The Department of English at the University of North Carolina at Greensboro has been generous in providing a research assistant, Susan Underwood, whose care and diligence were essential in preparing the manuscript.

For permission to quote manuscript letters and a notebook of Robert Browning Sr. I am grateful to John G. Murray. The Harry Ransom Humanities Research Center of the University of Texas at Austin granted permission to quote the manuscript notebook of Browning Sr. A section of chapter 3 appeared in *Studies in Browning and His Circle*, and portions of chapter 6 were first published in *Victorian Poetry*. I am grateful to the editors for permission to reprint this material.

Every book has a family history, and mine is no exception. My mother, Lorene M. Gibson, was patient and encouraging when the manuscript came with me on holidays, and Emily Orzech allowed herself to be bounced with one hand while I wrote with the other. The greatest intellectual and personal debts, finally, are the hardest adequately to acknowledge. I thank Charles Orzech for argument, encouragement, and ideas I'm not even aware I've stolen. This is his book too.

CHAPTER ONE
INTRODUCTION: BROWNING AND HIS READERS

IN 1856 JOHN RUSKIN CREDITED ROBERT BROWNING with putting "more vitality into the shadows of the dead than most others can give the presence of the living."[1] Browning's shadows brought live from the dead have power and vitality still to move the student, the critic, and the casual reader. A recollection of Browning's poems is always peopled: paging through *Men and Women* or *Dramatis Personae* we glimpse this petty tyrant, that painter, this cleric. Though the poet rarely describes them, we create faces to go with the words; even without their paintings to clue us, Fra Lippo Lippi and Andrea del Sarto look nothing alike. The very profusion and individuality of Browning's characters often lead us in a curious way to forget that each one brings a whole set of historical circumstances with him. Much has been said about Browning's historical characters, yet surprisingly little has been written about Browning's view of history and still less about the connections between his historical understanding and the form of his poetry.[2] Few of Browning's readers have asked directly how his historical imagination works within and against poetic tradition; none has taken the full measure of the historical imagination that so impressed Ruskin.

1

My purpose here is to show how Browning's struggle with historical questions is inscribed in his poems. I argue in the following chapters that Browning's understanding of history is inextricably linked with his understanding of the poet's role and with the poet-personae, narrative structures, figurative strategies, and language of his poetry.

To read Browning's poems well and to see clearly their importance for modern poetics, we must situate them in both historiographical and literary tradition. To examine Browning's poet-personae is to ask how the poet can be an interpreter of history; to examine narrative structures is to ask how in Browning's long poems a historical account can be ordered; to examine Browning's ironies or his language is again to consider the poet as historian. Browning's poetry of history assumes historicity as the given through which poet and reader must work toward religious, moral, or aesthetic meaning. The effort to account for the importance of historicity in Browning's poetry requires a new approach to the critical categories through which poetry and history generally are understood.

The study of Browning's historical poems calls for a new approach to historical poetry, and it also suggests a reassessment of Browning's poems that frankly values the creation of poems like "My Last Duchess" as highly as the creation of "Childe Roland." Browning's appeal to modern poets and readers lies equally in his experiments with poetic form, particularly poetic language, and in his view of history as compelling and difficult. Obviously, Browning's poetry does not speak to every modern historical view; his understanding of history is uncongenial both to a narrowly conceived Marxist view and to the view that history is a nightmare, a necessary evil, to be ignored at worst and transcended at best.[3] Browning's poems appeal, nonetheless, to the modern sense that the past is essential to the present but never perfectly recoverable. Although his encounter with the problematic nature of history can be seen as "multitudinousness" or linguistic chaos, Browning's importance remains rooted in his particular imagining of an opaque past.[4]

The portions of the past Browning was most often bent on recovering were the world of late antiquity, the Greece of Euripides, and the Renaissance, early and late. In recovering late antiquity and the Renaissance, Browning presented his nineteenth-century readers with the ineluctable individuality of each era and, at the same time, with antecedents of their own culture. A striking number of his historical poems had contemporary point, and he often treated contemporary or recent events and his older historical materials with the same strategies. The stance of looking back to Renaissance forebears who in turn looked back to the world of antiquity was not Browning's alone. Pater much more elaborately exploited this triple focus; to different ends than Browning's, Arnold juxtaposed the present time with the ages of Sophocles and Shakespeare; and Ruskin in *The Stones of Venice* developed a "criticism based on historical self-consciousness" as he contrasted medieval architecture (a growth from the Greek) to the moral and aesthetic deficiencies of Renaissance Italy and Victorian Britain.[5] But Browning was much less interested than Ruskin or Arnold in representing a historical or aesthetic ideal as a measure of his own culture's deficiencies. He too challenged his readers and criticized their culture, but largely by indirection, by presenting them with a new and unmusical poetic language and with a succession of historical characters who are, for the most part, criminals, failures, or dim precursors of some future knowledge or achievement. So Browning chose Sordello not Dante, Andrea del Sarto not Raphael, Karshish not Lazarus, Cleon not Paul, and he embedded his more exemplary historical figures, the Pope and Euripides, in a sordid murder story. In *Sordello, The Ring and the*

Book, and the historical monologues Browning frequently drew on the historical preoccupations of his time—the vogue for all things Italian, the burgeoning of classical studies, the debate over the Higher Criticism.[6] Browning's purposes in using historical materials were neither antiquarian nor escapist nor directly didactic. His interests were at once psychological and analytical. He strove to see the present in the past and yet as different from the past, and he sought in the Renaissance or antiquity the lineaments of times anterior to but also related to his own.

To his contemporaries the interest of Browning's historical poems lay in their detailed historical particularity and in their challenge to Victorian conventionalities. Browning's admirers, like Ruskin, praised his ability to catch the contradictions of the Renaissance, the mixtures of motives in his characters, and the implied comparison between historical and Victorian perspectives. Browning's Victorian detractors decried his depictions of evil or what they saw as the crabbed obscurity of his verse.[7] By the turn of the century, of course, Browning's obscurities were being vigorously explicated and his moral and religious uprightness defended. In response to this late Victorian veneration, Browning's modern critics have been as embarrassed as his Victorian readers were inspired by the certainties the poet achieves. Those who find Browning's poems still readable and important emphasize more than Browning's contemporaries did the play of perspectives in his poems. They delight in the way his texts unravel the very historical webs they weave, and they praise his poetry's historical self-consciousness and linguistic density. Browning's skepticism chimes with the skepticism of his modern readers even while the faith it made possible has lost its power to move.[8] The Browning of the 1980s differs from the Browning whose last volume was published on the day of his death in 1889 by the measure of the historiographical debate and poetic experimentation that have come between. Fifty years after Browning's death most critics were no longer complaining of his obscurity; obscure was an adjective reserved for Joyce or Pound or Williams. And yet even now after numerous explications, Browning's poems have not become altogether translucent. These texts more than many other Victorian writings even now cause their readers to reflect on the possibilities of history and on what poetry has possibly to do with it.

The opaqueness of Browning's poems, their resistance to explication, is not simply the common resistance of text to reader; the difficulty we encounter at interpretive cruxes—in judging, for instance, the significance of Browning's epilogue to "Bishop Blougram"—is also the opaqueness that is the legacy of historicism. In Browning's view both the historical individual and historical events in general can never be understood completely. One tries to write history in spite of the obstacles history itself presents. This understanding of history, its emphasis on the individual and on the difficulty of historical knowledge, is attributed by Ortega y Gasset to the "historical school."[9] In Browning's England a striking example of this consciousness that history is difficult was Thomas Carlyle's declaration that each man's "existence" was to himself "a problem." The perfect historian who could fully understand such existences was a "faultless monster which the world is not to see."[10] For Browning, similarly, historical individuals were to themselves problematic, enmeshed in connections virtually impossible to explain. So Browning's monologuists, even the least reflective ones, are in some measure confronting the puzzle of their lives. Even Cleon, limited as he is, recognizes these difficulties, and imagining the perfect historian he is forced to imagine God. Only God or the "fiction" of God, as Cleon calls it, can show simultaneously what never can be shown, the "worth both absolute and relative / Of all his children from the birth of time."[11] As we watch Cleon justifying himself and puzzling out the nature of his historical moment, Browning's irony resonates, for we realize that no more than Cleon did we choose our own historical moment. The force of Browning's poetry, and the legacy of historicism generally, compel the reader to consider himself or herself a historical individual attempting, through limitations, the interpretation of history.

The relationship between Browning's modern readers and the legacy of historicism is assuredly complex; for any approach to historical poetry is significantly shaped by historical premises as well as by critical vocabulary. Among those who have discussed Browning's poetry of history there has been a tendency either to confine Browning's texts within a narrow compass of definitions and particularly within a narrow understanding of nineteenth-century historicism or to abandon Browning's historical poems in a retreat from historicism.

In the first place, Browning has been located in a historicist tradition that is reduced to scientism or to a positivist notion of critical objectivity and historical causation.[12] On this basis Morse Peckham has argued that Browning's poems move from a romantic treatment of history à la Carlyle, to the objective critical approach of Ranke in *The Ring and the Book,* to a rejection of history altogether after *The Ring and the Book.* Only a limited notion of Rankean and Carlylean historicism can ground such an argument. That Browning recognized in critical history what Peckham calls its "extremely equivocal foundation" is no argument that he subsequently turned away from history altogether. On the contrary, as I argue in detail in the next two chapters, the skepticism implied by critical historiography—and important to Carlyle's view as well as to Ranke's—was exactly what drew Browning to historical materials again and again. History becomes the given within which a poet finds and makes whatever order is possible. As James Loucks and Richard Altick have pointed out, Browning's protestations of objectivity in *The Ring and the Book* do not mean Browning became a Rankean historian of the narrowest kind.[13] I shall argue that Browning's texts themselves in their poet-personae and narrative structure present a much more complex historical situation than narrow historiographical distinctions can compass. The poet like the historian may be aware of the "equivocal foundation" of his efforts and yet persevere. The same ocean that may overwhelm the mariner also supports the ship.

Browning's situation as a historical poet can best be represented, not by a restrictive opposition between Carlylean or Rankean historiography, but by recognizing the complexities of historicism. We cannot conflate the critical historical emphasis on facts with a narrow or positivistic belief in the historian's access to truth. The complexity of Browning's position as a poet of history was very like that of Peckham's own representative of the "new" Rankean historiography in England. J. A. Froude, Carlyle's disciple and the critical examiner of the Simancas archives, described the necessary limitations and biases of historical knowledge and yet remained committed to the centrality of history. In "The Science of History," a lecture delivered at the Royal Institution in the year Browning began *The Ring and the Book,* Froude systematically dismissed the 'philosophy of history' as a series of distorting interests. In the face of such philosophies, history stands "in its passive irony":

> Like Jano, in Goethe's novel, it will not condescend to argue with you, and will provide you with abundant illustrations of anything which you may wish to believe.
>
> 'What is history,' said Napoleon, 'but a fiction

agreed upon?' 'My friend,' said Faust to the student, who was growing enthusiastic about the spirit of past ages; 'my friend, the times which are gone are a book with seven seals, and what you call the spirit of past ages is but the spirit of this or that worthy gentleman in whose mind those ages are reflected.'[14]

Having admitted the inevitable distortions of worthy gentlemen's minds, much as Browning does in *The Ring and the Book,* Froude concludes his attack on Buckle's positivistic history with a defense of dramatic poetry. As Froude presents it, the assumptions of critical history are not antithetical to poetry about the past; rather the best of critical history aspires to the status of poetry.

A second, and more subtle, way of narrowing or even deflecting the examination of Browning's historical poems arises in the encounter of the antihistoricist modern reader with the difficulties of Browning's historical view. The 'crisis in historicism' and modern reactions to nineteenth-century notions of progress have had immediate consequences for the ways we read historical poetry. The revolt against historicism is readily apparent in modern praise of the mythic or mythopoeic as over against the historical in nineteenth-century poetry. Although definitions of the mythic are extraordinarily various, the most powerful notion of myth in readings of Victorian and modernist poetics is what Mircea Eliade has characterized as the desire for a cosmic circularity and an escape from history. In *Cosmos and History* Eliade describes the longing for an eternal return as a "revolt against historical *time,* an attempt to restore this historical time, freighted as it is with human experience, to a place in time that is cosmic, cyclical, and infinite." Eliade goes on to say that this "horizon of archetypes" is "artificial, because decreed" and thus is a "nostalgia for the myth of eternal repetition."[15]

The nostalgia for the mythic can govern judgments as to which of Browning's poems are most valuable or successful; it can lead directly to antihistorical readings of Browning's narrative structures; or it can shape the outlines of literary history as it traces Browning's connections to modernism. For example, Robert Langbaum, the most influential modern critic of Browning's poetry, has concluded that Browning's importance and his defects are proportional to his achievement of the "modern mythical method." Though Langbaum describes this method as one that establishes mythic pattern through realism and psychology, he argues that Browning's idea of progress prevents "a complete reliance on mythical pattern." Browning remains, for Langbaum, an interesting rather than a great poet because for the most part he fails to achieve the "double vision" of myth. Browning cannot maintain the "continuous parallel between contemporaneity and antiquity."[16] As I shall argue in chapter 4, a similar critical position underlies the notion that circularity or simultaneity in narrative structures is fundamentally ahistorical.

A nostalgia for the mythic leaves us in the precarious position of valuing, as Langbaum sometimes does, Browning's "Childe Roland" more highly than poems like "The Bishop Orders His Tomb" or "Andrea del Sarto."[17] But a self-consciousness about "myth" as a category of value allows us a toehold for interpretation in Browning's texts. It allows us to see how these texts systematically historicize the mythic.

Rather than glorifying common eighteenth- and nineteenth-century notions that primitive language is poetic language and that the mythopoeic is the essential quality of poetry,[18] Browning's poems explicitly present myth as subsumed by history. Browning's view of myth is most complex when he considers the Higher Criticism and the relationship among myth, history, and belief. In 1845 Elizabeth Barrett wrote to Browning that although classical stories were too worn-out for poetry, Christianity was a "worthy myth, & poetically acceptable."[19] In *Christmas-Eve and Easter-Day* and in *The Ring and the Book,* Browning evidently agreed; in both poems, as well as in "A Death in the Desert," he refuses to oppose myth to history or history to faith. In *Christmas-Eve* Browning criticizes a "virginal minded rationalist" (probably modeled on David Strauss), and yet his doubts about the historical evidences for Christianity recall Strauss's "mythical theory."[20] In *Easter-Day,* moreover, Browning goes on explicitly to defend the truth of fable. The speaker in *Easter-Day* is admonished, "highest truth, man e're supplied / Was ever fable on outside" (*Easter-Day,* 925–26).[21] Still more clearly than in *Easter-Day,* in *The Ring and the Book* the choice between myth and history is delineated as a false dichotomy. Browning's Pope will not be forced to choose between myth and history, "God's gloved hand or the bare" (*RB,* 10.1401). In the Pope's monologue as in Browning's poetry generally, historical time is the medium through which symbolic or mythic forms appear; myth is in history, not outside the necessary succession of historical time.

Browning's most explicit treatment of myth and history is the "Epilogue" to *Dramatis Personae.* In answer both to the biblical David and to Ernest Renan, who are the speakers of the first two sections of the poem, Browning creates a vision of how "heaven's height" with earth's low "should intertwine." He would explain historical individuality, how one man "differs from his fellows utterly." He imagines individuals as rocks in the currents of arctic seas, and he views these individuals as momentary monarchs, "kings of the current for a minute":

> When you see what I tell you,—nature dance
> About each man of us, retire, advance,
> . . . .

> When you acknowledge that one world could do
> All the diverse work, old yet ever new.
> Divide us, each from other, me from you,—
>
> Why, where's the need of Temple, when the walls
> O' the world are that?
> . . . .
> That one Face, far from vanish, rather grows,
> Or decomposes but to recompose,
> Becomes my universe that feels and knows.
>
> ("Epilogue," 87–101)

In the "Epilogue" symbolic forms, like historical individuals, appear and disappear in the currents of time. As E. S. Shaffer has persuasively argued, for Browning, as for many others, the "destructive" work of the Higher Criticism makes possible this notion of "progressive revelation"—a revelation achieved not in a retreat from history but through interpretation. The skeptical awareness that the fact may "look to the eye as the eye likes the look" leads to complex acts of interpretation, to a renewed Christian apologetics, or, in Shaffer's words, to an "elevating casuistry."[22] History itself becomes Browning's myth.

THE CHAOS OF HISTORY AND THE PRIVILEGE OF ART

Both the search for a poet who can be narrowly defined as a historicist and the antihistoricist nostalgia for the mythic deflect a serious reading of Browning's historical poetry. A richer reading of these poems becomes possible as we begin from the premise that fictions and histories are related forms of discourse[23] and as we place Browning against a cultural context in which historical questions have become paramount and poetry is no longer uncontested as a privileged form of discourse.

For Browning poetry is no longer, as it was for

Aristotle, "more philosophic" than history, dealing with the "probable and possible order of things" and with "universals" rather than with "singulars."[24] In wrestling with the singulars of history within the poem itself, Browning would achieve universals from historical occurrences in their most improbable aspect. Poetry cannot easily be privileged, for poetry, like theology, must come to terms with chaotic and resistant particulars. Browning's poems enact the conviction of his friend Carlyle that both poetry and history have their origin in a confrontation with the "Chaos of Being," and the "first idea" of both is the idea of time.[25] Yet Browning's notion of poetry, as I shall show, is more equivocal than Carlyle's vision of the historian-poet who finds athwart the stream of time the "bottomless Eternal." In Carlyle's view history itself strives toward the paradigmatic poetic ideal.[26] In Browning's poems a critical eye is turned on the paradigmatic status of poetry itself. Art is neither the mirror nor the lamp, but a convex glass or even a prism, the obstacle that splinters light to show us such truth as we are capable of seeing.

In attending to the "chaos" of history, Browning goes even further than Carlyle would have wished and allows the chaos of history to impinge upon the orderings of art.[27] Though Browning does not go so far in this direction as William Carlos Williams or Ezra Pound, both of whom present the welter of historical particulars in the poem and hope to see order emerge from them, I will suggest briefly in concluding that Browning prepared the way for these experiments by refusing to privilege poetry with a freedom from the chaos of history.

In order to understand any historical poem we must ask many of the same questions that have often been asked of prose fictions and histories. How does the poem suggest the poet can know history? What kind of knowledge is historical knowledge? How orderly or chaotic are historical events? Can one identify in a poem a political ideology or a theology that mediates questions of order and disorder, causes and ends in history? What kinds of historical causes are suggested in the poem? How is the individual connected to the causes, ends, or circumstances of historical events? Answers to such questions are not presented purely conceptually in the poem any more than they are in historical narratives. Rather, historical understanding leads to various formal choices that are themselves worked out through or against poetic traditions.

In the following chapters I trace such connections, and I argue that in Browning's texts historical materials give rise to a poetry of obstacles. For Browning historical interpretation and whatever knowledge poetry can yield are reached through the encounter with resistant matter; accordingly, the poet-persona is both powerful and limited, contending in Browning's words with "mediates" in seeking "ultimates."[28] The difficulty of absolute unmediated knowledge, the impossibility of a complete and permanent interpretation complicate the telling of historical stories; consequential narrative thus is less important in Browning's longer poems than patterned simultaneity. Just as the narrative strategies of Browning's longer poems situate individuals and events in historical contexts, so in the monologues historical context provides a basis for our judgments of Browning's dramatic speakers. Juxtapositions of historical perspectives create complex historical ironies. The difficulties of historical judgment, narration, and self-presentation are reflected in the language of Browning's poetry. As the poet's words speak rather than sing, walk rather than soar, the obstacles of historicity are encountered and even embraced.

Although this examination of Browning's personae, narrative structures, ironies, and language will answer a number of questions about Browning's understanding of history, it is obvious that some historical questions are more applicable than others to any one historical or fictional text. For poets, as for historians and philosophers of history, historical questions may be primarily epistemological, theological, teleological, psychological, or political. Discriminating among these sorts of historical questions allows us to characterize accurately a particular historical view and to describe the tensions within it. One could say, for example, that Walter Scott's Waverley novels exhibit a strong concern for the relationship of the individual to the ordered and inevitable progression of history from stage to stage.[29] Carlyle is even more concerned than Scott with the real possibility of disorder (the "Chaos of Being") and with the power of the historical individual to shape historical order. Browning and Pater are much less interested than Carlyle in questions of historical causation. Both Browning and Pater explore the individual's connection to a particular historical milieu by asking questions about historical knowledge; they often ask how the historical individual can understand his or her own time and how the poet or historian can understand individuals in the past. Seldom does the poet or the historian achieve a harmonious approach to history in which notions of historical knowledge, order, and causation are easily compatible. For example, I shall suggest in a concluding chapter that Pound's *Cantos* combine an imperative to explain the causes of historical change with a conviction that historical knowledge is necessarily limited. Other tensions are more important in Browning's poems and still others in Carlyle's works. As I argue in the next chapter, answering systematic questions about Browning's historical view allows us to characterize it as contextualist. Within this general characterization we can locate the complexities of Browning's historical understanding and his similarities to and differences from such other contextualists as Pater and Burckhardt.

HISTORICAL POETRY IN THE BROWNING CANON

In focusing on Browning and history, I have chosen to approach the poet's texts topically rather than chronologically and to emphasize those poems, the historical monologues, *Sordello,* and *The Ring and the Book,* that make the most direct appeals to readers' historical understanding. As the next chapter suggests, my emphasis is on what I see as Browning's contextualist historical poems. These poems, of course, only partially represent the range and variety of the poet's work. As the examination in chapter 2 of "Love Among the Ruins" indicates, Browning's lyrics also frequently explore the connections of past and present, sometimes exploiting historically significant settings. Often Browning's nonhistorical lyrics evince the same willingness to experiment with form and language that characterizes the historical poems; often these lyrics use dramatic strategies similar to those in the historical poems. Such similarities, of course, enable one to speak generally of Browning's style and to characterize his individual voice. Browning's later poems, too, the translations, *Red Cotton Night Cap Country,* and the *Parleyings,* among others, are poems of struggle against obstacles and experiments with form and language. Both the nonhistorical lyrics and the later long poems represent further reaches of Browning's art. To explore in detail the entire corpus of Browning's fifty-five year career is necessarily beyond the scope of a single study. Nonetheless, a new understanding of Browning's contextual historical poems has implications for the study of the lyrics and the other long poems; for such poems as *Sordello* and the historical monologues were central to Browning's art and have been central to his critical reputation and to his influence on his successors.

Even this concentration on Browning's contextualism does not easily offer itself as a story of the poet's development, as an account of systematic progression from one kind of poetry to another or from one view of history to another. The story of development, however, has been the most common approach to the Browning canon. Numerous studies of Browning's poems through *The Ring and the Book* have described Browning's development as a search for an adequate genre or form; less usefully his art has often been described as a progression from subjective to objective poetry; and Clyde Ryals has recently suggested a tripartite division of Browning's career as moving from a mode of romantic irony, through a period of stasis and determinancy coinciding with his marriage, to a renewed ironic posture.[30] None of these approaches offers a systematic account of Browning's historical understanding. More helpful is John Maynard's biographical account of the poet's youth. Yet when we look specifically to the question of Browning's development as a poet of history it is difficult to arrive at a simple description of the poet's development. Indeed, it is remarkable how early and with what sophistication Browning embraced historical subjects. *Strafford, Sordello,* and "My Last Duchess" all were published in the decade after "Pauline." Rather than progressing from a simple to a complex understanding of history, Browning grasped even in the 1830s the historical matter that was largely to occupy him for the next thirty years, and he experimented with these materials in a way that critics were to characterize for years as harsh or obscure. Though one can divide Browning's career into three periods (early work to 1846, 1850 through the publication of *The Ring and the Book* in 1868–69, and later poetry), Browning's fascination with history and with Italian history in particular spanned the first two thirds of his career and recurred even in his later years. The story of Browning's development as a historical poet, then, is not one with a single narrative thread, not a clear movement from genre to genre or theme to theme; rather it is a story with many threads. In his historical poetry Browning repeatedly struggled with the problematic role of the poet-historian, with the problem of historical narrative, and with the nature of historical irony and of an inclusive poetic language. Each major historical poem is a fresh experiment or, as Herbert Tucker puts it, a new beginning.[31]

Although my focus here is on Browning's poetry, especially on what I call his contextualist historical poems, it is crucial to observe at the outset that Browning's training ground as poet and historian was not only the several revisions of *Sordello* but equally the seven plays of his early career. These plays offer evidence, not so much of a movement toward a mature and finished style, but of Browning's early confrontation with questions that shaped his historical point of view. In the theater, as in *Sordello,* Browning grappled with the historical materials in which he located themes that were to occupy him throughout his career. In the nine years between the performance of *Strafford* (1837) and the publication of *Luria* and *A Soul's Tragedy* (1846) Browning found his interest in history reinforced by the general Victorian enthusiasm for historical romances and historical drama. He himself experimented with the romance in a number of poems published in the 1842 volume *Dramatic Lyrics* and in the 1845 publication of *Dramatic Romances and Lyrics.* Of his seven dramas both *A Blot in the 'Scutcheon* (1843), with its vaguely realized eighteenth-century setting, and *Colombe's Birthday* (1844) with its more concrete seventeenth-century setting, partake of the romance. Both minimize complex historical questions. But even these two dramas are thematically akin to Browning's more serious historical plays.

All of Browning's plays reflect the social and political milieu of the 1830s and 1840s even as they rely on historical settings. Browning's Evangelical roots and his association with the liberal Unitarianism of W. J. Fox are evident in the plays' opposition to slavery and in their general, if problematic, antiaristocratic bias. Beyond these timely concerns the significance of the plays for Browning's historical poetry is that Browning engages more subtle questions about the viability of individual action and about the nature of historical or political change. Browning's plays return with remarkable persistence to a cluster of themes: the nature of heroism, its sources of inspiration and the possibilities of its perversion; the opposition between hierarchical and republican political structures; the possible failures of revolution or revolt.

Browning's debts to Byron, Shelley, and Carlyle are evident in his analysis of heroism, its possibilities and perversions. Yet his plays, like *Sordello*, are as often a dissection of failed heroism as a celebration of heroic action. As early as *Strafford* Browning analyzed this vexing mixture of success and failure; Strafford's great virtue—his loyalty—is also the source of his defeat, for in choosing the monarchical principle he must be loyal to the vacillating and inadequate monarch. Strafford's loyalty indeed is touching, but neither the principle nor the man whom he serves is shown to be worthy of his loyalty. It is this conflict as much as the deficiencies of dramatic action that makes *Strafford* problematic. A similar problem of loyalty afflicts the less able protagonist of *King Victor and King Charles*. Charles's heroism is compromised by his weakness, and his loyalty to his tyrannical father only escapes disastrous consequences by his father's timely if improbable death. In Djabal of *The Return of the Druses* and in Luria Browning attempts the creation of tragic heroes, though Djabal is far the more interesting of the two.

Although Browning makes Luria a kind of second-rate Othello, he is unable to make Luria's nobility as persuasively probable as the pettiness and corruption Luria faces from the Florentine council. Browning and Elizabeth Barrett laid the weakness of the play to his lack of success with Domizia, who was supposed to be a much more persuasive and passionate villain than she actually is. Luria himself is a greater weakness. Despite Elizabeth Barrett's praise for the "noble" Luria, the subtle policy and hypocrisy of the Florentines is ultimately more dramatically powerful than what Domizia calls Luria's faith, "loyalty and simpleness" (5.268). Luria's heroism is finally unconvincing; for unlike Othello he is not the dupe of extraordinary evil and of his own passions, but of Italian politics and his own simplicity. Luria, it is clear, is not intended as an exemplar of failed heroism; his failure must have been instructive to his creator, however, for Browning never again attempted so simple a hero.[32] Ironically *Luria*, published last of Browning's plays, works less well than Browning's first play *Strafford*. In *Strafford* the hero himself is made more plausible by the historical Strafford; in *Luria* the hero constructed out of Browning's own imagination (and his reading of Shakespeare) seems less plausible than the historical and political realities on which Browning drew for the background of his play.

Browning's other tragic hero, Djabal, is a more interesting case than Luria, for like Sordello and like many of Browning's historical monologuists he is divided against himself. Though like Luria Djabal has no historical antecedent and though the entire play rests on Browning's conjecture as much as on his research, Djabal achieves a more convincing complexity than Luria. He is one of Browning's earliest and most interesting imposters; he is trapped in a messianic role which at first he glories in and then renounces, only to be caught in a political trap. Djabal both confesses himself to be merely human and continues his imposture in order to assure his people's freedom; the sole way

Djabal can assure the Druses' freedom without continuing to compromise himself is suicide. In Djabal Browning emphasizes the difficulties of political and moral choice characteristic of *Sordello* and many of the monologues, and he moves his hero from the messianic to the merely, but nobly, human. But even Djabal's nobility is accompanied by the ironic recognition that his triumph is also his last imposture. In Strafford, in Charles, in Chiappino of *A Soul's Tragedy*, and especially in Djabal, Browning goes beyond the simplicities of dramatic romance; he begins to create a density of historical and political circumstances and a complex world of moral choice in which heroism is more often than not compromised and hedged about with difficulties.

A second concern in Browning's plays and in his historical poems is the recurrent opposition of aristocratic to republican values. The conflict is obviously important in *Strafford:* though the compromised republican Pym detracts from the purity of the republican cause, Charles himself still clearly exhibits all the worst traits of aristocratic absolutism. In *King Victor and King Charles* republicanism is scarcely a possibility, and King Charles at least avows that he has modeled himself on his absolutist father. Nonetheless, though Browning presents Victor as a representative of eighteenth-century despotism, he endows Charles with an unhistorical interest in the welfare of his subjects (*Handbook,* 100). *A Blot in the 'Scutcheon,* derives its sole, if limited, importance as an example of Browning's interest in 1842–43 in aristocratic tyranny and obsession with lineage. "My Last Duchess" and a number of the other poems in *Dramatic Lyrics* confront this matter more powerfully than either play. The most interesting treatment of republicanism comes in Browning's last play, *A Soul's Tragedy:* here the simple liberalism of *King Charles* and the antiaristocratic impetus of *A Blot in the 'Scutcheon* are replaced by a more sophisticated though more cynical political view. *A Soul's Tragedy* examines in detail the hypocritical misuse of republican ideology for selfish ends. Chiappino begins as a fiery republican and ends ready to assume the office of Provost, which he once despised, and to swear allegiance to the Pope's legate Ogniben. Without demonstrating any political ideals himself, Ogniben manages to draw out Chiappino's real motives; as Chiappino rationalizes his change of heart, he reveals a consistent dedication only to his own self-interest. In this final play Browning explores the corruption of republican idealism, a theme of obvious importance during a decade of revolutionary ferment. Though Browning's predisposition was clearly liberal and relatively egalitarian, at each end of his career as a dramatist Pym and Chiappino stand as warnings of how political expediency can undermine even the worthiest causes.

As Browning examined the conflict between republican and aristocratic values and the nature of heroism in his plays he focused at first on the possibilities of revolution and revolt, on decisive shifts in political power. Such moments, of course, naturally lend themselves to drama—witness the intensity of dramatic action in Shakespeare's history plays. But more often than not Browning shows revolt, rebellion, or dramatic political change to be complicated or compromised. Only *The Return of the Druses* and *Luria* present dramatic and sudden changes in political power; and ultimately even Luria himself appears to be merely the instrument of preserving the Florentine status quo. It would be more accurate, then, to suggest that in the plays, as in *Sordello,* Browning presents *possibilities* for change. In *Strafford, Sordello, Luria, A Soul's Tragedy,* and in part 3 of *Pippa Passes* the moment of possible political change, even the moment of rebellion or revolt, is a moment of failure; or as Browning quotes Voltaire to introduce *King Victor and King Charles,* we are presented with "a terrible event without consequences." With all its emphasis on sudden political change, the political vision in Browning's plays is a far cry from Shelley's revolutionary idealism or Carlyle's visions of the phoenix-like political conflagration.

Browning's scrutiny of heroism, of aristocratic and republican values, and of the possible failures of revolt in the plays presages the shift in his later writing toward an examination of the social and political fabric. Rather than emphasizing sudden political change in the major historical monologues and *The Ring and the Book* Browning examines broader shifts and changes in cultural and historical climate. Individuals may still have their moments of spiritual crisis and of sudden inspiration, but their personal resolves and actions do not in themselves make for revolutionary social and political change. Rather, like Fra Lippo Lippi, they participate in or, like Andrea del Sarto, they attempt to hold themselves aloof from the great cultural or social changes of their times. In this shift from examining revolt to examining broad patterns of cultural change, Browning deemphasizes one aspect of romantic historiography—the centrality of the hero—in favor of another—the spirit of the age. This emphasis underlies the poet-personae, the narrative structures, the historical ironies, and the language of Browning's historical poems, and it makes possible what I call Browning's contextualist understanding of history.

Both the characterization of Browning as a contextualist and the study of connections between Browning's historical understanding and poetic forms make possible a necessary rereading of Browning as a poet of history. Such a rereading at once looks back to Browning through the modern poetry of history and points to a reassessment of Browning's importance for modern poetry. We see Browning's poems most accurately when we read them as part of a dynamic process of historiographical speculation and of poetic experimentation. But we need not ask that Browning's historical poems conform to a completely consistent historiographical system. It is enough to value Browning's historical understanding for what it allows him to see and to show. The vivid particularity, the freshness of language, the historical ironies, and above all the sense of intricate connections between the individual and a historical moment give Browning's poetry its special quality of making the past immediate to the present.

CHAPTER TWO
CONTEXTUALISM AND HISTORICAL POETRY

HISTORICAL INDIVIDUALS IN BROWNING'S POEMS ARE often vividly representative of their times, whether or not they can see beyond the necessary limits of their historical situations. In order to situate historical persons or events in their contexts, Browning wrestles with words and with facts. He makes us see individuals as so enmeshed in their historical circumstances that their very possibilities for thought are shaped in ways they can only partially understand. The vividness of "My Last Duchess" or *The Ring and the Book* does not depend on Browning's investigation of causal laws or historical ends; rather Browning welcomes the chaotic particulars of his rags and scraps (*RB*, 1.746) and traces varied connections among them. This emphasis on tracing connections is at the heart of Browning's understanding of history, an understanding that can best be characterized as contextualist. Browning's contextualism has more affinities with cultural history than with the common forms of political and military history, and it is elaborated in his most important figuration of history, the metaphor of historical circumstance as web.

Although the weaving of a contextualist web is not

the only mode of Browning's historical poetry, it is by far the most important. It is common to poems so apparently diverse as the historical monologue "Cleon" and the lyric "Love Among the Ruins." The examination of Browning's contextualism not only reveals the characteristic obsession with historical time in poems as different as these two, it also challenges us to go beyond source studies or historiographical categories and to pursue the implications of contextualism for historical understanding and poetic form. An understanding of Browning's contextualism allows Browning's own reading of history to enrich our reading of his poems.

To characterize his historical conceptualization as contextualist, however, is not to argue that Browning ordered his art according to a philosophy of history. Nor is it to say that Browning's attitudes toward history were altogether systematic and harmonious. On the contrary, the contextualist conceptualization of history creates difficulties for those like Browning who would at once explore the complex interconnections of psychological and social fabric and assert the validity of Christian teleology.

BROWNING IN CONTEXT

Among others Hayden White has defined a contextualist approach as one that apprehends history as a spectacle and accounts for events by a method of "colligation." The contextualist seeks a relative integration of phenomena. To explain a historical figure or occurrence, the contextualist picks out the "'threads' that link the event to be explained to different areas of the context. The threads are identified and traced outward, into the circumambient natural and social space within which the event occurred." These connecting threads may also be followed backwards or forwards in time. The contextualist mode of historical conceptualization defines "trends" or "physiognomies" of periods or epochs.[1]

Contextualist elements are common in many kinds of histories, but in some histories the organizing principle may be called contextualist. Though it appropriates poetic forms as well as historical models, Browning's historical poetry shares the organizing and explanatory strategies of contextualist history. The contextualist principle is no less important for Browning's poems than for Jacob Burckhardt's history or Walter Pater's criticism. In fact the nature of Browning's historical imagination can be seen with particular clarity in the context of Burckhardt's and Pater's cultural histories of the Italian Renaissance. In the texts of poet, critic, and historian, the colligation of particulars generates historical ironies while the spectacle of these connections, regarded by the poet, the historian, or the individual in history, gives rise to aestheticism.

Pater's criticism and Burckhardt's history of the Renaissance connect historical threads in ways that point up what Pater called "dramatic contrasts." The contradictions of the Renaissance and even more importantly the juxtapositions of the Renaissance with antiquity and with the present set up ironic reverberations. Burckhardt, for instance, builds his history on a historical irony when he describes the characteristics that caused the fall of the Renaissance humanists as making possible the culture of the ages that followed them. At the same time, Burckhardt's contemplation of the "state as a work of art," like Pater's "aesthetic criticism," leads to a reflection on history as spectacle.

The irony and aestheticism implicit in the contextualist approach to history are significant forces in Browning's poems as well as in Burckhardt's and Pater's historical essays. Browning's "Cleon" combines so clearly these aspects of contextualism that a reading of Browning's reading of history must begin with it and return to it. As Browning presents him, Cleon is in a thoroughly ironic situation: his vaunted knowledge returns to ignorance; he ages, yet his appetite for pleasure increases. Browning leads us to appreciate further ironies as he juxtaposes Cleon's historical context with the nineteenth-century context and reveals Cleon's spiritual deficiencies. In "Cleon" irony and aestheticism are grounds for a retreat from the active life.[2]

Yet "Cleon," like many of Browning's poems, reflects on aestheticism without indicating a full acceptance of ironic detachment. Clearly a young man who began surrounded by Evangelical piety and who moved on to the less orthodox excitements of Shelley and *Sartor Resartus* was not likely to accept fully the aesthetic tendency of the contextualist approach. Neither could he escape it. Browning's poems return with remarkable persistence to the attractions and the dangers of aestheticism. With varying degrees of sympathy, we are led to examine the aesthetic impulse in "Cleon," "The Bishop Orders His Tomb," "My Last Duchess," "Andrea del Sarto," "Pictor Ignotus," "Bishop Blougram," "Bottinius" of *The Ring and the Book,* and even in the early books of *Sordello.* In these poems aestheticism takes a number of forms, from love of pure, perfect, and untainted art, to hedonistic or, worse, acquisitive desire for beauty. For Browning's aesthetes—and indirectly for the poet himself—the most tempting lure is to view history or society as mere spectacle, to achieve an aesthetic posture of questionable ethical value because it is disengaged.

The contextualist need not of course become another Duke of Ferrara or even a pessimist of Burckhardt's sort. From quite another point of view, for instance, Jerome McGann sees Byron's *Don Juan* as a movement away from the solipsism of high romantic tradition and toward a "contextual and socialized life." For Byron (as for Burckhardt) a contextual approach to society or to history militates against an overt absorption of particulars by a conceptual framework; details are not easily absorbed into the single narration of a consequential plot. Narrative in *Don Juan,* McGann suggests, seems "factive" rather than "fictive."[3] Phenomena appear within shifting or overlapping contexts, and these interconnections themselves serve as a corrective to the isolation of solipsism. Though one would hardly characterize Browning as a Byronic critic of romanticism, especially in his attitudes toward symbols and imagination, Browning does share the burden of connecting the aesthetic and the social. So Sordello fails because he cannot unite the poet with the polis. Though the contextual approach is developed much more completely in Burckhardt's *Civilization of the Renaissance in Italy* than in *Don Juan* or even in *The Ring and the Book,* both for the poets and the historian the nature of individuality and the relation of the individual to social and historical circumstances are central problems.

The method of colligation among particulars to situate an individual in social and historical circumstances is particularly useful in tracing the physiognomy of a culture. The very method of contextualism in Browning's poems as well as in Burckhardt's and Pater's histories is predicated upon both the meanings of culture Raymond Williams has described: culture as moral and intellectual activities *over against* "the driven impetus of a new kind of [industrial] society" and culture as a state or habit of mind, a "whole way of life."[4] Though it would be reductive to suggest that cultural history must always be contextualist and vice versa, it is clear that such seminal cultural histories as Pater's *Renaissance,* Burckhardt's *Civilization of the Renaissance in Italy* (*Die Kultur der Renaissance*), and Huizinga's *The Waning of the Middle Ages* share a contextualist method of organization. These histories, like Browning's historical poems, attempt to get at habits of mind and to describe the moral, spiritual, intellectual, or aesthetic preoccupations of an age.

Although the major texts of cultural history furnish significant analogies to Browning's poems, Browning's own leanings toward cultural history owe much to a historian who was not truly a contextualist at all. Carlyle's historicism, his skepticism and countervailing dedication to the ideal, gave rise to an emphasis on the heroic and to a form of history that traced through narrative the drama of historical cycles ascending phoenix-like from their own destruction. Despite their differences, Carlyle's historicism embraced much that became essential to Browning, and Carlyle's early essay "On History" (1830) was an exhortation to the practice of a cultural history much like Browning's. Carlyle advised the historian to seek "the inward condition of life" that is different in every age. Traditional military, political, or constitutional history cannot tell us enough, Carlyle says. Laws and political constitutions "are but the bare walls of the house: all whose essential furniture, the inventions and traditions, and daily habits that regulate and support our existence, are the work not of Dracos and Hampdens, but of Phoenician mariners, of Italian masons and Saxon metallurgists, of philosophers, alchymists, prophets, and all the long-forgotten train of artists and artisans; who from the first have been jointly teaching us how to think and how to act, how to rule over spiritual and physical Nature."[5] Carlyle's list itself reads like a subject catalogue of Browning's poems. Though Carlyle himself was to become increasingly concerned with Dracos and Hampdens, Cromwells and Fredericks,[6] nevertheless his effort in *Past and Present* was to define an "inward condition of life" over against which his readers might measure the machineries of modern England. Browning's own attempts to describe the inward condition of the Renaissance had a less immediate social relevance than Carlyle's histories; in Browning's poems, consequently, the relationship between the "long forgotten" and present society may be less clear. The past serves as an example to the present, but only indirectly.[7] Though Carlyle moves in the direction of distinguishing the sheeplike masses from heroes and from individual venerators of heroes, Browning frequently takes an interest in characters who are neither Johnson nor Boswell. These characters, though often insignificant from the perspective of political history, are more interesting from the perspective of cultural history.

One might argue, however, that such a historical view not only tends toward aestheticism but also becomes too personal or individualistic to account for meaningful historical change. Patrick Brantlinger, for example, suggests that Browning is so "intensely individualistic that it is impossible for him to think in genuinely historical terms." For Browning history becomes merely a means of "escaping from the present."[8] Brantlinger's view is consonant with his own historical premises, for he distrusts the liberal's tendency to identify individuals apart from their place in the economic structure, and he defines meaningful history as that which points to the inevitability of social change. To this view Browning's historical emphasis is hardly sympathetic, for Browning sees history as interesting in itself, aside from its political lessons, and he savors individual peculiarities for their own sakes. Though this cherishing of the particular could easily have led him into excessive aestheticism, antiquarianism, or even individualism, Browning seldom lost sight of the complex relations of the individual to the larger historical and social milieu.

Though Browning seeks to account for an individual's relationship to the larger historical milieu, his contextualism is not without its inner tensions. A central tension is the tension between determinism and individual choice or action. If individuals are enmeshed in historical circumstances that necessarily limit their knowledge and their actions, are they then controlled by an exterior fate? A second and related source of tension in Browning's contextualism is the problem of unifying a contextualist understanding of history with a Christian theology and particularly with a Christian teleology.

Whereas Carlyle's belief in divinely inspired heroes was his way of asserting individual choice and action within the virtually deterministic drama of historical cycles, Browning, as I have argued, was more ambivalent about the possibility of heroes singlehandedly bringing about historical change. Even as early as the plays, *Paracelsus,* and *Sordello,* Browning steered a course between hero worship and determinism; it is rare that a Browning hero actually succeeds in effecting social or political change. Browning's most systematic attempt at a tragic hero—his Luria—is as much trapped by his political circumstances as he is freed by his own (suicidal) choice. Revealingly, Browning himself confessed that in the contest between Luria's simplicity and the Florentine's "Tuscan shrewd ways," he unfortunately sympathized "just as much with these as with him."[9] It is no accident that this early exploration of a hero enmeshed in historical circumstances is shot through with the metaphors that characterize Browning's later treatment of historical determinism—puppets, chess pieces, and the gloved hand of God.

Both in his plays and in the contextual historical poems Browning returns repeatedly to the problem of how historical circumstances constrain individual knowledge and choice. Rather than making a case for inevitable historical change, either cyclical or strictly progressive, Browning explores how individual action, indeed individual consciousness itself is determined by and determining of historical circumstances.

Browning's ambivalence toward hero worship and toward historical determinism is but one form of the deeper tensions in his historical contextualism: tensions between the human-centered nature of his historical view and the demands of Christian theology and between the contextualist emphasis on the moment and the demands of Christian teleology. Browning inherited, strayed from, and to an extent returned to a religious tradition both Calvinist and Evangelical. His mother, one of the more important influences on his religious beliefs, was by birth a Scots Presbyterian and by affiliation a member of the York Street Congregational Church whose minister could be characterized as "Calvinistic." Yet the Calvinism of Sarah Anna Browning and of the York Street Church was, as John Maynard describes it, more worldly and more humanized than early Calvinism.[10] Although it encouraged the introspective examination of conscience, it moderated a strict notion of divine election, deemphasized the hellfire and brimstone vision of divine judgment, and gave precedence to moral action over more extreme forms of other-worldliness and renunciation. This moderate, even genteel, Calvinism provided no compelling necessity for the view that all historical events are providentially determined, though it of course encouraged a general belief that God works in history.

Browning took Christianity seriously enough that it was impossible for him to conceive of history solely in human terms. Thus Browning struggled with the question of the intervention of God in history and with the correlative question, very troubling to his contemporaries, of the historical evidence for Christianity. Although in the most general sense Browning had a providential view of history, his definition of providence was bounded by the importance he attached to the necessary limitations of human knowledge and understanding. Rather than emphasizing decisive breaks in history and direct divine intervention in human affairs, Browning emphasized both the necessary limitations of historical circumstances and the possibilities for divine inspiration in every age. In one of Browning's most explicit treatments of historical time, the Pope's monologue in *The Ring and the Book*, neither Euripides, nor the Pope, nor the skeptics who will follow the Pope can have a complete understanding of the providential order of history. This order, moreover, is not progressive strictly speaking. Browning does metaphorically present a movement from Euripides' predawn era, to the dawn of Christianity in the time of St. Paul, to the full light of noon in the Pope's day. But the progression is not simple; the Pope sees sufficient darkness in his own time, and he predicts that the skepticism of the next age will, paradoxically, beneficially challenge the complacency characteristic of his own time. In short, Browning's claims for progressive and providential history, at its most confident in the Pope's monologue, is hedged about with questions.

Providential order and divine intervention may be thought to operate on the individual level as well as on the level of whole societies and historical epochs. Browning's understanding of divine intervention on the individual level is no simpler than his understanding of Christian teleology in history. In fact, glib claims about general or special instances of God's operation in history are in Browning's poems a litmus test of shallowness, insincerity, or worse. Andrea del Sarto's false resignation is only the most obvious example of the glib invocation of providence. Andrea's confidence that "all is as God overrules" is the measure of his failure.

Though wary of individual claims of divine intervention, Browning follows his Calvinist heritage in recurring to moments of individual conversion and revelation. These moments of conversion, revelation, or inspiration to action are most often presented as the special experiences of dramatically particularized characters; for the most part, the poet presents or alludes to the visions of his characters rather than writing a visionary poetry. He focuses, for example, on Karshish's report of Lazarus's vision rather than on that vision itself; thus the visionary experience is firmly set in a historical context. Claiming less direct revelation than Lazarus, the Pope is shown groping toward a divine purpose in history through a process of historical as well as spiritual reflection. The common form of individual conversion or revelation in Browning's poetry comes not, as in Lazarus's case, with a miracle, but through the working of human love in a concrete human situation. Caponsacchi and Pompilia both experience the impetus to action through the medium of human love and compassion: Pompilia's determination to save her child is, according to the Pope, both natural and divine, and Caponsacchi's determination to rescue Pompilia is an awakening of faith through the medium of Pompilia's faith in him. The moment of conviction, of will to action, is for each of them a personal, revelatory experience, but it is not a moment of apocalyptic vision, of the timeless and divine breaking into and somehow annihilating history.

Although the baseline of Browning's understanding of religion and history is an emphasis on human action and human love, Browning's grounding in Evangelical Protestantism made especially perplexing the problem of revelation in history. The most striking of Browning's poems that directly present a vision of the revelation are *Christmas-Eve and Easter-Day*, "Saul," and "A Death in the Desert." In *Christmas-Eve and Easter-Day,* Browning confronts directly the problem of revelation and the possible abolition of time, and in *Easter-Day* he engages with the Calvinist dichotomy of the this-worldly and the other-worldly. The poem should carry the weight of the poet's religious conviction, but many readers have remained unconvinced by its claim to vision. *Christmas-Eve and Easter-Day* embodies the personalist vision of Evangelical Protestantism, and yet the speakers of both halves of the poem are curiously compromised by the circumstantial particularization of their characters. We may take the poem as a pair of testimonials, but neither speaker attains the authority to compel the reader's assent. There is something facile, if not a little ridiculous, in the first speaker's claim to be transported to Rome and to Gottingen by touching the robe of the imaged Christ; the poem itself undercuts this vision by suggesting that the speaker has nodded off amongst the motley congregation of a dissenting chapel. The realistic particularity and the comic tone of the verse itself (which Browning feels it necessary to defend explicitly) undercut what might otherwise seem a serious effort to present a revelatory experience as a religious vision annihilating time.

Easter-Day is equally problematic. The speaker of *Easter-Day* claims a personal revelation, even an apocalyptic vision, but the speaker's own ambivalence in the poem's closing section and the strength of his asceticism are disturbing. The deep dichotomy of the this-worldly and the other-worldly in *Easter-Day* cuts against the grain of Browning's usual understanding of the relationship between the historical and the divine. Even the speaker's belated understanding of love is balanced by his declaration that he will go on to a "Better Land," "Be all the earth a wilderness!" (*Easter-Day*, 1003). Love, in this definition, would seem to work outside the "wilderness," not within it. Through these dramatic speakers and through the compromised or uncharacteristic ways he allows them to reach truth, Browning hedges about the nature of revelation and allows realistic detail to remain more convincing than the claim to a vision of truth beyond history.

Browning's "Saul" is a more convincing attempt at unmediated vision, partly because Browning's choice of a biblical subject lends credence to the poem's claims. David attains a prophetic vision of the coming Christ and claims this Christ will resemble himself, while Saul stands as a prefiguration of the crucifixion. In contrast to *Easter-Day,* the prophetic vision in "Saul" is not reducible to an other-worldly asceticism. Rather, the natural world seems to smile on David's triumph, and the prelude to David's vision of Christ is a vision of God in the "soul and the clod." Browning presents even David's moment of vision in the context of human love, and he relies on the biblical narrative to establish the authority of David's vision. Again in "Saul," Browning's vision is personalist, emphasizing individual revelation rather than the sweep of history and presenting Christian teleology in service of that individual vision.

The connections between revelation and history are explored more directly by a play like *The Return of the Druses* or a poem like "A Death in the Desert" than they are in *Christmas-Eve* or in "Saul." In *The Return of the Druses* Browning takes up what was to become for him an important theme—the nature of incarnation. Significantly, Djabal's claim to be the messianic Hakeem is treated with psychological subtlety. When Djabal recognizes the folly of his messianic claim, he is able to succeed in leading his people and in altering history on a human level. Paradoxically, Djabal is transformed sufficiently to rise above his human failings by Aneal's human love.

The question of revelation in the course of human history is still more complex in "A Death in the Desert" than in the *Druses,* particularly since Browning's imagining of early Christian history inevitably raised questions among his audience. More than *Christmas-Eve and Easter-Day* or "Saul," "A Death in the Desert" is a product of Browning's contextualist encounter with history. And as E. S. Shaffer has shown, it is also Browning's most powerful encounter with the historical apologetics of the Higher Criticism. The most striking aspect of Browning's defense of John and of John's defense of Christianity in "A Death in the Desert" is that neither defense claims to be a complete vision of future history or to be an apocalyptic vision of the end of history. Instead, as Shaffer argues, Browning makes a case for progressive revelation, which is essentially a higher critical response to historical questions about John's identity. Like the Pope's monologue, "A Death in the Desert" argues for a Christian teleology in history, but it refrains from envisioning some final end to the shifting stress of historical circumstances. According to John's notion of progressive revelation, the reality of Christianity and the questions directed to Christianity shift over the course of time; each new answer or newly founded faith will be tested by new questions and new circumstances. Such a process is necessarily "tortuous," as Shaffer argues, and "in the view of history based on perceptual skepticism, progressive revelation is accomplished by interpretation, and is in no way patent to the simple observer of the course of events."[11] The interpreter of events, even as he has a prophetic vision of past and future, is characterized by doubt as much as by confidence in his powers.[12] In John's vision of Christian teleology, then, and in Browning's defense of John, history is teleological, but its end, or telos, can never be completely grasped by the struggling prophet or by the historian poet. Both prophet and poet are necessarily rooted in and, to a great extent, limited by their historical circumstances. Each person can only seek to understand the enmeshing historical web and to divine, however tortuous the process, the larger movement of which it forms a part.

HISTORY AS WEB

In choosing the web as the central trope for history and historical experience, Browning chose a figure that has been central to historicist and contextualist histories. In Browning's poems the figure stands for history in both its senses—historical individuals and events and historical texts themselves. Not content with simple or single references to webs, Browning twists, turns, and reweaves the figure to a variety of ends.

The most elaborate of Browning's webs is woven in the music of Master Hugues of Saxe-Gotha. As the organist plays, the composer's fugue becomes as uselessly complex as the Danaides' sieve (a first web), and the organist, groping for another metaphorical equivalent, chances upon the spider-webs covering the church ceiling. The organist first sees the web as a figure for the fugue; it strengthens and thickens until "we exclaim—'But where's music, the dickens'?" (100). Next he interprets the web as a figure for experience:

XXII

Is it your moral of Life?
    Such a web, simple and subtle,
Weave we on earth here in impotent strife,
    Backward and forward each throwing
      his   shuttle,
Death ending all with a knife?

XXIII

Over our heads truth and nature—
    Still our life's zigzags and dodges,
Ins and outs, weaving a new legislature—
    God's gold just shining its last where that lodges,
Palled beneath man's usurpature.
. . . .

XXV

Ah but traditions, inventions
    (Say we and make up a visage)

> So many men with such various intentions,
>   Down the past ages, must know more than
>   this age!
> Leave we the web its dimensions!
>   ("Master Hugues," 106–15, 121–25)

The speaker distrusts Hugues's web and has difficulty grasping the composer's intent. He has the misgiving that "Truth's golden o'er us although we refuse it— / Nature, thro' cobwebs we string her" (134–35). In "Master Hugues," as in a number of Browning's other poems, we find historical earth-bound life figured as a web; or in the Bishop of St. Praxed's platitudinous phrase, "swift as a weaver's shuttle fleet our years." Hugues's web is not just the weaving of a single life; it is also the intertwining of numerous lives, "backward and forward each throwing his shuttle." The dimensions of the web, furthermore, stretch back in time as the web itself is made by so many men "down the past ages." Thus the web serves as an image of an individual's life, of his relation to his circumstances, and of the historical complexity of those circumstances.

Browning employs this figure for experience both positively and negatively. For Rabbi Ben Ezra, the web is a "rose-mesh"; it represents a synechdochal relationship of the body with the larger dance of "plastic circumstance." In *The Ring and the Book,* on the other hand, webs have predatory and ensnaring power. Guido, Pompilia, and Caponsacchi all are caught in webs. Guido spins lies until at his death we see "left bare the metal thread, the fiber fine / Of truth i' the spinning" (1.1271–73); and even Pompilia is caught in the "vapory films," the "web of circumstance" (12.553–59).[13] In other instances Browning's web of circumstance is not malevolent or predatory; it is simply the condition of life. In "An Epistle Containing the Strange Medical Experience of Karshish," Browning uses the figure to explore the tension between aspiration and finitude. Lazarus is the man of all men who has had the most direct experience of a reality beyond the historical web. And yet even he must continue to weave the thread of historical life:

> He holds on firmly to some thread of life—
> (It is the life to lead perforcedly)
> Which runs across some vast distracting orb
> Of glory on either side that meagre thread,
> Which, conscious of, he must not enter yet—
> The spiritual life around the earthly life:
> The law of that is known to him as this,
> His heart and brain move there, his feet stay here.
> So is the man perplext with impulses
> Sudden to start off crosswise, not straight on,
> Proclaiming what is right and wrong across,
> And not along, this black thread through the blaze.
> ("Karshish," 178–89)

For Lazarus, the only approach to life in this world is "not straight on." Despite the ideal he can fitfully discover or imagine, the artist or historian is like Lazarus in having to pull a thread "crosswise." As part of the historical world he interprets, the poet must "tell a truth / Obliquely" (*RB*, 12.855–56).

Of course Browning is not alone in figuring experience as a web; the motif appears in Blake with negative emphasis and in Shelley's work as an emblem of mortality, and it is developed with historical implications by Carlyle, George Eliot, Pater, Dilthey, and Collingwood. The web metaphor frequently offers itself as a figurative model to those who would explain individual action or larger historical events through the combination of forces in a particular context. Terry Eagleton has suggested, for example, that George Eliot's "web" in *Middlemarch,* indeed that "realism" as Eliot conceives it, "involves the tactful unravelling of interlaced processes, the equable distribution of authorial sympathies, the holding of competing values in precarious equipoise." From Eagleton's perspective, a

Marxist model of historical change, Eliot's webs "dehistoricize" social and historical reality.[14] Even from a less teleological perspective, the web metaphor seems to imply static conditions. Does the figure actually undermine the liberal and teleological notion of progress? Browning's modern critics have been particularly quick to point out that his optimism and his notion of progress are significantly tempered by skepticism, and I would add, by his insistence on "proving the Past," as he calls it in "Rabbi Ben Ezra."[15] The web as an emblem for present finitude or for historical connections, although not directly contradicting the idea of progress, does make it difficult to account for historical change.

A similar problem was encountered by Wilhelm Dilthey who systematically developed his notion of historical understanding by using similar metaphors. For Dilthey the web is a proper figure for historical connections, and the wave or stream is the trope for historical change. The coincidence in Browning's and Dilthey's choice of metaphors is not merely fortuitous, I believe, but indicates a more fundamental similarity of historical conceptualization. Dilthey understands the individual as a bearer of historical development and as a crossing-point (*Kreuzungspunkt*) of various systems of social interaction.[16] Understanding of individuals is made possible by an understanding of context: "In understanding we proceed from the context of the whole (*Zusammenhang des Ganzen*) as given in its vitality, in order to make the parts comprehensible on the basis of it. . . . All psychological thought contains the basic feature that the apprehension of the whole makes possible and determines the interpretation of the individual."[17] To articulate the process of understanding an individual's relation to a context, Dilthey conceives of history as a musical web. For Dilthey, values or individuals are "notes" from which the "web of melodies" of the historical world emerges, and each individual is placed according to relations with others. At the same time, each is "something indefinable, unique, not only according to the relation in which he stands but also of himself."[18] This "web of melodies," then, is at once the historian's conception and his object. As the historian moves from recollection to interpretation he begins his history, and even with a limited subject "a thousand threads lead on and on into the infinity of all the memories of mankind." Like Browning's poet in Book 1 of *The Ring and the Book* who finds his inspiration in a ruin "left / By the roadside 'mid the ordure, shards, and weeds" (1.666–67), Dilthey's historian "stands in the midst of the ruins, of the remnants of things past, the expressions of minds in deeds, words, sounds, and pictures of souls who have long ceased to be. How is he to conjure them up?" The historian, Dilthey says, "supplements" the remnants, interprets expressions, and lifts "the accounts of deeds from isolation back into the context in which they originated."[19] In interpreting human interactions Dilthey faces a tension between the individual existing in the connecting "flow of life" and the values, "universal and forever" that the historian seeks: "It is as if we had to draw permanent lines and figures on an ever-running stream.... But the flow of life is everywhere unique, every wave in it rises and dies away."[20]

Browning, too, turns to the web and the stream as providing a satisfactory figuration of historical life. So Pompilia is "enmeshed" in the web of circumstances in *The Ring and the Book,* and she is virtually a "drowning orb," who is not vindicated by man's law but, for once, by God acting through the Pope (10.579–81). The Augustinian friar, however, reminds us that even in God's covenant with Noah, the innocent are destroyed. "No wave rolls by, in all the waste" without beauty being "made blank." Only Pompilia in this instance is finally extricated from "the welter" (12.490). Guido is more desperately caught in the world's welter. Just as he perverts the web metaphor, so Guido presents a still darker version of the rock in the stream. The waves for Guido are all rushing on to death:

> I see you all reel to the rock, you waves—
> Some forthright, some describe a sinuous track,
> Some, crested brilliantly, with heads above,
> Some in a strangled swirl sunk who knows how,
> But all bound whither the main-current sets,
> Rockward, an end in foam for all of you!
> (*RB*, 11.2346–51)

But the figuration of historical life as the web in the stream need not be so bleak a prospect as it is for Guido. In the "Epilogue" to *Dramatis Personae*, the web and the stream combine: individuality and time meet in a universe of change that is also a universe of positive knowledge and feeling. In the "Epilogue" Browning confronts history as a spectacle of disappearing forms. He answers Renan's historical questions and perhaps replies obliquely to Matthew Arnold's elegy for the withdrawing "Sea of Faith." "Heaven's high" with "earth's low" intertwines in the current of changing form.

HISTORICAL POEMS

The web, then, is the central figure for Browning's contextualist view of history. It presents the individual necessarily enmeshed in circumstances and moving through historical time as the web of circumstance dissolves and is rewoven. Though the web figuration is at the center of Browning's historical understanding and though the encounter with history is at the center of Browning's poetry, not all of Browning's poems are, strictly speaking, historical and not all of his historical poems are contextualist. It is useful to discriminate among Browning's poems as historical or contextualist, as I implicitly do here in choosing some texts for discussion and in omitting others. But the formulation of such categories may also be misleading, for historical poetry can no more be considered a separate genre than the historical novel can.[21] One may use reference to historical events and appeals to verification as indexes of historical seriousness, but such an approach should not exclude historical poems referring to contemporary events or ignore lyrics that take history seriously even though they are not obviously based on historical sources.

The pastness of the past would seem a not altogether satisfactory criterion for identifying a poem as historical. As Lukács has argued, a writer may well treat contemporary or recently past events in the same way he treats more conventionally 'historical' subjects. Thus Lukács suggests one would be hard pressed to distinguish between the novels of Scott and of Balzac as historical and nonhistorical respectively. Lukács characterizes the shift from the novels of Scott to the novels of Balzac as a shift from past history to the present as history, and he praises Balzac for going beyond Scott in historical concreteness.[22] Similarly, I think it pointless to argue that Browning's "My Last Duchess" is historical but "Prince Hohenstiel-Schwangau" is not: though the Prince (Napoleon III) was still living in 1873, Browning's "Saviour of Society" is caught up in the same difficulties that plagued Sordello, and Browning's method of displaying character is similar to the techniques of characterization in his more obviously 'historical' poetry.

Though categorical distinctions are neither obvious nor infallible, clearly those poems in which Browning's historical concerns are most important are those that appeal to external verification of facts or circumstances. Browning's appeals to external verification began early in his career. In *Paracelsus*, though he eschews the "external machinery of incidents," Browning attaches another kind of machinery in the form of a long note beginning, "The liberties I have taken with my subject are very trifling. . . ."[23] In the case of *Sordello*, we learn from Harriet Martineau's diary that Browning did consider the issue of explanatory notes, and in writing his poem he consulted the historical works of Verci and Muratori as well as more general sources.[24] In the poems of the fifties, Browning often included chronological tags and date lines to fix the poems firmly in time and place. But of course the most debated of all Browning's appeals to verification is in *The Ring and the Book*. Browning consulted a variety of sources, and he declared within the poem and in his letters to Julia Wedgwood that he had been faithful to them. In addition to citing sources, in many of his poems Browning also assembles relevant details in order to create the sense that specific circumstances of events are essentially accurate and subject to external verification. A poem like "The Bishop Orders His Tomb" is successful in part because we feel, as Ruskin did, that the poem's temporally conditioned details refer to an actual historical situation. The power of the poem is not only in the successive revelation of character but also in the revelation of a historical milieu that we are involuntarily testing for accuracy with reference to our own notions about the Renaissance.

Not all the poems that appeal to verification could be called contextualist. "Gold Hair: A Story of Pornic," for example, is instead a moral fable. Its conceptualization is overtly didactic. In writing it, Browning drew upon Carou's *Histoire de Pornic* and possibly also on oral tradition. Significantly, Browning changed the subtitle from "A Legend of Pornic" to "A Story of Pornic" in the second edition of *Dramatis Personae*.[25] The poem implicitly would turn the saint's legend into a story by revealing the acquisitiveness concealed by the "saint's" gold hair. "Gold Hair" is more of a moral fable than most of Browning's poetry, yet it is not at the same time a rejection of historical method. Browning explicitly locates his poem in the context of "Our Essays-and-Reviews' debate," and his reasons to "suppose" Christianity true lie in a revisionist theology rather than in an outright rejection of the Higher Criticism. Browning suggests that Christian faith is the answer to the "corruption of Man's Heart," while this corruption is itself revealed by the historical (or quasi-historical) debunking of a legend. Despite the implicit historiographical debate, in "Gold Hair" Browning's didactic end is more important than an examination of motive or of historical context.

A second alternative to the contextualist mode of historical conceptualization is fundamental to a poem like "Hervé Riel." For his facts Browning used a Croisic guidebook and an unidentified source. In 1881 Dr. Furnivall called Browning on some of his facts, and the poet had to confess he had mistaken the hero's ultimate reward (*Handbook*, 408). A heroic ballad, "Hervé Riel" like "Incident of the French Camp" or "How They Brought the Good News from Ghent to Aix," is a more conventional 'historical' poem than a poem like "Andrea del Sarto." In "Hervé Riel" and "Good News," historical and geographical circumstances provide occasions for heroism or adventure; and as a result of this emphasis, the narrative development is as forceful as in any of Browning's works. The reader asks not how or why something happens, but what happens next. Historical circumstances, the number of forces impinging upon the characters, are conceived in a fairly simple way; and the characters themselves respond accordingly—their motives are either simple or treated simply. They act; they do not pause for complex rumination.

Neither the overtly didactic conceptualization of history nor the conceptualization of history as heroic adventure is central to Browning's major achievements. A contextualist and more complex relation of the present to the past unfolds in many of Browning's poems, and we see Browning's characters respond adequately or, more often, inadequately, to the challenges of life in time. A close look at two such poems will serve to suggest the poet's characteristic concerns with the individual enmeshed in his history. Though it is not obviously a 'historical' poem, "Love Among the Ruins" is one of Browning's most explicit treatments of the individual in time. "Cleon" is more obviously a poem obsessed with history and historical questions. Taken together, these two poems move from the—perhaps—glorious past to the modern recollection of it.

"Love Among the Ruins" seems at first glance a poem commending present love and condemning past glories. Browning may have placed it first in *Men and Women* from a combination of motives: it provides an accessible and familiar beginning because it treats a pastoral theme; it introduces several issues that will be important in both volumes—the country and the city, the vagaries of love, the proper value of classical civilization. Most important, however, "Love Among the Ruins" is a poem obsessed with time. Past, present, and future are intimately connected in the speaker's mind, and his attitude toward the past makes possible his famous assertion that "Love is best."

As a number of readers have noted, only the simplest reading of "Love Among the Ruins" takes the speaker's conclusions at face value. John Maynard, David Shaw, and Eleanor Cook have suggested that the poem does not simply reject the past; rather the speaker rejects the past, while the reader sees the speaker's assertion in the context of the past he has called up. As Eleanor Cook puts it, the speaker "assumes and loudly asserts that his love makes him essentially different from and better than the dead city-dwellers. What earth will return for him he forbears considering."[26]

Examining the possible sources for "Love Among

the Ruins" reveals still more clearly the ironic possibilities in the speaker's assertion. First, it seems virtually certain that Browning had a particular historical context in mind when he originally titled the poem a "Sicilian Pastoral." The ruins may well be the ancient Sicilian cities of Syracuse or Agrigentum combined with details from Edmund Spenser or John Dyer.[27] That Browning changed his title from "Sicilian Pastoral" to "Love Among the Ruins" indicates an effort to generalize, but it also has the effect of sharpening the antithesis between "love" and "ruins." We quickly find that the speaker has more difficulty than he knows in laying the past to rest. Indeed, the speaker is caught between recollection and anticipation; past and future alike are products of his imagination.

The speaker asserts that love may redeem the "folly, noise, and sin" of the past, but it is difficult to see how this redemption or escape is possible. The contrast with Spenser's "The Ruines of Time" is instructive. In Spenser's pastoral lament the yellow-haired spirit of "Verlame" laments the vanity of "earthly princes." The pastoral speaker of Spenser's poem, moreover, sees even natural beauty "wasted quite," and the envoy ends the poem with the admonition: "So vnto heauan let your high minde aspire, / And loath this drosse of sinfull worlds desire."[28] In his pastoral Spenser attempts, paradoxically, to make the poem a monument in the ruins of time. Browning's speaker is caught in a yet more cruel paradox: the attempt to make love endure the ruins of time. Despite his concluding exclamation, Browning's speaker anticipates extinction even in imagining his beloved. He figures the passionate moment to himself:

> When I do come, she will speak not, she will stand,
>   Either hand
> On my shoulder, give her eyes the first embrace
>   Of my face,

> Ere we rush, ere we extinguish sight and speech
> Each on each.
> ("Love Among the Ruins," 67–72)

In this passage the speaker imagines his lover imagining him. The focus is on her anticipation rather than his own. In this imagined union, half the senses—sight and speech—are extinguished. The speaker's paradoxical situation is even more pointed in the final stanza. His recollection of past glories reaches a hyperbolic climax, and the distinction between his own love and past glories becomes unclear:

> In one year they sent a million fighters forth
> South and North,
> And they built their gods a brazen pillar high
> As the sky,
> Yet reserved a thousand chariots in full force—
> Gold, of course.
> Oh heart! Oh blood that freezes, blood that burns!
> Earth's returns
> For whole centuries of folly, noise and sin!
> Shut them in,
> With their triumphs and their glories and the rest!
> Love is best.
> ("Love Among the Ruins," 73–84)

In the last three stanzas, the careful alternation of past and present becomes more and more complex, until here in the final stanza past and present are no longer easily distinguished. It is unclear whether the speaker refers to his own heart or to the hearts of those million fighters he finally would pass judgment upon. Is the "heart," the "blood that freezes, blood that burns" his own "return" on the glories and follies of the past? Does such a lover of "quiet-colored" eves deceive himself into imagining his blood freezes and burns, or is he himself implicated in the past he condemns? In either case the speaker is hardly condemning his own "world's desire" (as Spenser's speaker does) however willing he is to pass judgment upon past "folly, noise and sin."

One other possible source also provides an interesting contrast to "Love Among the Ruins." Poe's "To Helen" presents an earlier version of the woman in the tower, and Browning's admiration for Poe makes it likely that he would have known the poem, probably in the 1845 collection of Poe's poetry.[29] Characteristically Browning creates a more limited and equivocal view of past glories than Poe does. Though Helen herself is as vague and shadowy as the girl in "Love Among the Ruins," unlike the girl in Browning's poem she is a beacon of inspiration. She draws the poet home "To the glory that was Greece / And the grandeur that was Rome." An early version of "Love Among the Ruins" echoes this view of the past, but with the difference that the speaker is not drawn home to the past. He would shut it away. In the Houghton manuscript of "Love Among the Ruins," Browning originally concluded:

> Shut them in,
> With their grandeur and their glories and the rest!
> Love is best![30]

The substitution of "triumphs" for "grandeurs" in Browning's final version emphasizes conquest rather than greatness, and the revision seems ironically appropriate to a speaker who would condemn the past while pursuing his own conquest in love.

Browning's girl with eager eyes and yellow hair is also a more limited and equivocal figure than Poe's Helen. The woman in Browning's poem seems to be identified in the speaker's mind with the gold of the past and with inevitable extinction. As she looks where the king looked, the present is superimposed upon the past. The girl would seem to substitute for past grandeur. She would become like Helen the one bright spot in this twilight piece. We see her, however, only in the speaker's imagination. Unlike Helen she holds no agate lamp of inspiration. As the speaker of "Love Among the Ruins" imagines the girl imagining him, she can hardly be said to exist at all, for she exists only in his conjecture. The women in the two following poems, "A Lover's Quarrel" and "Evelyn Hope," exist more concretely though one is absent and the other dead. Browning's treatment of love destroyed and love unfulfilled in these next two poems in *Men and Women* provides a context in which the assertion "Love is best" sounds too absolute to be true. Neither the sources, nor the context, nor the internal logic of "Love Among the Ruins" allows us to interpret the poem as a condemnation of a glorious but sinful past. The poem in fact suggests that such a view of the past shapes the anticipation of the future, and between glory behind and glory before the speaker is left, like Andrea del Sarto, "all in a twilight."

Cleon too struggles with the burden of an all too glorious past, and like Browning's pastoral lover, he too fails. If the lover among the ruins is obsessed with time, Cleon is obsessed with history. In fact, Cleon might be seen as a contextualist historian gone bad. I have noted already the dangers of Cleon's aestheticism, and in discussing Browning's method in the dramatic monologues I will examine the ironies of "Cleon" in some detail. Here it is enough to suggest that Cleon cannot accept himself as a being in time or in history. He imagines Zeus as the perfect historian, but the perfection of history is necessarily its end. Cleon boasts about man's perfecting of nature and extols the grape of "culture" as superior to the "savage-tasted drupe," yet of course Cleon cannot halt his own natural decay. His thirst for perfection extends even to his arrogant good wish for Protus. Cleon hopes Protus's tower will provide, not a view of folly, noise and sin, but an ascent or retreat into "the eventual element of calm." Both for Browning's pastoral lover and for Cleon, however, to seek calm is to seek extinction. Whereas Browning's pastoral lover increases the vitality of the past in his imagination, Cleon attempts to reduce the vitality of ancient Greece until its heroic age becomes as gray as he is himself.

Despite his limitations, Cleon is in several ways a Browningesque historian. He advocates seeing from multiple perspectives. As he tells Protus,

> We of these latter days, with greater mind
> Than our forerunners, since more composite,
> Look not so great, beside their simple way,
> To a judge who only sees one way at once,
> One mind-point and no other at a time,—
> Compares the small part of a man of us
> With some whole man of the heroic age,
> Great in his way—not ours, nor meant for ours.
> ("Cleon," 64–71)

Here Cleon's sense of his own diminution to a "small part of a man" contradicts his belief in his own "greater mind." Cleon asserts the importance of multiple "mind-points" and would allow each age its own character. Yet unlike his creator, Cleon feels diminished by the heroic perfections of the Hellenes whom he follows. Here Cleon might be compared with his Roman analogue, Protus, in *Men and Women*. In "Protus" heroism is found not in the perfect type of Hellenic beauty but in the rough vigor of John the smith. As DeVane and, more recently, Herbert Tucker have noted, Cleon's failed perfections are Browning's answer to the Arnoldian admiration for Greece.[31] Ironically, Cleon advocates multiple mind-points for studying history, though he himself is limited to one.

Cleon is also a Browningesque historian in his progressive and contextualist view of the past. He figures history as a mosaic:

> See, in the chequered pavement opposite,
> Suppose the artist made a perfect rhomb,
> And next a lozenge, then a trapezoid—

> He did not overlay them, superimpose
> The new upon the old and blot it out,
> But laid them on a level in his work,
> Making at last a picture; there it lies.
> ("Cleon," 82–88)

The mosaic, however, is a less satisfactory contextualist metaphor than the web, or the web in the stream, for the mosaic is a picture in mortar. It does not move. As Cleon's respect for ancient heroism undercuts his pretension to "greater mind," so his idea of progress is betrayed by his figure for history. As Tucker has noted in a stimulating reading of "Cleon," the Greek poet would freeze time and stop history with himself at the pinnacle of historical achievement.

Even when Cleon takes up Browning's pervasive image—the thread of life—it is only to reduce it. Cleon laments life's insufficient capacity for joy, and he takes as his example the Naiad fountain in his garden. The Naiad's "water-bow / Thin from her tube" is her water of life; but in Cleon's view it is too little. So Cleon asks:

> What if I told her, it is just a thread
> From that great river which the hills shut up,
> And mock her with my leave to take the same?
> The artificer has given her one small tube
> Past power to widen or exchange
> ("Cleon," 254–58)

As Tucker suggests, Cleon is a reductive interpreter of signs. In his "profound discouragement," he is no better than his own stone Naiad; he refuses his own potential to "widen or to change" as he refuses the possibilities offered by Paul, the "barbarian" Jew. Despite his potential for seeing history properly, Cleon misestimates the value of the past, mistakes his own present merit both absolutely and relatively, and finally denies the future.

"Cleon" and "Love Among the Ruins" reflect Browning's persistent concern with the ways the past may impinge upon the present. There is evidence here surely of what Harold Bloom calls the strong poet's obsession with overcoming precursors. There is also the sense that misinterpreting the past may imperil the present; it may lead to a complacent grayness or to the pursuit of illusory perfection.

In their preoccupation with time and with history, "Cleon" and "Love Among the Ruins" represent the dominant concerns of Browning's poetry. At its most complex, Browning's understanding of history was not that history provides only moral lessons or heroic narratives. Rather, Browning saw history as a subtle interweaving of the individual and a social milieu. Browning's contextualism, his skeptical attitude toward the poetic ideal, and his belief that individuals—including poets—are enmeshed in history were essential to his historical understanding. This understanding of history, in turn, is reflected in the shape of Browning's poetry. As we shall see, narrative structure in the long poems, historical irony and judgment in the dramatic monologues, and even the language of Browning's historical poems owe their form to Browning's historical concerns. Perhaps most striking of all is the relationship between Browning's historical understanding and his poetic theory and poet-personae. In Browning's view the poet faces the same challenges and limitations as the historian or the historical individual. Like them, the poet can only seek the infinite in the pattern of finite forms.

CHAPTER THREE
POETIC PERSONAE AND THE INTERPRETATION OF HISTORY

"Without immediate delight in concrete reality and its gross and subtle complexities of causality, the exposition of ideal values loses contact with the soil in which it is nourished and becomes vacuous and arbitrary."
—Friedrich Meinecke

"THE BUSINESS HAS BEEN, AS I SPECIFY, TO EXPLAIN *fact*," Robert Browning wrote to Julia Wedgwood in 1868, "and the fact is what you see, and worse, are to see. . . . the black so much—the white no more."[1] Defending "Guido" against his correspondent's desire for pleasant poetry, Browning makes the claims of the realist and the historian. It is not enough for him simply to present the facts; the poet must also explain them. Facts do not interpret themselves. The poet like the historian must ask what a "fact" is, how it is known, how it should be interpreted, and what it has to do with values.

The matter of fact and its interpretation are essential both to Browning's view of the poet's role and to his poetic practice. As he developed his understanding of poetry and his characteristic subject matter, Browning had to come to terms with both historical and poetic traditions.[2] His father, his friend Carlyle, and the critical history of Niebuhr and Ranke presented the question of fact in compelling ways. In his own aesthetic theory and in his poetry Browning, like these historians, entered the nineteenth-century discussion of individual subjectivity and objective historical knowledge; and like many historians, Browning could neither accept an extreme subjectivism nor claim complete objectivity. Browning's most explicit aesthetic statement, the "Essay on Shelley," is characteristically ambivalent about the poet's ability to know the "facts" and to make judgments about them. In the long poems, particularly *Sordello* and *The Ring and the Book*, these difficulties are again apparent, this time in Browning's metaphors for the process of seeing the ideal in the actual. Browning's figures for the poet are drawn from the traditional imagery of inspiration. Metaphorically, the poet joins the company of biblical prophets; he burns with the fire and light of knowledge or truth; he is consequently a seer. Yet Browning uses biblical parallels in a carefully circumscribed way; he modifies fire and light into sparks and wicks, and he transforms seeing into optics. This characteristic reduction of the vatic to the historical corresponds to the characteristic role of the poet-personae in *Sordello*, in *The Ring and the Book*, and even, to some extent, in "Pauline." The poet-persona becomes a presenter, a commentator, and finally an artist of juxtaposition who claims to have disappeared.

BROWNING'S HISTORICAL TRADITION

Browning conceived the poet's role in connection with questions that applied equally to the historian, and it is clear that he became acquainted with historical research and historiographical controversy in a number of ways. The poet certainly shared his father's historical interests; he was cognizant of the school of critical historiography; and his closest friendship with Carlyle coincided with the period in which Carlyle was at work on *The French Revolution* (1837), *On Heroes and Hero-Worship* (1840), and *Past and Present* (1843). These influences bore fruit in a number of poems for which Browning borrowed particular historical materials or interpretations. As interesting as these particular debts are the general analogies between the crucial problems in Browning's aesthetics and in nineteenth-century historiography.

Certainly the earliest source of Browning's historical interests was his father, an ardent bibliophile and amateur historian. Most probably, of course, such influences worked in both directions, with the father taking his cue from his son and the son from the father. One passion the son surely inherited, however, was an interest in historical and antiquarian books. Browning Sr. no doubt collected many of the books that were auctioned after Pen Browning's death. The poet himself acquired a collection of standard histories from Macaulay to Prescott, in addition to more specialized historical esoterica.[3] Browning Sr.'s addiction to bookstalls was, if anything, stronger than his son's. In a series of letters to the poet and Sarianna Browning, written from Paris where he had moved perforce in 1857, he describes "walking among the books" as the only recreation he experiences.[4] In addition to recommending books to his son, Browning Sr. offered his assistance as a researcher. In an undated letter from Paris he mentions a favor he has done for the poet and remarks "how pleased I am that anything I could have had to communicate should have afforded you any useful information. I might perhaps be of further use in ferreting out any dates, facts, or names you may wish to be more particularly acquainted with."[5]

Collecting books and ferreting out facts do not in themselves make history, but Browning Sr.'s researches do seem to have provided his son with both specific historical material and with some degree of self-consciousness about historical method. The most striking parallel in Browning's and his father's historical interests is between Robert Sr.'s historical researches of the 1850s and the Pope's monologue in *The Ring and the Book*. Browning seems, in fact, to have found in his father's researches an important perspective on his own pontiff, Innocent III. In his letters to his son, Browning Sr. returns insistently to his research on Marozia, a tenth-century Italian woman who was the daughter of an unscrupulous and powerful Roman family, mistress of Pope Sergius, and by him mother of Pope John XI. Sergius, of course, is the anti-Formosan whom Browning's Pope describes in his recapitulation of papal crimes, intrigues, and perversions of justice. Browning's Pope, moreover, shares the historical authorities and the general historical judgment of the poet's father. Both the Pope and Robert Browning Sr. find their documents at once fascinating and dismal.[6]

Browning Sr.'s view of tenth-century Italian history provides a clue to the poet's choice of this period as the beginning matter of Pope Innocent's monologue. In one of this letters, Browning Sr. asks his son to find a "young man" to write Marozia's history, and he takes pains to explain the significance of his subject: "The narrative (if I may call it so) takes up but about 30 years—yet in that short space of time what wonderful events occurred. In that period are included—The rise of Modern Europe—The foundation of the Roman Hierarchy—the ascendancy of tyranny of the nobility—and the murder of several popes—as this period is allowed, by every historian, to have been the darkest period of the dark ages—we have, as might be expected, a continual record of the most atrocious crimes."[7] Browning Sr. thus points to the thirty years' narrative, probably 895-926, as comprising at once atrocious crimes and the rise of modern Europe. In having the Pope begin his monologue by focusing on nearly the same period, Browning too is accounting for a continuity of Italian history—from Marozean tyranny on a grand scale to the decline and petty tyranny of the Franceschini. The Pope's sense of his own fallibility is made more believable by his initial meditation of an age Browning Sr. characterized as the "darkest" of dark ages of the church; for neither Formosus nor his enemies provide shining examples of papal justice. Though Browning apparently never found a "young man" to take up his father's tenth-century researches, he indirectly fell heir to them himself in writing the story of the Old Yellow Book, which after his father's fashion he had tried to give away.

In addition to their common interest in medieval Italian history, Browning Sr. and his son shared an interest in questions of historical method. Despite his obvious antiquarianism and fascination with detail for its own sake—as evidenced in the care he expended on his "Nomenclator of Old Testament Genealogy"— Browning Sr. was not a simple empiricist or fact collector.[8] He was acquainted with the method and the theoretical problems of the new critical history. His concern with such questions is evident in the way he envisions a history of Marozia. He longs for a young man to "try his hand on Marozia—But by no means to make a novel of it—I have collected material enough to form a 'truthful' history of her, which as it is not a hackneyed subject might be read with interest.... I am certain an entertaining as well as useful biography might be made of it—The great difficulty lies in the willful misrepresentations many writers of ability have been guilty of—but there is great difference between omitting and misrepresenting facts—and also a great pleasure in being able from authentic sources to clear up any difficulty arising from carelessness or any other less reputable sources." In his directive for a proper history of Marozia, Browning Sr. shows himself to be undertaking the central task of the critical historian—evaluating the biases of his sources. He is also sensitive to the problems in selecting material to represent a historical event fairly. Finally, his remark—in quotations—that he desires a 'truthful history' indicates he is aware of the competing claims of history and fictions to present the 'truth' about the past.[9]

Although Robert Browning Sr. was clearly important for the development of his son's historical interests, the poet had a number of other opportunities to become acquainted with the historical method of Niebuhr and Ranke, and, at first hand, with the historical researches of Carlyle. The German tradition of critical history was certainly known to Browning through his father's researches, but Ranke's work was no doubt familiar to the poet well before Browning Sr. consulted the 1860 edition of *The History of the Popes*. Publication of Ranke's third major work was completed in German in 1836, and the first English edition followed in 1840.[10] Several years later, when Browning was living in Italy, his friend William Wetmore Story attended a course of Ranke's lectures in Berlin.[11] Niebuhr's work on Roman antiquities was surely known to the poet as well, both directly and perhaps also indirectly through Wordsworth's *Memorials of a Tour in Italy*. It is unlikely, however, that Browning could have shared Wordsworth's judgment of Niebuhr. While Browning's Italian journey of 1838 produced *Sordello*, Wordsworth's travels in 1837 led him to "Musings Near Aquapendente" in which he laments that his age is cut off from "ennobling impulse from the past." In Wordsworth's view the history of Niebuhr and his school is "lifeless fact to fact / Minutely linked by diligence uninspired / By godlike insight."[12] As we shall see, such a critical view of critical history is weighted too heavily toward insight and away from fact to be altogether congenial to Browning.

The person who raised the question of fact and insight most forcefully for Browning, however, was not Wordsworth or even Ranke, but Thomas Carlyle. The history of Carlyle's friendship with the Brownings is most fully and entertainingly recounted in Charles Richard Sanders's two-part article on the "Carlyle-Browning Correspondence."[13] This is not the place to recapitulate the vicissitudes of their long friendship, but it is interesting to note that the warmest period of their intimacy began in 1840 when Browning was attending Carlyle's lectures "On Heroes." In addition to their discussions of poetry, in which Carlyle exhorted Browning to try his hand at prose, Carlyle also requested Browning's help in locating a letter and books for his use in the *Life of Cromwell*. A few years later Carlyle again asked for Browning's assistance, this time in researching the biography of Frederick the Great.[14] In the end, however, Browning, like Tennyson, was unsympathetic to Carlyle's latest hero, and could not finish even the first volume of *Frederick*.[15] Carlyle's earlier production, *Past and Present*, was more congenial to both the Brownings. In 1846, three years after the publication of *Past and Present*, Robert wrote to Elizabeth approving the general principle of Carlyle's view of the past: "Carlyle has turned and forged, reforged on his anvil the fact that 'no age ever appeared heroic to itself,' and so worthy of reproduction in Art by itself."[16] However accurate this comment as a reading of Carlyle, it indicates the impetus toward history that he and Browning shared.

Browning seems also to have shared Elizabeth Barrett's view of Carlyle's general strengths. Certainly both poets warmly admired Carlyle, and like his wife Browning singled out *Sartor Resartus*, not the histories, as Carlyle's greatest achievement.[17] In an essay she wrote with R. H. Horne for *A New Spirit of the Age* (1844), Elizabeth Barrett calls *Sartor* "the finest of Mr. Carlyle's works in conception and as a whole." For similar reasons she adds that *Past and Present* is undoubtedly "his finest work, as a matter of political philosophy." Carlyle reaches general principles, Elizabeth Barrett says, through a distinguished power of "individualization." Ultimately, she praises *Past and Present* on a basis she and Robert could equally approve. Carlyle, at bottom, is a poet: "And when he casts his living heart into an old monk's diary, and, with full warm gradual throbs of genius and power, throws out the cowled head into a glory; the reason is not, as some disquieted readers have hinted, that Mr. Carlyle is *too* poetical to be philosophical, but that he is *so* poetical as to be philosophical in essence when treating of things."[18] Elizabeth Barrett concludes that Carlyle is no "mere historian." Although Browning clearly agreed with Elizabeth Barrett's assessment of Carlyle's strengths—poetry, the power of making the past live, moral force—he was also sympathetic to the details of Carlyle's historical research.[19]

Browning was a good deal less likely than Elizabeth Barrett to set poetry and philosophy in opposition to "mere history." No more than Carlyle could Browning wholly approve the "Dryasdust" historian; no less than Carlyle, Browning found him necessary. Despite his admiration for Carlyle's passion and his "intense radicalism,"[20] Browning could not follow him in his apocalyptic vein. One has only to imagine a Browningesque version of Mirabeau or Napoleon or a Carlylean version of Sordello or Guido to appreciate their differences in approach. At the same time, it is not perhaps fanciful to see the monks of St. Edmundsbury and Fra Lippo Lippi as distant cousins.

The significance for Browning of his father's studies, of the rise of critical history, or of Carlyle's work is not, in any case, that he came to share wholly in any of their attitudes toward history. Nor is it entirely necessary or ultimately even possible to know how heavily Browning was indebted to German historiography, to his father, to Carlyle, or to some other source for his understanding of history. It is true, nonetheless, that nineteenth-century historical controversy provides a necessary context for understanding Browning's poetry, for Browning developed his characteristic approach to aesthetic questions by struggling with historical materials. The real question for Browning as he worked within and against the historical thinking he came upon in his father, in the critical historians, and in Carlyle was equally an historical, aesthetic, and epistemological one. How can one know history? How can the poet or the historian shape and connect facts, meanings, and values?

KNOWING THE FACTS: THE ANALOGY TO HISTORY

For Browning as for the historians contemporary with him, epistemological, aesthetic, and historical questions were inevitably framed in terms of objectivity and subjectivity. The general importance of this dichotomy is evidence of the growing conviction in the nineteenth century that fact and the interpretation of fact are fundamentally inseparable.[21] In working through the dichotomy of objectivity and subjectivity, of fact and its inevitable interpretation, Browning's poems become accessible to a reading that finds them resolutely modern. His poems even flirt with the postmodernist possibility that language is an endless interplay of signs and real historical knowledge is impossible. But Browning's poems never ultimately claimed purely objective knowledge of "facts" or supported a purely subjective self-referentiality. Rather than retreating from history or claiming pure objectivity, Browning sought in his view of aesthetics and in his poetic forms a middle ground. The nature of subjectivity in history and the possibility of objective historical knowledge are recurrent concerns in Browning's poetry, and the synthesis Browning attempted can best be understood in the context of Ranke's and Carlyle's grapplings with similar difficulties. Like Ranke and Carlyle, Browning emphasized the particular, the individual, and the individual character of historical periods, and for him as for Ranke and Carlyle the question became how or whether the historical individual or event is connected with some overarching pattern, meaning, or value.

Common to the historical thinking of Ranke, Carlyle, and Browning is their attention to the subjectivity of the historical individual. In various ways they ask how any participant in or witness to an event can be expected to see clearly the truth, or even the particulars of experience. Ranke of course insisted upon the historian's obligation to account for the biases of his sources. The historian must allow for the individual subjectivity that has produced the document he is using. Thus, for example, in the appendix to the *History of the Popes*, which Browning consulted in writing *The Ring and the Book*, Ranke reproduces the accounts or *relatione* of several Venetian ambassadors to the court of Rome; and he discusses the Venetians' biases and the discrepancies among their records.[22]

Though he insisted less strongly than Ranke upon a detailed critical apparatus, Carlyle was equally concerned with the subjectivity of the historical individual. Carlyle's critique of bias extends even to the individual's perception of the historical event of which he is a part. In "On History," for instance, Carlyle portrays the process of perceiving, selecting, and recording the historical event as fraught with opportunities for distortion:

> The old story of Sir Walter Raleigh's looking from his prison-window, on some street tumult, which afterwards three witnesses reported in three different ways, himself differing from them all, is still a true lesson for us. Consider how it is that historical documents and records originate; even honest records, where the reporters were unbiased by personal regard; a case which, were nothing more wanted, must ever be among the rarest. The real leading features of a historical Transaction, those movements that essentially characterise it, and alone deserve to be recorded, are nowise the foremost to be noted.[23]

On the simplest level, Carlyle contends that no two witnesses ever perceive an event in precisely the same way. Moreover, these witnesses cannot be trusted to grasp the significance of the event they have seen. What is needed, Carlyle concludes, is a seer.

Analogously, Browning explores the problem of subjectivity, both in general and specifically in history. Like Carlyle, Browning is aware of the power of subjectivity to control perception, and he examines the quintessential romantic duality between solipsistic subjectivity and action in the world. Sordello, for example, is torn by the difficulties of subjectivity and by the implications of subjectivity for moral choice. At the very end of his life, Sordello must choose between Ghibelline and Guelf though neither faction is entirely to his liking. His new Guelf sympathies have been frustrated and his circumstances have been complicated by Salinguerra. Sordello is left with only his own divided mind:

> I feel, am what I feel, know what I feel;
> So much is truth to me. What Is, then? Since
> One object viewed diversely, may evince

> Beauty and ugliness—this way attract,
> That way repel,—why gloze upon the fact?
> Why must a single of the sides be right?
> What bids choose this and leave the opposite?
> Where's abstract Right for me?
> *(Sord.* 6.440–47)

Faced with a choice of compromises and viewing each diversely, Sordello is unable to act. He is paralyzed by his unwillingness to accept earthly impurities. As Carlyle would say, he is unable to do the work nearest at hand. Sordello is surely not the historical seer Carlyle commends. His failure, nonetheless, is understandable. If he were less of a relativist action would be simple; if he could bring himself to accept the imperfection relativism implies, action would be possible. As it is, the poet judges that he has missed his historical moment: "Sordello's chance was gone."

The Ring and the Book is even more complex than *Sordello* in exploring how individuals, enmeshed in their circumstances, must be limited interpreters of history. These limitations, in documents or in the traditions associated with historical events, must be taken into account by the historical poet. Accordingly, Browning begins by questioning the reliability of sources. The reader, he says, will receive only such food as he is fit for:

> —No dose of purer truth than man digests
> But truth with falsehood, milk that feeds him now,
> Not strong meat he may get to bear some day—
> To-wit, by voices we call evidence,
> Uproar in the echo, live fact deadened down,
> Talked over, bruited abroad, whispered away,
> Yet helping us to all we seem to hear:
> For how else know we save by worth of word?
> *(RB,* 1.821–829)

Having raised the question of historical evidence, Browning goes on to describe some of the least worthy words in his poem, namely Half-Rome's view of the

Franchesini case. Half-Rome, we're told, indulges in the "instinctive theorizing whence a fact / Looks to the eye as the eye likes the look" (*RB*, 1.855–56). Half-Rome is thoughtlessly biased; he theorizes from false and unexamined premises. In his description of Half-Rome, Browning rejects sheer relativism even while he admits the near impossibility of establishing objective truth.[24]

But how can the poet recognize sheer relativism when he sees it? And how can he select significant details from among the insignificant? The poet and the historian are, like their historical subjects, enmeshed in history; how can they judge the worth of word? Carlyle, Ranke, and Browning all formulate these difficulties with reference to subjectivity, objectivity, and imagination.

Carlyle, for example, framed such questions succinctly in a letter to John Stuart Mill on 28 October 1833. As Hill Shine has demonstrated, during this period Carlyle was feeling his way toward his characteristic approach to history.[25] In thinking through the problem of perception and objectivity that he began to formulate in "On History," Carlyle repeatedly asked himself how historical particulars are related to transhistorical values. He wrote to Mill:

> One of the questions that oftenest presents itself is, *How* Ideals do and *ought to* adjust themselves with the Actual. A vast question, as I take it up. On which ground our John Knox and Scottish Kirk is so peculiarly significant for me. A *genuine* Ideal, that did subsist in spite of men and devils, with Life in it, for a hundred and fifty years! On the same ground too, my value for the Actual (in all senses), for what *has realised* itself continues and increases: and often I ask myself, is not all Poetry the essence of Reality (could one but get at such essence), and true History the only possible Epic? What limits my affirmative answer should have, are yet nowise clear.[26]

Carlyle's vast problem is the relation of the actual to the ideal, of historical events to values; and his solution takes poetry as the third term mediating the dualism. Poetry is the ideal in the actual.

At the same time that he defends poetry on these grounds, Carlyle is reluctant in his own works to cross over into fiction and to embrace the realistic particularity of the Victorian novel.[27] As George Levine puts it, Carlyle's attitude toward time and "the limits of man's possible knowledge about the past" was not in harmony with the leading conventions of the novel; it was for Carlyle, rather, to anticipate Jamesean experiments with a point of view that theoretically "absolve[s] the narrator from the overwhelmingly difficult responsibility of knowing all."[28] Carlyle attempts at once to overcome the limitations of subjectivity and to connect the actual to the ideal, first in the more explicitly visionary and more obviously fictional mode of *Sartor Resartus* and then in the historical visions of *The French Revolution, On Heroes,* and *Past and Present.*

Whatever his differences from Carlyle and from Browning, Ranke, too, formulated the challenge of history as the confrontation of the historian, himself limited by his subjectivity and circumstances, with the value or significance of particulars. As numerous readers of Ranke's works have pointed out, his insistence on particulars is balanced by an emphasis on values—values not in the sense of abstractions, but as the understanding of how particulars become significant.[29] In an illuminating study of Ranke, Leonard Krieger argues that Ranke's approach to history implied a theoretical dichotomy between subject and object, and a resulting emphasis on the "priority of particulars in the method of knowledge and the priority of universals in the substance of knowledge."[30] As Ranke himself phrased it in the 1830s, the discipline of history, at its best, "is itself called upon, and is able, to lift itself in its own fashion from the investigation and observation of particulars to a universal view of events, to a knowledge of the objectively existing relatedness."[31] As Krieger argues, however, this ideal harmony of subjective historian and objective value remained a theoretical dualism for Ranke which was resolved only in the practice of his mature history. While believing "objective historical truth" to be possible and desirable, Ranke "also acknowledged throughout his career both the undeniable actuality of each generation's imposition of its own values upon history and the welcome actuality of present influences upon the historian."[32] Though his historical practice side-stepped this theoretical dualism and though he was hostile to the truth claims of historical fiction, Ranke nevertheless insisted upon the historian's empathy with his materials, and he saw this engagement of the historian with his materials as essential to writing history. Thus the picture of Ranke as a scientist dispassionately dissecting the knowable object is countered by Friedrich Meinecke's argument that to Ranke the "artistic-intuitive" approach was an "essential and indispensable technique" in view of the "never completely, decipherable" interpenetration of mechanistic, morphological, and individualistic causes in history.[33] In his own way Ranke, like Carlyle, acknowledged the necessary subjectivity of historical individuals, including historians, without giving up a belief in larger and objectively existing patterns or values.[34]

Like Carlyle and Ranke, Browning too acknowledged the historian's or the poet's subjectivity without giving up his claim to a measure of objective truth. We see both in Browning's poetics and in his poet-personae the same kinds of dualistic tension that also informed Carlyle's and Ranke's visions of the historian. Browning's view of the relationship between objectivity and subjectivity, between facts and values is nowhere so explicitly developed as in the "Essay on Shelley"; less explicit but equally important are Browning's encounters with similar dualisms in *Sordello* and *The Ring and the Book.*

As we have seen, Sordello is beset by the perils of his own subjectivity; the narrator tells us that Sordello misses the proper links to "out nature." In Book 5 Sordello himself hears an oracular voice advising him that a complete view of history is available to human beings only in brief glimpses. The steady sight of "time's completed plan" is reserved to God alone (5.84–97). Neither aspiration nor recognition of limitation, neither god-like objectivity nor a self-circling subjectivity offers Sordello a solution to his political and poetical difficulties. One well might argue that the problem of Sordello is the problem of the poem, that neither the poet nor his troubadour has successfully answered the question of vision—of how the poet can see value or truth in history. To this extent the poem might be said to raise theoretical questions that it cannot concretely solve.

Interestingly, just this aspect of the poem drew the most telling criticism from Browning's friend Alfred Domett. Browning sent a presentation copy of *Sordello* to Domett in February 1840, and at the poet's request Domett in turn lent him the annotated copy in 1842 when he was reviewing his work.[35] Domett was less troubled by the complexity of plot in *Sordello* than by a quality of abstraction that he describes in his comment on Book 4: "As you take from thought the need of expressing itself by its own *deeds*—actions i.e. *corporeal* actions—so take from mind the need of expressing itself by thought—i.e. mental actions—and you love Good and hate evil—So doing the Germans get their pure Reason."[36] In Domett's view *Sordello* is a progressive refinement from action, to thought, to mental states, to "pure Reason"; thus refined the connections within the subject and between subject and object become unclear. Both in Sordello's mind, and perhaps in the poem itself, the proper connections between inner and outer are missing.

Such problems are formulated more clearly in *The Ring and the Book* than in *Sordello*, because they are presented as historiographical problems and as questions about the proper relationship of fiction and history. *The Ring and the Book* in this respect is closer than *Sordello* to the problem of historical knowledge as Carlyle and Ranke conceived it. Even *Sordello*, however, presents the subject / object tension in the context of historical questions; the poet makes clear that he is not writing a mere chronicle of particulars but is seeking to connect them meaningfully, insofar as he is able.[37] In *The Ring and the Book*, the connections between objective and subjective and between fact and value are examined still more explicitly in the context of historiography. Book 1 is at once Browning's prologue and his defense of method. Browning explains in detail the process of mixing fancy and fact; like Carlyle and Ranke, though to a different end, he weighs the relationship between fiction and history.

At the same time, the poet is aware that the reader may be weighing him. There is in his tone more than a hint that he suspects he may have sought a middle path and pleased no one.[38] He wonders whether he has pleased antiquarians and fact lovers, but he fears he may have disappointed readers looking for contemporary true stories. "Lovers of dead truth, did ye fare the worse?" he asks. "Lovers of live truth, found ye false my tale?" (*RB*, 1.690–91). Replying to his own query, the poet assures us that his tale is both adequate to its facts and adequate as "live truth." Thus he arrives at the further implications of his ring metaphor:

> Well now, there's nothing in nor out o' the world
> Good except truth: yet this, the something else,
> What's this then, which proves good yet seems
>   untrue?
> This which I mixed with truth, motions of mine
> That quickened, made the inertness malleable
> O' the gold was not mine,—what's your name for
>   this?

Are means to the end, themselves in part the end?
Is fiction which makes fact alive, fact too?
(*RB*, 1.692–98)

In its tone this passage is rather closer to Ranke's prefaces than to Carlyle's essays, though it defends a thesis Ranke could never wholly accept. The self-effacing almost casual tone and the repeated use of questions are the poet's way of avoiding dogmatism. The interrogative allows him to evade the systematic defense of a thesis that might land him in a muddle of logical contradictions. He begins with a self-evident proposition—there's nothing good except truth—and he concludes by defending the inseparable connections of imagination, fact, and truth. Neither the historian nor the poet simply discovers truth in the facts; rather, both make truth from the facts.

The facts, nonetheless, have an importance of their own. Thus having shaped his ring through the alloy of imagination, the poet tells us that only the pure gold is left; and similarly he claims to have disappeared behind the documents of the Old Yellow Book. "I disappeared," he says, "the book grew all in all" (*RB*, 1.681). This disappearance behind the document is an ideal first described, though not attempted, in *Sordello*. Yet it must remain an ambiguous claim if we take seriously the poet's necessary subjectivity. Ranke, interestingly, makes an analogous and equally ambiguous claim in describing his *English History*.[39] For the poet and the historian alike the goal of objectivity is a compelling one. Yet the very documents behind which they claim to have disappeared are haunted by the individual subjectivities responsible for their selection.[40]

THE "ESSAY ON SHELLEY": UNEASY COMBINATION

Equally haunted by subjectivity and an elusive poetic ideal, Browning's "Essay on Shelley" is his most explicit examination of the subjective and objective as aesthetic terms. But even as he defends Shelley, Browning cannot resolve the tension between the actual and the ideal; he cannot dismiss the necessary limitations of subjectivity or ignore the necessity of connecting the realities of the objective poet to an ideal or overarching truth.[41]

In turning to the Shelley essay, one might easily be tempted to find in it a critical vocabulary for describing Browning's early poetry or an autobiography of his development as a poet. Like kindred historiographical discussion, however, the Shelley essay creates more difficulty than clarity. It is not the key to Browning's art, the outline of a developmental scheme in which we may watch him metamorphose from a subjective into an objective poet. The poet's ambivalence toward the artist as seer, however, is complex enough to have evoked interpretations ranging from the claim that Browning attempts in his own poetry "the synthesis of objective and subjective roles"[42] to the notion that Browning surely "would classify himself as an objective poet" and is "far from conceding that this is an inferior order."[43] It is difficult on the basis of the Shelley essay to say with certainty how Browning would classify himself—or whether he could categorize himself at all. Ultimately Browning does not describe a poet who creates a compound of the subjective and the objective. Nor does he enlist himself under either classification. Rather he suggests that even the ideal poet produces a mixture of subjective and objective in "successive perfect works."[44]

This dualistic approach was common to poetics and historiography in the nineteenth century, and Browning's essay is organized on the basis of this major theme in nineteenth-century aesthetics. Browning's theory of art, like those of many of his contemporaries, could fairly be called an aesthetics of antithesis.

In Germany the subjective / objective dichotomy as applied to the arts was proposed variously by

Schiller, the Schlegels, and Goethe, and it entered the English critical vocabulary in the works of Henry Crabb Robinson, Lockhart, DeQuincey, Carlyle, Coleridge, and others.[45] In different form we see the habit of classifying poets or their works into antithetical camps in the writings of Mill, Hallam, and, still earlier, Wordsworth.[46] The essays by Robinson and Mill may have been especially well-known to Browning, for they were published by W. J. Fox in the *Monthly Repository* in 1833, the same year Fox reviewed Browning's "Pauline."[47] While Crabb Robinson distinguishes the lyric from the epic and the subjective from the objective, Mill separates Wordsworth's poetry of "culture and thought" from Shelley's "poetry of feeling." Interestingly, however, like Browning after him, Mill takes Shelley's *The Cenci* as an exception, as a powerful example of Shelley's "feelings and imagery in subordination to the thought."[48] Predating the antithetical categories of Mill and Robinson is Wordsworth's division of poets into two classes. Although he himself is classified by Mill among the poets of thought and culture, Wordsworth opposes the poets of "enthusiastic and Meditative Imagination" to poets of "the human and dramatic imagination." The first group includes Spenser, Milton, and implicitly Wordsworth himself; the second is represented most importantly by Chaucer and Shakespeare.[49] As we shall see, Wordsworth's understanding of the "human and dramatic" poet is not unlike Browning's view that pure objective poetry is "dramatic" and is best exemplified in the work of Shakespeare.

Such antitheses as poetry of thought or feeling, poetry of dramatic or meditative imagination, and subjective or objective poetry may become the basis of a literary history, the tools of literary analysis, or the terminal values on a normative scale.[50] Browning's subjective / objective dichotomy, like the antitheses of his predecessors, combines these applications.

In coming to grips with the subjective / objective dichotomy, which M. H. Abrams calls the "primal fracture" in romantic poetics and philosophy, Browning does not propound a "metaphysics of reconciliation."[51] Nor does he move toward an apocalyptic view of knowledge and history. Rather, Browning embeds the distinction between subjective and objective poetry in historical time. The subjective and objective follow each other in cyclical alternation.[52] Though he feels obliged to admit that subjective poetry "might seem to be the ultimate requirement of every age," his historical emphasis allows Browning to defend the essentially equal value of both kinds of poetry.

Even in Browning's historical model, however, the terms *subjective* and *objective* have an important normative dimension. By definition, the subjective poet experiences the world and his own life with reference to the absolute; the value of his work needs no defense. On a normative scale, the subjective poet would appear to be the positive pole. The objective poet, in contrast, is not so obviously worthy. Browning does defend the historical importance of the objective poet, but it is the rhetoric of his defense as much as his historical scheme per se that attributes value to the work of the objective poet. The objective poet, Browning says, cuts for us a "fresh and living swathe"; he is "prodigal of objects" for our outer sight; he is concerned with the "manifold experience of man" (*ES*, 286). In Browning's view, then, the objective poet is generous, even munificent. His is a poetry of plenitude. The objective poet is necessary historically, for his "outer sight" has its intrinsic worth. Just as for Ranke every age is "immediate to God," so for Browning subjective and objective poets, if not equally immediate to God, are at least equally useful to him.

As Browning applies his partly normative and partly analytical and historical categories to individual poets, he begins implicitly to find the subjective / objective dichotomy inadequate. In the first place, Browning carefully emphasizes that his categories are not absolute. The basis for the subjective / objective division, he says, "seems not so much from any essential distinction in the faculty of the two poets or in the objects contemplated by either, as in the more immediate adaptability of these objects to the distinct purposes of each" (*ES*, 285). He cautions, further, that subjective or objective tendencies may be "pushed to an extreme and manifested as a deformity" (*ES*, 285). Finally, Browning is especially wary of the claims for subjective poetry even while he is attracted by the subjective poet's immediate access to the ideal.

In his definition of the two kinds of poets, Browning's ambivalence becomes clear. Browning calls the objective poet a fashioner or maker who may dispense even with narrative "as suggesting a describer" and write purely dramatic poetry. The objective poet is concerned with the "raw material" of the world. The subjective poet, in contrast, is the seer who refers "the thing he perceives" to Ideas, to the "supreme Intelligence which apprehends all things in their absolute truth." The subjective poet "digs where he stands"; he seeks the primal elements of humanity in his own soul and expresses them in an effluence from his own personality (*ES*, 284). The subjective poet selects that "silence of the earth and sea in which he can best hear the beating of his individual heart, and leaves the noisy, complex, yet imperfect exhibitions of nature in the manifold experience of man around him, which serve only to distract and suppress the working of his brain" (*ES*, 286). The risk of solipsism for the subjective poet is clear. In the context of Browning's repeated insistence on imperfection, moreover, one may see the difficulties in the subjective poet's turn from the "imperfect exhibitions of nature" to the "beating of his individual heart" and the realm of "Ideas." Perhaps equally, one can sense Browning's discomfort with a category that would seem to require a poet to reject the plenitude of the actual in order to pursue the highest achievement.

It is not surprising, then, that in describing Shelley, Browning is also driven to consider the possible unity of his two kinds of poetry. In contrast to Shakespeare, the great objective poet, Shelley would seem to be a great modern type of the subjective poet. Shelley's work should be considered "a sublime fragmentary essay towards a presentment of correspondency of the universe to the Deity, of the natural to the spiritual, and of the actual to the ideal" (*ES,* 289). Even in his subjective poetry, Shelley would appear to have achieved a synthesis of subject and object, actual and ideal. Nevertheless, Browning goes on to praise him for his "successful instances of objectivity," including such poems as *The Cenci,* "Julian and Maddalo," and "Ode to Naples." Having made a division between two kinds of poetry, Browning is at pains to heal it.[53] The individual subjective poet challenges Browning's aesthetic antithesis; Browning is no more comfortable in categorizing Shelley as a subjective poet, pure and simple, than he is in using "subjective" and "objective" as normative terms. A unity of the two categories remains an irresistible ideal.

Both his initial division of two kinds of poetry and his historicization of these categories, however, make it difficult for Browning to imagine the whole poet. Despite his praise for Shelley, Browning cannot actually envision a poet who synthesizes the objective and the subjective in a single work. The two qualities, in Browning's view, can never be fused. They can only be combined. As he explains it: "Nor is there any reason why these two modes of poetic faculty may not issue in successive perfect works, examples of which, according to what are now considered the exigencies of art, we have hitherto possessed in distinct individuals only. A mere running in of the one faculty upon the other is, of course, the ordinary circumstance" (*ES*, 285). The usual combination of objective and subjective faculties is, in Browning's view, a "mere running in," a dilution of both. In describing the ordinary attempt at unifying poetic faculties, Browning criticizes those in whom the original insights of romanticism or subjectivity have become solipsism or for whom poetry is mere imitation of conventions rather than of life. For such poets, as for the "Homerides" of the subjective poet, the world subsists "wholly in the shadow of a reality." Not even the ideal poet, however, can synthesize the two faculties. Rather, they issue in "successive perfect works." If he can attain such successive perfections, the ideal poet displays in himself the historical alternation of the subjective and the objective.

Even the ideal poet, then, cannot at once reproduce external things for the common eye and internal things for the eye of God. He cannot speak with the tongues of men and angels too. He can scarcely be said to speak with the tongue of angels, for like the subjective poet the ideal poet cannot actually see as God sees—he may "partially" attain this ultimate view. Toward this "he struggles."

Browning suggests that despite their differences, the goal is the same for the ideal poet and for those poets who cannot combine both poetic modes. All worthy poets, and implicitly Browning himself, are involved in a process of poetry that is more progressive than a simply cyclical alternation of subjective and objective. The nature of art, Browning says, is such that the very sufficiency of objective poetry "shall require, at length, an exposition of its affinity to something higher,—when the positive yet conflicting facts shall again precipitate themselves under a harmonising law, and one more degree will be apparent for a poet to climb in that mighty ladder, of which, however cloud-involved and undefined may glimmer the top-most step, the world dares no longer doubt that its gradations ascend" (*ES,* 286). As they alternate with each other, subjective and objective poets are at least ascendant, if not transcendent. As Browning implies, ideal unity like ideal transcendence is yet only a goal.[54]

In *The Ring and the Book,* the figure of the poet ascending retains its hold on Browning's imagination, and the essential ambivalence toward the possibility of transcendence, the edge of skepticism toward the imaginative unification of the actual and the absolute, remains. Though, as Kay Austen suggests, he may be criticizing a complacent audience in the first book of *The Ring and the Book,* Browning is also ruefully admitting that he is the butt of his own joke:[55]

> Shall not my friends go feast again on sward,
> Though cognizant of country in the clouds
> Higher than wistful eagle's horny eye
> Ever unclosed for, 'mid ancestral crags,
> When morning broke and Spring was back once
>   more,
> And he died, heaven, save by his heart, unreached?
> Yet heaven my fancy lifts to, ladder-like,—
> As Jack reached, holpen of his beanstalk rungs!
>   (*RB,* 1.1332-39)

Even as early as *Sordello* a self-consciousness about the poet's task issues in self-mockery. Like the comic hero before him, the narrator of *Sordello* commences a Quixotic attempt:

> for as the friendless-people's friend
> Spied from his hill-top once, despite the din
> And dust of multitudes, Pentapolin
> Named o' the Naked Arm, I single out
> Sordello
>   (*Sord.,* 1.4-8)

Jack and the Beanstalk and Don Quixote stand as Browning's self-conscious reminders of the folly possible in aspiration. In these comparisons we meet an ultimate seriousness tinged with skepticism or, perhaps, graced with a saving humility.

THE POET IN METAPHOR

A similar ambivalence toward the poet's aspirations and his powers is manifest in the metaphors Browning chooses for the poet's role. Again, we see the dialectic of aspiration and limitation, and we sense the tension between the actual and the ideal. If we allow Browning's poems, particularly *Sordello, The Ring and the Book,* and "A Death in the Desert," to provide a context for each other, three dominant and connected metaphorical patterns come into view. Browning defines the poet's relationship to the prophet in a number of biblical metaphors and allusions; he describes the power of the poet in terms of sparks and wicks; and he firmly ties the poet's vision to the actual in metaphors taken from optics.

Browning frequently develops his view of the poet's work through biblical allusion and through extended metaphors rooted in a biblical context. Despite his attraction to the image of the poet as prophet, Browning can no more espouse prophetic poetry than he can wholeheartedly praise purely subjective poetry in the "Essay on Shelley." The poet's possible connection to the prophet is explored in a literal way in "Pauline" and *Paracelsus* and in a figurative way in the later poems.

In "Pauline" the "sun treader" Shelley is explicitly god-like; the poet of "Pauline" has stood with him "as on a throne / With all thy dim creations gathered round" ("Pauline," 163–64). The poet of Pauline can only partially share these powers. The sun treader has gone, and the speaker dreams, not of emulating him, but of returning to England from his seclusion. The poet at once rejects and invokes the sun treader. Though the poet suggests he is dying, he also asserts, "I shall be priest and lover as of old."[56] In the 1888 revision of "Pauline" Browning amended this line to read, "I shall be priest and prophet as of old." Whether

Browning intended to increase the euphony of the passage or to underscore the ambitions of Pauline's poet, it is impossible to say. It is clear, however, that "Pauline" promises little success to such priestly or prophetic ambitions.

Paracelsus, too, is explicitly concerned with poetic and prophetic ambitions. The sage Paracelsus and the poet Aprile have mistaken the way to truth by seeking exclusively either knowledge or love. As Aprile dies he recognizes his own failure and sees for the first time that "God is the perfect poet, / Who in his person acts his own creations" (*Paracelsus,* 2.648–49). Just as in "Cleon" God is the perfect historian, so here he is also the perfect poet for whom creation is the bodying forth of life itself. Obviously, both Paracelsus and Aprile fall short of God's perfection; and ironically Paracelsus' failure is that he strives for immediate godlike power without having enough love and patience to bear with his fellow's dim "struggles for truth" and "poorest fallacies" (*Paracelsus,* 5.878). In "Pauline" and still more explicitly in *Paracelsus,* Browning is already uncomfortable with the heterocosmic analogy for the creation of art.[57] As he develops his own poetics, he modifies the proposition that God is to the world as the poet is to the poem; his poetics emphasizes equally the artist's powers and limitations.

In *Sordello* we first see the specifically biblical context in which Browning develops his metaphors for the poet. Allusions to Revelation and to St. John are particularly important as Browning defines the possibilities and limitations of the poet's role. In Book 1, Browning likens the poetry of Dante and his forerunner Sordello to "the sea whose fire was mixt with glass / In John's transcendent vision" (*Sord.,* 1.364–65). The allusion is to Rev. 15:2: "And I saw as it were a sea of glass mingled with fire; and them that had gotten the victory over the beast, and over his image, and over his mark, and over the number of his name, stand on the sea of glass, having the harps of God." The narrator proposes to separate the glass from the fire, to "disentwine" the contribution of Sordello from that of Dante, and the narrator is challenged by the poets (Dante, at least) "having the harps of God." For himself, he is properly modest, declaring, "I would do this! If I should falter now!" (1.371). In this passage Dante clearly has a divinely inspired role, for he is the "plucker of amaranths grown beneath God's eye" (1.371). Sordello, the argentine, is less clearly in touch with the absolute. The poet-speaker may be taken as a further declension from divinity.[58]

In Book 2, Sordello's own position is clarified by another explicit allusion to Revelation. Sordello has failed: the man and the bard have split because the man has sacrificed art for interest, fame, and popularity and because the bard has failed in pursuing the "ideal of song" (2.595, headnote). Finally the narrator characterizes this failure by alluding to the vanished ideal:

> But the complete Sordello, Man and Bard,
> John's cloud-girt angel, this foot on the land,
> That on the sea, with, open in his hand,
> A bitter-sweeting of a book—was gone.
> (*Sord.*, 2.690–93)

In Book 2, Sordello has fallen short of the prophetic role. Unlike Sordello, when John saw the cloud-girt angel, he was told to eat the book and to "prophesy again before many peoples, and nations, and tongues, and kings" (Rev. 10:11).

The image of duality unified, of heaven, land, and sea merged in prophetic vision, appears again at the end of *Sordello*. In Book 6, the poet is again connected to the prophet of revelation, and again with significant modification. Sordello has not become a prophet before nations, tongues, and kings, though he has tried to plead the Guelph cause with Salinguerra. He has scarcely even become the poet his early aspirations had promised. Ultimately, though at the point of death, Sordello comes to understand that "the soul's no whit / Beyond the body's purpose under it" (6.563–64).[59] Just as John's angel has one foot on the earth and one on the sea, so here heaven and sea and earth (soul and body) mirror each other and move in harmony:

> Like yonder breadth of watery heaven, a bay,
> And that sky-space of water, ray for ray
> And star for star, one richness where they mixed
> As this and that wing of an angel, fixed,
> Tumultuary splendours folded in
> To die.
>
> (*Sord.*, 6.565–70)[60]

Such harmonious visions, in Sordello's experiences, are glimpses of an ideal that touch the world and depart. Sordello is not quite John or John's angel either.

In fact, Browning most explicitly connects Sordello to John in the prophet's most human moment. In Book 3, the narrator appears, not as a disembodied voice, but in his own person, and he compares Sordello to John himself. The poet-speaker cautions us that we do not yet know Sordello as we should. He warns, "What seems a fiend perchance may prove a saint" (3.989). He illustrates his point with a parable in which John mistakes a portrait of himself for a devil (3.1012).[61] Implicitly, the narrator challenges us to recognize Sordello; but just as Sordello, like John, has difficulty recognizing himself, so we have difficulty discovering who Sordello really is.

It is almost as difficult in reading *Sordello* to say who the narrator really is or what powers he considers himself to have. In Book 3 the narrator is compared to angel, god, and archimage. "Nor slight too much my rhymes," the narrator admonishes us, for they "Dispart, disperse, lingering overhead / Like an escape of angels" (3.595–96). He compares himself to the archimage (Merlin?) who creates a "transcendental platan" for his lady's amusement, but he rejects his own metaphor and makes the transition to his actual seat on the Venice step by comparing himself to a god gliding from one world to another. As though in answer to this figuration of the poet as god of his creation, the narrator turns to the actual if ghost-like woman near him and immerses himself in the "murk lodgment of our building-time" (3.854). In *Sordello* the poet undoubtedly does have power over his own creation, but his poem is no escape from an actual world not of his own making. If he can prophesy he is like Moses "awkwardly" smiting the rock in the desert (3.826).

Browning's concerns with the poet and the prophet, the poem and truth are also taken up in the more clearly developed biblical metaphors of "A Death in the Desert" and *The Ring and the Book*. Motivating these metaphors is a defense of fiction in a world of fact and, especially in *The Ring and the Book*, a defense of poetry as a means of breathing life into history. In *The Ring and the Book*, Browning uses the prophet Elisha to explain the poet's function and his relation to divine truth; in "A Death in the Desert," the apostle John presents his own work in terms of the artist's.

In "A Death in the Desert," John articulates a poetic theory based on imitation, and he implies that a process analogous to mimesis is essential both to progress and to his prophecy. At the climax of his monologue, John compares the person seeking truth to the sculptor. The artist begins with clay, sees in it the "shape's idea," and begins to mold it, "changing what was wrought, / From falsehood like the truth to truth itself" ("A Death," 613–14). John praises the artist who is undaunted by inevitable imperfection, and he emphasizes the distinction between the artist and God. The sculptor, John says, should be commended,

> that he clapped his hands,
> And laughed 'It is my shape and lives again!'

> Enjoyed the falsehood, touched it on to truth,
> Until yourselves applaud the flesh indeed
> In what is still flesh-imitating clay.
> Right in you, right in him, such way be man's!
> God only makes the live shape at a jet.
>
> ("A Death," 617–23)

In John's view the artist touches truth, but his work remains "flesh-imitating clay." In "A Death in the Desert," the prophet's paradox is analogous to the artist's—he is a prophet of limitation.

Browning's most striking use of biblical allusion to create a metaphor for the poet's role comes in Book 1 of *The Ring and the Book*. John in "A Death in the Desert" likens himself to the artist; conversely in Book 1 of *The Ring and the Book*, the poet compares himself to the prophet Elisha. Again, Browning emphasizes imitation (or resuscitation) rather than creation *ex nihilo* or from his own subjectivity. On the basis of his own work, the poet generalizes about human limitation:

> For such man's feat is, in the due degree,
> —Mimic creation, galvanism for life,
> But still a glory portioned in the scale.
>
> (*RB*, 1.739–41)

As in *Sordello* the poet here compares himself to a "mage"—in this case to Faust—but again he rejects the comparison. Rather, he would compare himself to Elisha:

> Who bade them lay his staff on a corpse-face.
> There was no voice, no hearing: he went in
> Therefore, and shut the door upon them twain,
> And prayed unto the Lord; and he went up
> And lay upon the corpse, dead on the couch,
> And put his mouth upon its mouth, his eyes
> Upon its eyes, his hands upon its hands,
> And stretched him on the flesh; the flesh waxed warm:
> And he returned, walked to an fro the house,
> And went up, stretched him on the flesh again

And the eyes opened. 'T is a credible feat
With the right man and way.
                            Enough of me!
                            (RB, 1.754–67)

Browning's account of Elisha is virtually a paraphrase of the biblical story in 2 Kings 4. In choosing the story of Elisha, Browning simultaneously emphasizes the poet's extraordinary powers and his role as a resuscitator. More than a hint of divine empowerment is implicit in Browning's choice of biblical allusion. As if aware of the danger in overstating the poet's special abilities, however, the narrator quickly turns from meditating on his own powers and toward the "medicinable leaves" of the Old Yellow Book. Here, as in *Sordello* and "A Death in the Desert," the poet walks cautiously among the self-aggrandizing temptations of a prophetic poetics.

This emphasis on mimesis or 'resuscitation' also finds expression in a second group of metaphors which is important to Browning's view of the poet. The poet, and likewise the person who recognizes truth, serves as a spark to rekindle a burnt-out wick. Browning first develops this metaphor in "Pauline" (line 824) and in *Sordello*. Sordello himself is likened to a "half-burned taper" laid away at a marriage feast. In summarizing Sordello's career, moreover, the narrator chooses the metaphor of the spark to express a central problem in the poem. The narrator concludes that truth cannot easily be seized, but must be "casual truth" elicited in "mean sparks" through "chance blows." Such sparks of truth are "solitary" hints of "buried fire, which, rip earth's breast, would stream / Sky-ward!" (*Sord.*, 6.185–94).

In summarizing Sordello's career, moreover, the narrator chooses the metaphor of the spark to express a central problem in the poem. The narrator concludes that truth cannot easily be seized, but must be "casual truth" elicited in "mean sparks" through "chance blows." Such sparks of truth are "solitary" hints of "buried fire, which, rip earth's breast, would stream / Sky-ward!" (*Sord.*, 6.185–94).

> "A stick, once fire from end to end;
> Now, ashes save the tip that holds a spark!
> Yet, blow the spark, it turns back, spreads itself
> A little where the fire was: this I urge
> The soul that served me, tell it task once more
> What ashes of my brain have kept their shape,
> ("A Death," 105–10)

Like the artist molding clay, John himself is also a reluming spark of truth; his failing breath is the power which blows the spark to light.

In *The Ring and the Book,* Browning shapes this metaphor into a figure for the process of poetry. Again he emphasizes the gulf between the poet's power and the power of divinity. He declares in Book 1:

> Man's breath were vain to light a virgin wick,—
> Half-burned-out, all but quite-quenched wicks o' the lamp
> Stationed for temple service on this earth,
> These indeed let him breathe on and relume!
> (*RB*, 1.729–31)

A. K. Cook suggests that in calling the poet a temple watcher Browning refers to Samuel, who "ere the lamp of God went out in the temple," heard God's voice (1 Sam. 3:3).[62] Both here and in his allusion to Elisha, Browning points more to the poet's act of resuscitation than to his prophetic power for divine speech.

In expanding the figure of the poet as relumer, Browning establishes a motif that functions significantly in the remainder of *The Ring and the Book.* He explains in Book 1 that the poet of insight and outsight commissions forth half his soul which

> May chance upon some fragment of a whole,
> Rag of flesh, scrap of bone in dim disuse,

> Smoking flax that fed fire once: prompt therein
> I enter, spark-like, put old powers to play
> (RB, 1.175–78)

Calling the poet's vision a reluming spark, Browning subsequently uses this figure both for Caponsacchi and the Pope, the two characters in whose judgments we have implicit trust. Caponsacchi, for example, tells the court:

> Well then, I have a mind to speak, see cause
> To relume the quenched flax by this dreadful light,
> Burn out my soul in showing you the truth.
> (RB, 6.146–48)

> Let me, in heaven's name, use the very snuff
> O' the taper in one last spark shall show truth
> For a moment, show Pompilia who was true!
> (RB, 6.169–71)

The Pope, too, characterizes himself in terms of sparks and flaxen wicks at the beginning of his monologue. Two names, the Pope says, flash from mouth to mouth in Rome: "(Sparks, flint and steel strike)— Guido and the Pope" (RB, 10.290). We discover that the Pope is of course the true spark and Guido the ignis fatuus in the context of their own speeches and in the poet's introduction. This judgment is further strengthened when the Pope, like Caponsacchi and the poet-speaker, is seen as a relumed wick. The Pope meditates on his imminent death and characterizes himself as a frail man trying the truth of Guido:

> When a straw swallowed in his posset, stool
> Stumbled on where his path lies, any puff
> That's incident to such a smoking flax,
> Hurries the natural end and quenches him!
> (RB, 10.327–30)

The Pope becomes at once the smoking taper and the spark by which it is relumed. Later in his monologue, the Pope again calls himself a spark to explain a complex relationship to divinity. He is at the same time fallible and in touch with truth:

> Yet my poor spark had for its source, the sun;
> Thither I sent the great looks which compel
> Light from its fount: all that I do and am
> Comes from the truth, or seen or else surmised,
> Remembered or divined, as mere man may:
> I know just so, nor otherwise.
> (*RB*, 10.1280–85)

The Pope's spark, like the poet's, is a spark of knowledge—not an original Promethean fire to light a virgin wick, but limited light that has true light for its source.

In this linking by means of metaphor, Browning reinforces our positive assessment of the values of Caponsacchi and the Pope, and he emphasizes their special personal connections with the poet-speaker. Because of the connections in the spark / wick figure among the Pope, the priest, and the poet, we are led to feel that the poet's special gift, despite its limitations, is a connection to the absolute.

In the most complex metaphor Browning creates for the connection of finite and infinite, prophetic vision is reduced to optics. Browning's ambivalence toward the poet-as-seer becomes clear when he considers vision as interpretation of history, particularly in "A Death in the Desert" and *The Ring and the Book*.[63] In these two poems the seers, the Pope and John, are not actually poets, but as we have seen each is closely identified with the artist. Not surprisingly, then, Browning's metaphors imply that proper sight is equally difficult for the poet and for the man of God. In both poems, moreover, proper sight is defined as proper historical and spiritual point of view. Both John and the Pope share concerns that were also crucial to Carlyle and Ranke: they question the connection of the finite and the infinite, and they ponder how one finally establishes truth. Both the apostle and the Pope use the optical metaphor to explore the nature of "historic fact" or historic truth; and both are concerned with the way truth presents itself to men of limited faculties.[64] In short, Pope and apostle are interpreters of the seen.

The most famous of the Pope's optical metaphors is the "convex glass," a mirror for reducing an image:

> Man's mind, what is it but a convex glass
> Wherein are gathered all the scattered points
> Picked out of the immensity of sky,
> To reunite there, be our heaven for earth,
> Our known unknown, our God revealed to man?
> Existent somewhere, somehow, as a whole;
> Here as a whole proportioned to our sense,—
> There, (which is nowhere, speech must babble thus!)
> In the absolute immensity, the whole
> Appreciable solely by Thyself,—
> Here, by the little mind of man, reduced
> To littleness that suits his faculty
> (*RB*, 10.1306–18)

And the Pope continues, asking what does the form of truth matter so long as our intelligence is filled with it. Ultimately, the Pope declares truth may be mediate or immediate:

> —whether a fact,
> Absolute, abstract independent truth,
> Historic, not reduced to suit man's mind,—
> Or only truth reverberate, changed, made pass
> A spectrum into mind, the narrow eye,—
> . . . .
> What matter so intelligence be filled?
> (*RB*, 10.1383–87, 1394)

The spectrum of the mind's eye here reduces "abstract" "historic" truth of revelation to fit our capacity for comprehension.

Similarly, John in "A Death in the Desert" tells his disciples that (like all men who have not personally experienced revelation) they must see as through the wrong end of a telescope:

> —as I should use an optic glass
> I wondered at erewhile somewhere i' the world,
> It had been given a crafty smith to make;
> A tube, he turned on objects brought too close,
> Lying confusedly insubordinate
> For the unassisted eye to master once:
> Look through this tube, at distance now they lay,
> Become succinct, distinct, so small, so clear!
> Just thus, ye needs must apprehend what truth
> I see reduced to plain historic fact,
> Diminished into clearness, proved a point
> And far away: ye would withdraw your sense
> From out eternity, strain it upon time,
> Then stand before that fact, that Life and Death,
> Stay there at gaze, till it dispart, dispread,
> As though a star should open out, all sides,
> Grow the world on you, as it is my world.
> ("A Death," 227–43)

The Pope and John are clearly concerned with human capacity for knowledge; however, they seem to employ similar terms in somewhat contradictory ways. The Pope speaks of "abstract, independent truth / Historic"; John calls "plain historic fact" the optical *reduction* of truth. Taken together, then, these passages raise a variety of questions about what "historic" fact or truth is and how one knows it. John sees "historic" fact as a reduction, and yet in the process he describes—in the straining of sense upon time— the reduction becomes expansive. Finally the fact "disparts," "dispreads" and grows the world.

The double nature (eternal and temporal) of the historic fact is, of course, the paradox of incarnation, and therefore is a truth as "abstract" as that the Pope describes.[65] "Historic fact" and "historic truth" if properly known are ultimately the same, the central truth of incarnation. As Thomas Collins points out in discussing the Shelley essay and as we have seen with reference to nineteenth-century historiography, seeking the conjunction of finite and infinite is also significantly the artist's business.[66] John leaves no doubt that knowing "plain historic fact," though specifically a recognition of incarnation, is more generally a way of learning. Man, John says, lives "Set to instruct himself by his past self" ("A Death," 601). Like the artist who relumes the wick of history, the person who instructs himself through his past selves (or the pasts of others) learns most at the point of convergence in which plain historic fact and "abstract truth, historic" are identical. The perfect synthesis of the actual to the ideal comes only in incarnation; the artist in his imperfection and in his necessary and even affirmative embracing of the objects of "outsight" must make do with less.[67]

In the optical reduction of truth to fit human faculties, in sparks relighting old wicks, and in prophets turned resuscitators or mimetic poets, Browning explains metaphorically the limitations and possibilities of art. The possibilities, of course, remain significant. Loucks and Altick conclude, in fact, that Browning as artist "emulates the Pope and St. John by employing his superior gift of imagination to do what he is persuaded all men should do according to their capacity. . . . it is incumbent upon men to look behind appearances and contested motives; to find the symbolic, transcendental meaning behind deeds" (L and A, 361). This prophetic role retains a powerful force in Browning's imagination even though he may have to relinquish a claim to unmediated truth; similarly the poet remains an important presence in the longer poems, though like the objective historian, he may claim to have disappeared. The difficulty of knowing truth, absolute or historical, is further reflected in the functions of the poet-personae of "Pauline," *Sordello*, and *The Ring and the Book*.

POET AS PRESENTER

To become meaningful, objects for our "outer sight" must be rendered and interpreted. The poet's office, accordingly, is a complex one. In the historical monologues, as we shall see, the poet guides our judgment indirectly; in most cases he remains an implied author.[68] In "Pauline" and in the longer poems *Sordello* and *The Ring and the Book,* however, we find fully developed poet-personae who take on a number of roles, ranging from the commentator to the self-effacing narrator. The personae of *Sordello* and *The Ring and the Book* function at once as dramatic presenters, commentators, and interpreters of history. Their personal involvement in the poems' actions reinforces the connections between individual values and social and historical circumstances, institutions, or mores.[69] In these personae Browning provides interpreters of events; the more obvious technique of asides and parenthetical commentary and the subtler art of juxtaposition provide interpretations of events.

In some ways a simple developmental argument seems adequate to describe Browning's uses of poet-personae; one can with fair accuracy see Browning's development of poet-speakers as a shift from subjective to objective personae.[70] Certainly the poet-persona of *The Ring and the Book* differs sharply from the speaker of "Pauline" who hopes for rejuvenation as "priest and lover." Even the speaker of *Sordello* seems more "objective" than Pauline's poet: he would like to "body forth" his story with himself "kept out of view" (*Sord.,* 1.15). But despite his intentions, the material of *Sordello* resists pure dramatization, and the poet-commentator remains. Nevertheless, to see this series of poet-speakers as progressing from subjectivity to objectivity is to ignore the extent to which "Pauline" and *Sordello* criticize solipsistic subjectivity and to minimize the personal interpretations of historical action by the later personae. Moreover, if one simply categorizes the speakers of Browning's long poems as subjective or objective, one risks the same confusions Browning himself encountered writing the "Essay on Shelley."[71] Though Browning is obviously much concerned with individual subjectivity in "Pauline," we are more distant from and more judgmental of the poet-speaker in "Pauline" than in *Sordello* or *The Ring and the Book*. Reading "Pauline" suggests a reversal of the common view that Pauline's poet is closer to Robert Browning than is the narrator of *The Ring and the Book*.

In "Pauline," Browning follows Shelley's lead in *Alastor* by criticizing the radical isolation of solitude, and, as John Maynard points out, he may be playing with the stance of the Byronic poet as well. Though Pauline's poet may be a Shelleyan hero with a touch of Byronic guilt, he is not unequivocally identifiable with the poet himself. Even in creating a quasi-heroic speaker who goes into the dark to "fight giants," Browning is incapable of isolating him as thoroughly as Shelley does the hero of *Alastor*. Always, however shadowy, there are both Pauline and the prospect of returning to the world. We must set the speaker's isolation against the normative power of community. Maynard, like Philip Drew, sees Pauline herself as affording a kind of "realism" in the poem.[72] Browning's interpolation of Pauline's long note on the speaker's "examen de son âme" at line 811 provides us with the sole external vantage point for judging him.

"Pauline" also contains internal clues that lead us to feel a division between the poet-speaker and Robert Browning. Following Pauline's note, the speaker proclaims to her, "I am thine forever." He then describes her:

> —a Pauline from heights above,
> Stooping beneath me, looking up—one look
> As I might kill her and be loved the more.

> So love me—me, Pauline and nought but me,
> Never leave loving! Words are wild and weak,
> Believe them not Pauline!
> ("Pauline," 900–905)

The speaker's description of Pauline in the third person and his morbid sense that he might "kill her and be loved the more" is a startling prefiguration of the demented killer in "Porphyria's Lover," which Browning wrote at most two years after publishing "Pauline" (*Handbook*, 113).[73] It is difficult in this wild, weak, and demented lover to find an uncritically treated representative of subjective poetry. More probably the speaker's "unintelligibility," as Pauline calls it, is in itself a criticism of isolation. But despite the powerful indications that we are to judge the speaker critically and to feel distanced from his frame of mind, our standpoint for viewing the speaker is not clearly established. The poem provides few clues as to the proper perspective for understanding the speaker.[74] The difficulties of "Pauline," consequently, arise not from the reader's being asked to sympathize with the poet-speaker's "subjectivity" but from the reader's difficulty in finding a stable perspective for regarding Pauline's poet.

In *Paracelsus* and *Sordello,* Browning is careful to situate the reader more precisely with respect to his characters and his narrator. In *Paracelsus* the division of the aspiring figure into two—Paracelsus and Aprile—is a dramatic device that, in some measure, allows each character to provide a perspective on the other. In addition, the otherwise uninteresting figure Festus stands with us and helps to form our perspective on the alchemist. Festus functions rather like the narrator of *Sordello:* his judgments serve as a pointing pole. At the same time, Festus is the hollow core at the center of the dramatic action; though he provides a perspective on the poet, his own motives and actions do not advance the action of the play. Browning evades this difficulty of dramatization in *Sordello*, and he clearly establishes our perspective toward both the poet-speaker and the troubadour. In *Sordello* and *The Ring and the Book*, the poet-speakers become indispensable as interpreters of events.

As a presenter the narrator of *Sordello* is ubiquitous. He mediates Sordello's story for the audience, conjuring up Verona in the beginning almost as a godlike creator:

> Lo, the past is hurled
> In twain: up-thrust, out-staggering on the world,
> Subsiding into shape, a darkness rears
> Its outline, kindles at the core, appears
> Verona.
>
> (*Sord.*, 1.73–76)

The narrator has just finished conjuring a troop of poet-ghosts, and he directly addresses them, his readers, and even his own character Sordello. In an intriguing reading of *Sordello*, Daniel Stempel characterizes the narrator as a diorama narrator or lecturer who mediates between us and the scene, action, and character.[75] This narrator's function is to fix our relationship to the poem and to insure our sympathy with his story. In seeking to establish this sympathy, Browning's persona sets us and himself in direct relation to the characters. In Book 1, for example, he exhorts the Ghibellines to face "Our" Azzo, "our Guelf Lion" (1.293). By the beginning of Book 3, narrator and reader have presumably taken such a proprietary interest in Sordello that the narrator refers to the troubadour's discarded garland as "our laurels." Not only does the narrator address his readers directly (1.89, 237, 443, 584, 604, etc.), but he also commiserates with his character. He calls him in Book 1, "My poor Sordello." Again, in Book 5, the narrator declares, "Ah, my Sordello, I this once befriend / And speak for you" (5.590–91).

Still more interestingly the narrator characterizes

himself as a dramatic presenter, specifically a puppeteer. The poet of such a subject as his must take a stand "Motley on back and pointing-pole in hand." Cowed by the distinguished audience he has summoned, he asks, "What heart / Have I to play my puppets, bear my part / Before these worthies?" (1.71–73). Curiously, however, Browning also presents a critique of puppeteering in Book 1. In turning from nature to the world of men, Sordello passes through the unsatisfactory stage in which he "Betakes himself to study hungrily / Just what the puppets his crude phantasy / Supposes notablest" (1.80–81). Though certainly Browning's narrator in *Sordello* is a more skillful manipulator than the young troubadour, we do sense in the puppeteer metaphor a clue to the poem's complexities. Browning's puppeteer-narrator is reminiscent of Thackeray's puppeteer in *Vanity Fair;* he will burst the bubbles of Sordello's pretensions and expose the failings in political machinations. But the narrator's transparent manipulations of his character and of his audience (readers) are not altogether compatible with the pathos at which he ultimately aims; resuscitation of the past mixes uncomfortably with self-conscious manipulation of the past.

In *The Ring and the Book,* the poet again appears as a presenter of drama, this time not as a puppeteer but as a tragedian. Curiously, the two speakers of *The Ring and the Book* who present action as puppetry are Tertium Quid and Guido. In his marvelous perversity, Tertium Quid recounts the murder story through the court's first decision and then prepares his audience for the denouement with this analogy:

> Is it settled so far? Settled or disturbed,
> Console yourselves: 't is like . . . an instance, now!
> You've seen the puppets, of Place Navona, play,—
> Punch and his mate,—how threats pass, blows are dealt,
> And a crisis comes: the crowd or clap or hiss

> Accordingly as disposed for man or wife—
> When down the actors duck awhile perdue,
> Donning what novel rag-and-feather trim
> Best suits the next adventure, new effect:
> And,—by the time the mob is on the move,
> With something like a judgment *pro* and *con*,—
> There's a whistle, up again the actors pop
> In t'other tatter with fresh-tinselled staves,
> To re-engage in one last worst fight more
> Shall show, what you thought tragedy was farce.
> Note that the climax and the crown of things
> Invariably is, the devil appears himself,
> Armed and accoutred, horns and hoofs and tail!
> (RB, 4.1272–89)

Tertium Quid the puppeteer cannot distinguish tragedy from farce or know a devilish action when he sees one—in excusing Guido he unwittingly presents us with a Guido-devil whom we can recognize as more threatening than any puppet. And Guido himself describes men as puppets. He would excuse himself by exposing all goodness as a facade thin as his own pretensions to honor. All seeming goodness, Guido says, can be reduced to interest; for unbelief may work the wires of mechanical men (5.608–10).

Unlike Guido or Tertium Quid, the poet-persona in *The Ring and the Book* is more like a tragic dramatist than a puppeteer. Though the speaker describes Caponsacchi as a tangled coil of wires attached to earth and heaven, this figure is far less deterministic than Guido's. The poet-speaker's emphasis is on a drama with greater significance than a puppetplay. In recounting his progress from reading to imagining the contents of the Old Yellow Book, the speaker says:

> The life in me abolished the death of things,
> Deep calling unto deep: as then and there
> Acted itself over again once more
> The tragic piece.
> (RB, 1.514–17)

As the poet prepares to list for us the voices we will soon hear, he commands, "Let this old woe step on the stage again!" (1.816). Although Browning does not exploit the stage metaphor with the same attention he lavishes on his ring analogy, it nevertheless makes fitting the Pope's confrontation with the shade of a real tragic dramatist, Euripides. Whereas the poet's persona represents, for us, the encounter of the modern man with the conditions of a past age, Euripides provides the opposite temporal pole as he views the impending spiritual crisis of Innocent's time from the complicated perspective that is both the re-creation and the analysis in hindsight of the spiritual conditions of his own "tenebrific" age.

The poet-persona and Euripides are not the only dramatic presenters in *The Ring and the Book,* for the Augustinian whose sermon provides the summary judgment on the actions likens the murder story to a private play in which the proscenium wall has been jerked away:

> And preferably ponder, ere ye judge,
> Each incident of this strange human play
> Privily acted on a theatre
> That seemed secure from every gaze but God's—
> Till of a sudden, earthquake laid wall low
> And let the world perceive wild work inside.
> And how, in petrifaction of surprise,
> The actors stood,—
>
> (*RB*, 12.540–47)

Here, as in the metaphors for the poet's knowledge, we see figurative connections between normative characters (Euripides and the Augustinian) and the poet-persona. The parallel between the persona and Euripides as dramatic presenters mitigates, I believe, the possibly disruptive effect of the speech by the dramatist's ghost. The parallel between the Augustinian and the poet, similarly, increases our sense that the friar's sermon is something of a peroration for the poet himself. In contrast to *Sordello* and its puppetry, *The Ring and the Book* is not diminished but deepened by these analogies between characters and the actors of the tragic stage.

Although the persona as presenter provides a metaphorical context for our understanding of an action, in fusing his "live soul" with the inert stuff of history he also directs our judgment through his commentary. In *Sordello*, of course, the narrator as commentator is even more important than in *The Ring and the Book*. As Stempel astutely notes, the narrator must "communicate not only his attitude toward his listener but his attitude toward the work he is shaping for that listener. His ultimate judgment of his work and its protagonist is, indeed, the final cause, the end toward which the entire poem moves."[76] In *Sordello* the commentator does step forth with chalk and pointing pole; even more than Pauline to her poet, he provides the counterweight to Sordello's virtually solipsistic interiority. The commentator is responsible for attempting the fusion Sordello himself cannot make between private consciousness and public necessities. The narrator, in fact, provides us with historical "background" which is—from Sordello's own point of view—no more than decoration; for the struggles of the Italian city-states only impinge on Sordello's consciousness late in the poem.[77] The narrator's sometimes explicit commentary keeps before our eyes the broad context of political and institutional struggle to which Sordello himself is largely blind. In Book 2, for example, we hear Sordello imagining himself being worshipped and addressing himself, "So, range, free soul!—who by self-consciousness, / 'The last drop of all beauty dost express—" (2.405–6). The narrator follows this speech immediately with an explicit comment on the dichotomy between Sordello's aspiration and his will to action:

> (Dear monarch, I beseech,
> Notice how lamentably wide a breach
> Is here: discovering this, discover too
> What our poor world has possibly to do
> With it!
>
> (*Sord.*, 2.415–19)

This passage, moreover, is but one instance of that ubiquitous mark of Browning's style—the parenthetical aside.

It would be difficult to find a hundred lines of *Sordello* without at least one parenthetical remark. The parenthesis in Browning's hands is a flexible pointing pole, serving variously to indicate shifts in time or place, to add detail, to direct the reader's attention, or to present the narrator's commentary. In this regard, at least, there is a stylistic equivalent to Robert Columbus and Charlotte Kemper's conclusion that the "formal structure of the poem becomes the Speaker's awareness of the complexities of the past, of the present, and of the mind, as he grasps at understanding."[78]

Even in Book 1, in which the exposition is more straightforward than usual, the narrator is liberal with his parenthetical commentary. He describes the political skirmishes in Ferrara and tells us, "(Yourselves may spell it yet in chronicles . . . " (1.189). Next, to introduce a simile, he admonishes us, "(Conceive)" and concludes this comparison by asking (without parentheses), "See you?" (1.237). Further, the narrator adds details (1.294, 301) and calls our attention to them (1.340); he telescopes time parenthetically: "(Tis autumn)"; "('Tis winter with its sullenest of storms)" (1.450, 453). He even provides the physical description of Sordello and of Palma parenthetically (1.751–56). These parentheses, like the narrator's other commentary, serve both as exposition and as guides to our understanding and judgment.

Despite the disappearance of the poet-persona

from the central monologues of *The Ring and the Book,* the poet-speaker still provides us with an essential commentary in the first and last books. He would establish with us the same familiar relationship that the narrator of *Sordello* seeks. He entreats us, instructs us, telling us to "(Mark the predestination!)" in his discovery of the book and to hold fast to his ring figure (1.139). The speaker has the job of clarifying the story for us and thereby of preparing us to assess it correctly. Consequently, his quotations from his source, his imagining of the story (1.452–829), and his preview of the speakers in their order prefigure for us the path to our own judgments. He has labored, he tells us with some irony (referring probably to *Sordello)* so that "whoso runs may read" (1.1373), and his beginning commentary is an effort to that end.[79]

In several respects, however, Browning's search for clarity is not simplification, but an increasing subtlety. By the time of *The Ring and the Book,* Browning has become a master of juxtaposition. As a result Book 12 contains less direct commentary than one might expect, even though the poet-persona reappears and though this is a logical place for an epilogue or comprehensive authorial opinion. In *The Ring and the Book,* especially in Book 12, the poet's self-characterization as a historian becomes essential. The poet is still the man who blows the unquenched spark of the ember into flame (12.829–30), but, more concretely, he is the one who leafs through the documents for us (12.287, 396 ff.), who touches the pages themselves (12.218). The commentary of Book 12, then, is largely oblique. It is commentary by juxtaposition. We see the letter of the Venetian visitor (which places the action on the stage of international politics); a letter from Arcangeli; a letter from his opponent, the prosecutor who has just turned his coat and begun prosecuting Pompilia; the Augustinian's sermon interpreted in the prosecutor's letter; and finally the "definitive verdict of the court" vindicating Pompilia. By the beginning of Book 12 we have no need of much explicit commentary and summary judgment; the Pope has already provided it. Instead, these juxtapositions call forth our evaluations of those speakers whom the Pope has not judged—the social creatures of Books 2–4 (represented in another guise by the Venetian gentleman) and the lawyers. What for the Pope in Book 10 is spiritual history is also reintegrated in Book 12 as social history.

By the time of *The Ring and the Book*, too, Browning is in full control of the effects of his parenthetical asides. As in *Sordello* the poet-persona does use the parenthetical comment as a pointing pole, but in *The Ring and the Book*, as in a number of shorter poems, Browning uses asides to the greatest advantage when they force us to judge a character out of his own mouth.[80] The narrator-commentator of *Sordello* gives place in *The Ring and the Book* to implicit comment by juxtaposition. We often reach our judgments of characters by recognizing the ironic contrast between their public rhetoric and their parenthetical comments.

Nowhere is this form of characterization more skillful than in the lawyers' monologues. Hyacinthus de Archangelis's monologue is a patchwork of his written Latin, his comments upon it, and his ruminations over the evening's coming dinner celebration. Arcangeli parenthetically congratulates and coaches himself (especially in 8.170–217), and as his speech nears its culmination so do his parenthetical allusions to his dinner. He mentally gives Gigia a recipe for liver (8.534–41) and progresses to melon and lamb fry until he reaches "the juicier breast of argument" and finally lands his fish of a speech. Arcangeli's opponent, too, is exposed in his own parentheses. He congratulates himself. He likens Pietro's family to the Holy Family, compliments himself on the travesty (9.50), and finally finds it inadequate, "(I must let the portrait go . . .)" (9.170). More tellingly, Bottinius systematically gives

Pompilia's case away for the sake of argument and relegates the truth of the action to parentheses. He admits only parenthetically that Guido "never slept a wink" on the night of Pompilia's escape (9.636) and that Caponsacchi never left his "relegation-place" (9.1245, 1268). The sum of the characters' own self-interruptions provides a commentary by juxtaposition that makes unnecessary the intrusive narrator of *Sordello.*

Just as in his explicit characterization of the poet Browning describes a creature who is something of a prophet, yet very much a man, so too Browning's poet-personae function both as discoverers of truth in documents and actions, and as limited interpreters who must struggle with the limitations of their sources. The series of metaphorical connections between the narrator and Sordello or between the poet-speaker and various figures in *The Ring and the Book* reveal a significance of past events that is necessarily personal for the poet. It is as if Browning, like his subjective poet, "digs where he stands," and yet he finds, not the primal elements of humanity as he himself embodies them, but these elements embodied in an obscure troubadour or a seventeenth-century Roman murder case. Patricia Ball describes this process as one of "self-commentary" in *The Ring and the Book:*

> Browning shows here on a large scale, as he does countless times on a small, that his vitalizing inspiration is a grasp of relativity: first, in seeing that the truth of each set of circumstances depends on the individuals who live in and react to these circumstances, and, further, in recognizing that creative use of this insight must involve the poet with the poem, so that it incorporates the perceiving creator as an element in its make-up.[81]

In *Sordello,* likewise, the parallels between the narrator and the troubadour are quite explicit. Ronald Bush, in fact, draws a three-way connection among

Robert Browning, his "caricature" the narrator, and Sordello.[82] Just as Sordello, by Book 3, comes to recognize the importance of directing his attention to the needs of his fellow men, so the narrator "baulked" too in his poetry receives his inspiration, his will to proceed, from encountering the mixed humanity of the Venetian market. The connection is even more clearly drawn in Book 5. In his speech to Salinguerra, Sordello calls himself a presenter of "Life's elemental masque" who marshalls his men and women and then unveils the "last of mysteries," casts "external things away." At this point the narrator interrupts self-consciously to remark the parallel and to exclaim, "Why, he writes *Sordello!*" (5.619). Although these parallels between the narrator and the troubadour to some extent deepen our understanding of Sordello's difficulties, we do not have the same sense we have in *The Ring and the Book* that the poet is establishing for us as well as for himself the meaning in past circumstances. These very parallels, instead of deepening our understanding of historical conditions, have an ahistorical effect. The parallel between past and present seems forced—not from a lack of historical information or because it *is* a parallel—but because Sordello himself is too much essence and not enough concretely realized man.[83] In *Sordello* we have only what Browning's John would call the "shape's idea"—the clay of history has not been formed into an individual historical gesture.

Unlike the parallels between the poet-speaker and various characters in *Sordello*, these parallels in *The Ring and the Book* help to establish the proper relation of the present and the past. Browning draws analogies, both metaphorical and narrative, between the poet and Caponsacchi, changing the date of Caponsacchi's rescue of Pompilia to coincide with St. George's day and thus identifying himself with his "knight." As DeVane has noted, Browning repeatedly identifies his marriage to Elizabeth Barrett with Perseus's rescue of

Andromeda and the later myth that assimilates Perseus to St. George.[84] For readers aware of this parallel, the "lyric love" invoked in Book 1 becomes perhaps a fitting muse rather than a merely personal intrusion.

I have already examined the metaphorical connections between the poet, Caponsacchi, and the Pope. Many readers of *The Ring and the Book* have in addition pointed to the close resemblance between the doctrine of imperfection the Pope preaches and the poet's sketch in the first book of man's limited capacity for knowledge. This resemblance between the poet and the pontiff has led to what is perhaps the most serious criticism of Browning's achievement as a poet of history: the charge that the Pope's philosophy is an anachronism, an unwonted intrusion of Browning's own views. After all, critics argue, the Pope's views on infallibility, his tolerance for the Molinists, his belief in the positive use of an age of doubt seem scarcely credible in a pontiff at the turn of seventeenth century. John Killham, for example, believes that Browning's modest estimate of the poet's role is false modesty and that there "is something embarrassing in having the Pope in the poem shown to come right in his judgment of Guido by courtesy not of God but an intuition like that Browning himself claims."[85]

I think for several reasons, however, that these discordancies do not seriously weaken our belief in the Pope as a historical character or as an agent of judgment. First, the identification between the Pope and the poet (and the poet's characterization of Innocent in Book 1) immediately elicits our sympathy for the Pope and his views. That the Pope should be limited by his mortality and circumstances is, at least for a Protestant or skeptical audience, not an embarrassing assumption. Second, one can make a real and not merely anachronistic comparison between the Pope's problem of maintaining a balance of civil and ecclesiastical power and the infallibility debate that was still at issue while Browning was writing *The Ring and the Book*. The nature and extent of Papal fallibility and authority was the central issue in the controversy that concluded in the 1870 Dogma of Papal Infallibility; prior to 1870, of course, the dogma of infallibility was not official church doctrine. Third, as Isobel Armstrong notes, the Pope's monologue must be understood in the context of the poem as a whole, and the poem itself examines assumptions about intuitive insights.[86] Finally, Browning carefully balances the Pope's unorthodox theology with an array of historical detail.

Early in the Pope's monologue, Browning is careful to create an appropriately detailed historical context for his hero; by the end of the monologue the Pope has become both a historical man and an interpreter of history. The Pope begins by giving us a bit of his own biography (*RB,* 10.382) and letting us know just who Antonio Pignatelli is; he characterizes his opposition, the forces for "civilization and the emperor"; and he recounts, for purposes of contrast, one of the duties of his tenure—to settle the Dominican and Jesuit dispute over the proper Chinese translation of the name of God. We discover, too, in Book 12 that this same pontiff has censured Fénelon. More importantly, however, the Pope's anachronistic theology is balanced by his historical view. The Pope and the poet-persona are the two speakers who place the events they resuscitate in a proper context; and in this respect the identification between the Pope and the poet is not simply a coincidence. As I have noted, the Pope begins his monologue with an account of the broils of his medieval predecessors Formosus and Stephen. He also reiterates the dates of these histories and of the present case to strengthen our conception of the poem's chronology. In the Pope's monologue, moreover, the question of temporal perspective is explicitly raised by Euripides. The Pope then concludes by imagining the future and by identifying himself with the passing of time. He asks, "Do we not end, the century and I?" (10.1906). Of course, the Pope's history is a history of the spirit, and specifically a history of the vicissitudes of Christian belief, but just this ability to view events in relationship to time past and to come separates Innocent from Caponsacchi who is guided, for all his goodness, by "mere impulse" (10.1917). It is this reintegration in their historical context of events rescued from oblivion that makes the Pope's speech central to the vision of *The Ring and the Book*.

In the parallels between the Pope and the poet-persona of *The Ring and the Book*, Browning establishes for his readers a perspective from which to understand the rags and scraps of the past that he would resuscitate, for the Pope like the poet considers the questions of how we can know history and how we can interpret its meanings. The Pope himself is not a prophet or unambiguously a spiritual seer; his capacity for knowledge is firmly rooted in his historical circumstances. The Pope like the poet-persona is called on to be at once a man of insight and an interpreter of history. Browning calls on his readers in turn to create a coherent vision of the case's circumstances by placing the Pope's judgment in the wider context of Books 11 and 12. In order to understand this web of circumstance, we focus finally on the mix of aspiration and limitation that Browning defines as the necessary lot of the poet as historical being.

In *Sordello* and *The Ring and the Book,* we see Browning's poet-speakers become commentators or presenters of drama who are themselves situated concretely in history. Insofar as these speakers mediate historical circumstances for us and make conscious the complexities as well as the significance of historicity, Browning's works may be said to overcome perspective through perspective.[87] Insofar as they show the perceiver inseparable from the thing perceived, the interpreter inseparable from historical fact, these two poems describe their own undoing. *Sordello* and *The Ring and the Book* present themselves as problematic attempts at histories toward which the poet can only struggle.

Yet the gestures toward transcending perspective in *The Ring and the Book* remain an embarrassment for many twentieth-century readers. The poet-persona's identification with the Pope, the Pope's optimistic prediction that the coming age of doubt may be medicinal, even Pompilia's instinctive goodness send the skeptical reader scurrying for cover to the thickets of *Sordello*'s complexities. The spectacle of the poet himself regarding the spectacle of history in *Sordello*, Book 3, makes us more forcibly aware of how tenuous a claim to true history must always be than does the Rankean poet-historian who says he has disappeared in *The Ring and the Book*. For all his protestation, however, the disappearing poet, not the Pope, has the last word in *The Ring and the Book,* and he articulates again the double message of the "Essay on Shelley." The poet says plainly he would "save the soul"; yet it is salvation against the odds, for he concludes, "our human speech is naught, / Our human testimony false, our fame / And human estimation words and wind" (*RB,* 12.834–36).

CHAPTER FOUR
SIMULTANEITY IN BROWNING'S LONGER POEMS

THOMAS CARLYLE WRITING "ON HISTORY" IN 1830 DEscribes what, for him, is a central paradox:

> The most gifted man can observe, still more can record, only the *series* of his own impressions; his observation, therefore, to say nothing of its other imperfections, must be *successive*, while the things done were often *simultaneous;* the things done were not a series, but a group. It is not in acted, as it is in written History: actual events are nowise so simply related to each other as parent and offspring are; every single event is the offspring not of one, but of all other events, prior or contemporaneous, and will in its turn combine with all others to give birth to new: it is an ever-living, ever-working Chaos of Being, wherein shape after shape bodies itself forth from innumerable elements.... For as all Action is, by its nature, to be figured as extended in breadth and in depth, as well as in length; ... —so all Narrative is, by its nature, of only one dimension; only travels forward towards one, or towards successive points: Narrative is *linear;* Action is *solid.*[1]

The historian confronts the Chaos of Being and finds he has walked into perplexity; he is an inadequate observer and an inadequate reteller of history, for though in isolated impressions he may perceive simultaneity, when he observes and records his impressions he must reduce the simultaneous to the linear. Ten years later Browning's poet Sordello is caught in an analogous dilemma. The poet forges a new language and attempts by a process of empathetic identification to clothe an action and its actors in the "harness of his workmanship." But in spite of his powers of perception and identification, Sordello fails:

> Piece after piece that armor broke away,
> Because perceptions whole, like that he sought
> To clothe, reject so pure a work of thought
> As language: thought may take perception's place
> But hardly co-exist in any case,
> Being its mere presentment—of the whole
> By parts, the simultaneous and the sole
> By the successive and the many.
>
> (*Sord.*, 2.588–95)

Like Carlyle's historian Sordello finds a gap between perception and language, for language in Sordello's view is by nature successive. Sordello's predicament, of course, is not precisely the same as Carlyle's, and it is only by extension the dilemma of Browning himself. Nor can we specify exactly what kind of "whole" Sordello perceives. Clearly, though, Browning's poet and Carlyle's historian have examined actions that are best seen as complex convergences of numerous forces. As Carlyle plainly says, this view of action has consequences for the creation of narratives, particularly for historical narratives.

By taking Carlyle's historical paradox as a starting point for examining the notion of historical simultaneity, we can in some measure account for Browning's experimental narrative forms in *Sordello* and *The Ring and the Book*. I have already discussed briefly the implications of a contextualist view of history for narrative form and have suggested that Browning's contextualist historical poems differ from his poems of history as heroic adventure. Although the latter, such as "Hervé Riel," emphasize narrative succession, the contextualist poems emphasize pattern. I have noted, too, the similarities between Browning's work and that of Byron and, more especially, of Burckhardt; all three writers often seek a colligation among particulars that refuse to be absorbed into consequential plots. For Browning such particulars are the plenitude of the actual, and the poet in his allegiance to such plenitude must become both a presenter and a mediator of historical circumstances. He must interpret for us the complexities of historicity. Just as his poet-personae are a practical answer to the questions he asked about interpreting facts and to the questions he raised about the relationship between fact and fiction, so Browning's narrative strategies answer the question of how one is to connect and present the 'facts.' Although the narrator or persona provides connections among historical particulars in *Sordello* and *The Ring and the Book,* in these poems, as in historical narratives, an even more basic coherence is created in the structuring of the narrative itself.

Browning's favorite metaphor for historical experience—the web and the stream—already suggests the elements in tension in his experiments with narrative forms. The relationship between pattern and sequence, repetition and succession, though essential to any fictional or historical narrative, is itself, sometimes uncomfortably, at issue in *Sordello,* in *The Ring and the Book,* and in a number of Browning's longer monologues.[2] Browning's concern with the possibilities of narrative in poetry was complemented by his sense of the varying complexities of historical narrative. Thus his observation to Ruskin that prose is to poetry as "chronicling is to history," poetry requiring leaps and prose walking in a straight line, indicates Browning's willingness to differentiate between simple and complex forms of organization in histories. Browning's view of chronicling and history, moreover, supports Paul Ricoeur's claim that historical and fictional legends and chronicles are more "naive forms of narration" than narrative forms in which sequence and pattern are connected through a "spiral movement" bringing us back "to the almost motionless constellation of potentialities that the narrative retrieves."[3]

In examining narrative in Browning's historical poems, I shall argue that they often seek to realize the constellation of potentialities—for good and evil—inherent in the complexities of character. Such realization is achieved more often through completion of pattern than through succession of actions and consequences.

In *Sordello* and *The Ring and the Book,* Browning develops forms analogous to those of contextualist history; he rejects linear progression and creates instead circularity and repetition or patterns requiring us to consider at once all parts of a work and to place them in historical, social, or moral contexts. A brief examination of the possibilities of historical narration will establish a basis for a more detailed analysis of the ordering of events in these long poems. The analogy with historical narrative also provides a fresh perspective on Browning's experimentation with form in several of the longer dramatic monologues. As he develops the narrative structures of a contextualist historical poetry, Browning's "simultaneous" poetic forms depend upon such technical devices as quotation within quotation and ellipsis. The analysis of Browning's narrative technique has more general implications as well. It opens the question of Browning's modernism by suggesting a reconsideration of recent arguments about spatial form and the narrative and temporal natures of myth and history. If we suggest, as I do here, that Browning attempts a poetry of simultaneity, must we then conclude that his is "spatial form"? If we find that he often establishes circular patterns in his long poems, must we discover that Browning is centrally preoccupied with myth rather than with history?

THE MOMENT IN CONTEXT

Returning to Carlyle's concerns in "On History" we discover the seeds of various approaches to narrative. Despite his irony, for Carlyle the chaos of boundless, even infinite, interconnections is what the historian "will depict, and scientifically gauge, we may say, by threading it with single lines of a few ells in length!"[4] Although maintaining that no historical narrative is completely adequate to the action it purports to depict, Carlyle assumes the primacy and necessity of sequential narrative; history in a basic sense *is* narrative.[5] In Carlyle's description we see at least two possibilities: in the first the historian must follow a connecting thread and virtually abandon the attempt to represent the chaos of interconnection; by extension of Carlyle's notion of "solidity," a second alternative is the effort to capture simultaneous convergence in a history. In the first approach, Carlyle's stated choice if not always his method in practice, we see the historian creating a thread. In the second we see him patterning threads into a tapestry that has a depth and texture approaching solidity.[6] The distinction between these two approaches, though a simplification, provides a key to what Lukács calls "forms of historical consciousness."[7] To put it schematically, we can say that the historian's job is to "freeze" the past, to establish patterns of coherence from temporal flux and confusion. This coherence, at least by the nineteenth century, can take at least two basic shapes, which I call for convenience the sequential and, following the broader definition already suggested, the contextual. Such a dichotomy, of course, does not presume that all sequential or contextual histories are alike; it points only to a broad distinction between narrative strategies.[8]

The backbone of sequential history is narrative as we usually think of it, a "chainlet," in Carlyle's phrase. We feel familiar with the sequence of cause, of conflict and denouement, or of development in the most elementary of historical textbooks and in the most complicated of historical dialectics. We need not feel a catharsis in the tragic demise of Italian liberty, but in Sismondi's *History of the Italian Republics* we do indeed follow a thread—the rise, development, and demise of republican freedoms. Or, again, a connecting thread may be more strictly a chain of causes and effects, as in the dialectic of class consciousness in Trotsky's *History of the Russian Revolution*. In other cases a historical connecting thread need not be such a clearly specifiable sequence or a working out of explanatory causes to anticipated effects. In Book 2 of *Past and Present,* Carlyle focuses our interest and expectations on the unfolding of Abbot Samson's story; we follow Samson's fate as the thread connecting Carlyle's observations on social order and personal morality. In *Past and Present,* Carlyle would give his "chainlet" solidity too by confining Samson's story to Book 2 and building around it an edifice of social and moral commentary. Nonetheless, what such obviously different histories have in common is a method of sequential narration in which the sequence itself is found to cohere in a particular way so that we must follow the sequence to understand the history.

If the sequential history is a thread of a "few ells length," the contextual is a head-on collision with the Chaos of Being. Although in Hayden White's analytical scheme contextualism is a "mode of argument," the term as he uses it refers directly to problems of narrative organization. The historical contextualist, as I have already suggested, presupposes that events "can be explained by being set within the 'context' of their occurrence."[9] The contextualist makes connections by a process of colligation that can best account for patterns and interconnections, or states of affairs. Consequently, contextualist history represents "an ambiguous solution to the problem of constructing a narrative model of the *processes* discerned in the historical field." The contextualist history tends to be "synchronic."[10] It preserves something of the solid quality of the past that so baffles and challenges Carlyle.

This creation of pattern to explain a state of affairs is particularly striking in the contextualist history of Jacob Burckhardt. Beginning the decade that Browning's *The Ring and the Book* closed, Burckhardt's *Civilization of the Renaissance in Italy* offers a curious analogy in its narrative shape to Browning's complex narrative patterns. In assembling a variety of historical particulars, Burckhardt deemphasizes connections of chronological sequence in favor of presenting a group of particulars that together prove to be facets of a unified whole or cultural phenomenon. Even in his discussion of the Italian political situation, Burckhardt claims, following a brief chronological introduction, that "as states depending for existence on themselves alone, and scientifically organized with a view to this object, they [the Italian governments] present to us a higher interest than that of mere narrative."[11] Indeed, Burckhardt's discussion of the Venetian and Florentine republics and his description of the fall of the humanists provide only attenuated sequential narratives. As Maurice Mandelbaum has suggested in describing Burckhardt's 'interpretive' history, sequential and interpretive histories are the converse of each other. Whereas the sequential historian must provide an interpretive view of the state of affairs at the outset of a history, the interpretive (or contextualist) historian must supply "a sequential background that sets the stage for the patterns of life with which he is to be concerned."[12] The sequential history initially requires a context; the interpretive history initially requires a chronology. Interestingly, such chronological expositions are equally important in Book 1 of *The Ring and the Book* and in Burckhardt's introduction to the *Renaissance*.

Though after his introduction he deemphasizes sequential narrative, Burckhardt produces a followable history, a focused whole that begs to be characterized as tapestry or tableau. Calling Burckhardt's method a composition of equivalents, Karl Weintraub observes that for Burckhardt culture is a "composite and coordinate reality." According to Weintraub, in writing history Burckhardt found "practical limitations were set by the 'successive course of speech, narrating gradually, while things actually were a largely simultaneous great one.' The ideal of the image-like composition thus determined the historian's ordering process, but the use of words restricted him.... It demanded a vision which related the parts to the whole. How does the historian acquire this? Burckhardt emphasized the hard work of learning to see."[13]

Both in his history of the Renaissance and in the historiographical speculations of his later years, Burckhardt emphasized the historian's vision and described the course of history in terms of waves, mosaics, and threads. Like Browning in his use of similar metaphors, Burckhardt explored the limitations of historical knowledge and the importance of seeing any particular moment, especially the present moment, in a wider context. Burckhardt stressed the importance of "standpoints" for nineteenth-century historical thought for the same reasons that Browning experimented with points of view. "We have a standpoint for everything," Burckhardt argued, "and strive to do justice even to the things that seem to us most strange and terrible." We judge each individual "from his own premisses, in his own time."[14] This effort to judge individuals from their own premises complements an understanding that, despite our natural inclination to think otherwise, our own present is simply one wave or thread among the rest (*Force and Freedom,* 358). History is constant flux, and consequently "true skepticism has its indisputable place in a world where beginnings and end are all unknown" (*Force and Freedom,* 86). Only religion offers us any "amelioration," any refuge from the skepticism that comes of following the threads of history into the darkness of past and future (*Force and Freedom,* 86–87). The double task of history, as Burckhardt defined it, is very like the task of poetry as Browning defines it—seeing the infinite in the finite. One must remember, Burckhardt warned, that "the spiritual . . . has a historical aspect under which it appears as change" and that "every event has a spiritual aspect by which it partakes of immortality" (*Force and Freedom,* 83). The contextualist historian, like Burckhardt, follows the threads of history, connecting an event to the context of its time, judging the individual from his own premises, remaining skeptical about claims to complete historical knowledge, even as he attempts to understand the connectedness of the historical and the immortal. The complex task of the historian is, in Burckhardt's view, not reducible to a narrative emphasizing succession; rather it demands a vision of intricate interconnection.

Like Burckhardt, Browning, as I have noted, repeatedly resorts to the optical metaphor; poetry, like history, involves learning to see. And Browning's readers, like Burckhardt's, again and again characterize his long poems as attempts at "simultaneity." Michael Mason, for example, points to Browning's comment on the simultaneous in *Sordello* already quoted, and he analyzes the poem as a pursuit of the simultaneous in syntax, argument, and narrative structure.[15] Similarly, Loucks and Altick introduce their discussion of *The Ring and the Book* by commenting upon it as a structure that should be perceived as a simultaneous whole despite the sequential analysis they must use in describing it (L and A, 37–40). The characterization of Browning's poetry and Burckhardt's history in terms of simultaneity is not surprising; for their works share general assumptions about what is historically significant and about temporal succession. The congruence between Browning's contextualist historical poems and Burckhardt's *Kulturgeschichte* is based on a shared conviction that the important past is the uncertain realm of personal motivation, world view, and representative spirit. In the Renaissance Burckhardt, like Browning, finds his historical telescope's perfect range (or he learns to see in his own way by examining the Renaissance). For Burckhardt, the Renaissance defines itself as the age of the individual, as the advent of the modern Western complex individual. To distinguish the unique character of the Renaissance, Burckhardt describes the end of the group identity of the Middle Ages: "In Italy this veil first melted into air; an *objective* treatment and consideration of the State and of all the things of this world became possible. The *subjective* side at the same time asserted itself with corresponding emphasis; man became a spiritual *individual,* and recognized himself as such."[16] Culture becomes a manifestation of personal beliefs, motives, and habits of mind and often of the possibilities in art that these attitudes create. Burckhardt, the student of Ranke, shares with Browning (and with Pater) the historicist understanding of the uniqueness of past cultures. A possible corollary to this view is to see history not so much as process but as a series of moments. The consequences for the development of a narrative, as Weintraub points out, are problematic.

In a real sense for Browning as for Burckhardt, the historical world is a series of moments. Even when the moment is explicitly described as transitional, it is treated not as a consequence of or a prelude to other events but as a moment made all the more complex by its transitional nature.[17] Sordello, for example, comes at the first "efflorescence out of barbarism." Sordello's life coincides with a cultural transition, and if he could only seize the opportunity it offers, his actions would be crucial for shaping a new age in politics and art. Like Sordello, the Pope in *The Ring and the Book* stands on the edge of a new age. His death and Guido's will close the century and will make way for the new voices of "culture," skepticism, and enlightenment. St. John in "A Death in the Desert" also feels himself to be the physical sign of the transition to a new age, and even Prince Hohenstiel-Schwangau (Napoleon III), as we finally learn, is literally on the eve of the Franco-German war and the end of the Second Empire. In each of these poems and in others as well, the transitional moment is remarkable for the complexities of character it reveals and for the incongruities of belief or attitude it carries with it. We ask, not what happens next, but how or why the transitional moment is so complicated.

If even the transitional is seen as a complex of interrelations, what has become of Carlyle's insistence that the basis of history is narrative sequence? Are Burckhardt and Browning attempting to write nonnarrative narratives? At this point we should recall that neither in history nor in Browning's long historical poems is the contextualist view of history completely independent of the sequential. Analytic dichotomies after all generally *presume* the existence of pure states. Certainly *Sordello* and *The Ring and the Book* involve sequences of events. What I have called the contextualist position, nevertheless, has been criticized precisely because of the difficulties it presents for narrative. In developing his philosophy of history, Dilthey, as we have seen, views history as a "system of interactions," but with reference to Ranke he warns against "disregarding the interrelations between the causal and chronological movements of history."[18] Of Burckhardt, Dilthey was even more critical, for he felt that in Burckhardt's aesthetic approach to the past, history was dissolved into "atomic elements" which were then regrouped into fundamentally unhistorical categories.[19] Dilthey's observation on Burckhardt reveals also the congruence between Browning's historical assumptions and his narrative experiments, though Dilthey himself cautions that in literature, as opposed to history, "another kind of context prevails"—this being the connections in the completed work, a unity which "lifts the beginning and the end out of the causal chain [of history or the course of life] and links its parts into a whole."[20]

NARRATIVE EXPERIMENTS

In reading Browning's historical poems, then, we find connections between treatment of narrative and larger historical views, yet we must account for the "unity" and effectiveness of each not as history but as a poem. I have already characterized Browning's historical view as an emphasis on the moment, on context rather than sequence, and I have indicated affinity between a contextualist view and cultural history; it is logical then to find Browning experimenting with narrative in an effort to achieve the "simultaneous and the sole." The results of this experimentation are forms which are not the consequential plots we are familiar with in most novels and drama,[21] and yet these experiments are plotted in a way that a lyric is not. The lyric, nevertheless, is Browning's true strength, and his longer works are most interesting as they experiment with new forms and struggle to take shape in the hazy world between the lyric and the consequential narrative. Certainly the late narratives *The Inn Album* and *Fifine at the Fair* are predictably sequential narratives, but they do not engage us in the unraveling of their plots. Much earlier, the plot of the historical drama

Strafford utterly fails to achieve the kind of inevitability its subject requires. Even in the drama (or closet-drama), Browning's development of the consequential plot is less interesting than the descriptive or pattern plot of a dramatic poem like *Pippa Passes* in which incidents are not interdependent except as aspects of a complete description of Pippa's village. Both *Sordello* and *The Ring and the Book* may in one sense be seen as consequential plots: the unfolding of self-knowledge and the subsequent death of Sordello; the trial, conviction, and execution of Guido Franceschini. These descriptions, however, ignore the highly patterned nature of these poems. A look at the pattern of *Sordello* reveals a difficult palimpsest in which tableau is laid upon tableau and the whole is then, forcibly, implanted in a broader historical perspective. *The Ring and the Book,* in a different way, is also as much a patterned as a consequential narrative, for Guido's death concludes the "story" while the Pope's judgment and the accounts of the execution complete patterns of moral judgment and social description.

This is not the place for a detailed exploration of the complex relationships among length, narrative structure, and generic conventions. I shall suggest, however, that Browning's longer historical monologues stretch the dimensions of the lyric, and yet in them the poet pulls back from fully developing a narrative. The reader in consequence reaches uncomfortably for the appropriate conventional clues to guide his or her expectations. *The Ring and the Book* in this respect is even more problematic than the long monologues. Its novelistic aspects seemingly invite us to bring to it the expectations we bring to consequential plots; its poetic conventions establish its kinship with the epic tradition; and its patterning of monologues demands yet a third kind of reading. *The Ring and the Book,* it seems to me, remains even for modern readers a disconcerting poem, both in its sheer length and in its combination of conventions. *Sordello* is perhaps less disconcerting, for at least it brings us a single teller narrating a tale, and in important respects it draws upon the conventions of romantic narrative poems. In *Sordello*, nonetheless, ellipses and repetition combine to give us a complex sense of what it means to "hear Sordello's story told," so much so that many readers have questioned whether they have heard a "story" at all.[22]

The difficulty of *Sordello's* form is glimpsed in Ezra Pound's address to Robert Browning in the early version of "Three Cantos." Pound resorts to several descriptive terms in order to capture the complexity of Browning's history of a soul:

    And you had a background,
Watched "the soul," Sordello's soul,
And saw it lap up life, and swell and burst—
"Into the empyrean?"
So you worked out new form, the meditative,
Semi-dramatic, semi-epic story,
And we will say: What's left for me to do?[23]

In a more specific way, Michael Mason finds the key to *Sordello* in the idea of simultaneity, and he points to the poem's two-part arrangement as making possible a "more significant selection and juxtaposition of elements than serial narrative would permit."[24] As Mason notices, the first part of *Sordello* is the opening scene at Verona and the details explaining its importance; the second is the story of Sordello's new interest in political action.[25] Between them the poet appears *in propria persona*. When we begin to investigate this division and to examine, for example, how Browning develops the scene of Sordello's meeting with Palma at Verona, the poem quickly begins to seem circular. Indeed Browning himself calls the first half a circle when he interrupts his story in Book 3:

    For thus
I bring Sordello to the rapturous

> Exclaim at the crowd's cry, because one round
> Of life was quite accomplished.
>
> (*Sord.*, 3.561–64)

In the headnotes to this section Browning declares, "Thus then having completed a circle, the poet may pause and breathe, being really in the flesh at Venice." As the poet himself suggests, his procedure in *Sordello* is to make circles out of linear chronologies and to focus our attention on moments that in themselves are much like tableaux.

The first of these scenes is Sordello's meeting with Palma at Verona. Book 1, after a rhetorical flourish, begins, or tries to begin, with the poet's words, "Appears Verona." Then the poet digresses, describing his strategy, summoning and selecting his ghostly audience. At length, he tries again to begin and this time succeeds in bringing us to Verona as "the past is hurled in twain." What follows is a historical summary and an overhearing of Ghibelline and Guelf partisan views. Finally we are brought to Count Richard's palace where we must be reminded that "the same night wears" (1.231) before we meet our hero and his friend. At last, at line 328, we see Sordello, if we could know it is Sordello—Browning does not identify him for another twenty lines. Instead, two of the poem's three central characters are introduced anonymously, even mysteriously:

> Nor mutes nor masquers now;
> Nor any . . . does that one man sleep whose brow
> The dying lamp-flame sinks and rises o'er?
> What woman stood beside him?
>
> (*Sord.*, 1.327–30)

From the beginning we must confront Browning's indirection; we are presented pieces of a puzzle and must suspend them unconnected until the picture is finally completed in Book 3. For the moment, the significance of the scene, like Palma's identity, remains mysterious, literally a question. This initial scene quickly gives way to an address to Dante, and finally the poet launches into the midst of his matter and begins almost halfway through Book 1 the account of Sordello's early life that continues through Book 2. We begin, then, at Verona, circle back thirty years, and arrive again at Verona.

When Sordello himself appears on the scene in Book 3, the poet again exclaims, "Appears Verona" (3.261). At last the opening tableau is explained: "I' the palace, each by each, / Sordello sat and Palma" (3.273–74). Even the imagery is repeated, and we discover the meaning of the tableau in Sordello's new resolution to enter the political world:

> Though no affirmative disturbs the head,
> A dying lamp-flame sinks and rises o'er,
> Like the alighted planet Pollux wore
> Until, morn breaking, he resolves to be
> Gate-vein of this heart's blood of Lombardy
> (*Sord.*, 3.553–57)

This patterning of narrative, the clearest doubling back in *Sordello,* is worth following in such detail as but one example of circular patterning throughout the poem.

The principal action of *Sordello* occurs during three days in 1224. The scene at Verona takes place on the first day; on the second day come the journey to Ferrara and Sordello's first meeting with the Ghibelline leader (and his father) Taurello Salinguerra; the last day is the afternoon of the father-son recognition and of Sordello's death after he rejects the Ghibelline leadership. In addition to the moment of initial resolve at Verona, the recognition scene and Sordello's death are particularly important, and both scenes, like the initial tableau, involve careful, if confusing, narrative repetitions and variations.

The recognition of Taurello and Sordello comes at the climax of no fewer than four repetitions of the account of the Ghibellines' expulsion from Vicenza in 1194 when Taurello's son was thought to be killed.[26] We do not get the truth about Sordello's parentage until Palma's revelation of Adelaide's secret at the final meeting of Sordello and Salinguerra. In Book 2 we have heard the story of Sordello, Elcorte's son, being rescued; presumably this is the account Adelaide wished Sordello to believe. In Book 2 the true story of the Vicenza seige is almost recounted by Palma, but she thinks better of her impulse. Palma describes Adelaide's death and how the old woman told secrets:

> Secrets, more secrets, then—not, not the last—
> 'Mongst others, like a casual trick o' the past,
> How . . . ay, she told me, gathering up her face,
> All left of it, into one arch grimace
> To die with . . .
>
> *(Sord., 3.393-96)*

The poet will not disclose the significance of Palma's ellipsis. Our suspicions may, possibly, be aroused, but this omission, like the initial view of Sordello and Palma, can only be explained when the narrative finally circles back on itself. Our reconstruction of these events, however, is not the sort of detective work that allows one to follow the plot of a suspense story.[27] The recognition of father and son, after all, does not depend upon Palma's revelation, and her tale merely allows us to readjust our assessment of the relationship among important characters and political factions.

In a similar way we are given numerous accounts of the seige of Ferrara and its cause, Ecelin's withdrawal to Oliero and abdication of power. Browning does not develop these events as sequential narrative; instead, accounts of them appear over and over with some variation in detail. Again, the reader is virtually required to conceive the poem as a simultaneous whole. Detail is added to detail as Browning toys with history in the beginning of Book 1, in Book 2 (868), twice in Book 3 (239, 507), and in Book 4 (630). In

Book 6 the narrator steps in a last time to complete our picture of Taurello's service to Ecelin and his sons (633). These repetitions generally do little to further the major plot line. Like the long account of Salinguerra's past, they serve chiefly to provide a specific, if confusing, sense of the complexity of political action. The accounts of the background to the seige of Ferrara along with the conflicting references to the Vicenza episode are difficult to put together, and yet to begin to grasp the poem at all we must unravel at least some of these quarrels and intrigues. Again, the sequence of these events is blurred by variation and repetition; sequence is subordinated to historical situation developed by accretion.

Like the revelation of Sordello's lineage, the last major incident of the poem is also circular. At the end of Book 5 Browning anticipates himself. The conclusion of Book 5 is simultaneous with the events of Book 6. Again, the ellipsis of Book 5 can be completed only as the poem circles back on itself in Book 6 and the details of the two tableaux—Sordello's death and burial—are filled in. Book 5 concludes with Sordello's "own foot-stamp" and Taurello and Palma's investigation of his fate. Hearing Sordello's final gesture, Taurello is immediately affected, and his "spirit's flight sustained thus far, / Dropped at that very instant" (5.1008–9). At this point the poet telescopes time and gives us at once an indication of Sordello's death and a description of his burial. He turns to the caryatid at Goito who

> remains't
> Like some fresh martyr, eyes fixed—who can tell?
> As Heaven, now all's at end, did not so well,
> Spite of the faith and victory, to leave
> Its virgin quite to death in the lone eve.
> While the persisting hermit-bee . . . ha! wait
> No longer: these in compass, forward fate!
> (*Sord.*, 5.1020–26)

Book 6 backtracks to fill in the conflict we know has killed the troubadour and to describe Palma discovering Sordello's body. At this point we have returned to Goito's hermit bee and tomb. We return, also, to the conclusion of Ecelin's sons' doom, to the definition of the moment Sordello has missed. From Book 1 Dante again rises among a troop of ghosts, and, despite the persistence of a snatch of song, the circle of Sordello's fate is complete.

Browning develops the simultaneous narrative of *Sordello* by establishing the chief incidents of the principal action in a circular way; the set of tableaux he creates seems particularly appropriate for a protagonist whose fate is a failure to act. The repetitions of historical material, moreover, reinforce our impression that everything happens at once or at least must be understood at once. This effect is not simply a consequence of repetition; it also results from the way Browning's narrator establishes transitions. The poet-speaker frequently introduces historical material with what we might call the meanwhile-back-at-the-ranch formula. In Book 2, for example, we follow Sordello's degradation as a poet until the narrator finally steps in to reacquaint us with developments in the world Sordello ignores:

> Meanwhile the world rejoiced ('t is time explain)
> Because a sudden sickness set it free
> From Adelaide.
>
> <div align="right">(<i>Sord.</i>, 2.868–70)</div>

At the beginning of Book 4 the narrator brings us back from considering Sordello's plight and his own similar situation to the city that is by now the troubadour's goal. We do not follow Sordello into the city; rather, the narrator leads us along showing us "meanwhile" Ferrara's "rueful case." He allows us to overhear partisan complaints; and finally we realize, nearly two hundred lines later, that we have followed Sordello to see him "paused beside the plinth / Of the door-pillar," for all the world like another of Taurello's garden statues. Like these sketches of historical events and situations, the reiteration of historical material especially in the first three books is designed to make us see Sordello's private history as developing simultaneously with Salinguerra's and the Ghibellines' public history.

Parallel to these events is the poet-persona's own situation. The pattern of his awakening is, as we have seen, an analogue to Sordello's. We do not see the persona's self-awareness develop in the process of his telling Sordello's story; rather, the Venetian scene is a moment, complete in itself, that is set beside the scenes of Sordello's recognition and death.[28] Browning's radical interruptions of chronology in *Sordello* leave us with a set of scenes to which we return again and again, supplying more of their proper context each time. As Elizabeth Barrett said of *Sordello* when Browning was contemplating a revision, "I think that the principle of association is too subtly in movement throughout it— so that *while* you are going straight forward you go at the same time round & round, until the progress involved in the motion is lost sight of by the lookers on."[29] Though certainly the bare bones of a sequential presentation of history and of a consequential plot can be discerned in *Sordello,* in this early poem narrative fights not to be consequential narrative.

Despite Elizabeth Barrett's comments, Browning's revisions of *Sordello* in 1863 served not to make the forward motion of the narrative more visible but to explain or comment on the poem's circularity. The most significant revision of *Sordello* in 1863 was the addition of running heads (these were dropped in the 1888 edition). The obvious purpose of the running heads is increased clarity; however, they actually add a further dimension of patterning. They provide another temporal dimension to the obvious temporal complexities of *Sordello*. In the main text we have the time of Sordello's birth and childhood, the virtual present of a day in Sordello's life, and the poet's present in the poem as he sits on the palace step at Venice; the running heads add the time of commentary—the editorial moment. Frequently these running heads pose questions that the text presumably answers, or they rephrase the questions that the text itself raises. Additionally they may serve as ironic commentary on the poem's action. The heads to Book 5, for example, tell us that Sordello is revealed as Salinguerra's son and comment: "How the discovery moves Salinguerra, and Sordello the finally-determined—the Devil putting forth his potency: since Sordello, who began by rhyming, may, even from the depths of failure, yet spring to the summit of success, if he consent to oppress the world. Just this decided, as it now may be [*as it now may be* not in 1863 edition but in 1868], and we have done."[30] Browning's revisions here add not only the time of commentary but of ironic commentary. Sordello's success, we see, will not be the fulfillment of noble aspiration but the oppression of those he wished to help. Drawing our attention to such ironies, the running heads complicate rather than simplify the text.

Browning's revisions to the text of *Sordello* are as problematic as his running heads. Many minor emendations clear up ambiguities of phrasing or punctuation. The most significant revisions, however, are those that underscore the presence of the poet-persona. Revisions to Books 3 and 5 create an obvious parabasis. In Book 3 the poet particularizes his own situation, adding that he awakes "being at Venice"; and he shifts the emphasis from Sordello to himself in saying that Sordello's song will never be "more than dreamed." In the fifth book Browning adds the most remarkable interruption of all: Sordello discourses on the nature of poetry, and the poet breaks in to exclaim, "Why, he writes *Sordello!*" (5.619–20) These emendations along with the running heads shift the poem's emphasis toward the present of the poet-persona. The first version of *Sordello*, in contrast, emphasizes more strongly than later versions the burden of the past on Sordello. Book 6, for example, concluded in 1833 that Sordello's despair was most imminent when he was most aware of "greatness in the past." Later editions deemphasized the weight of the past and the inexorable character of Sordello's destiny.[31] The 1833 version of *Sordello*, with its burden of past poets and its sometimes ambiguous syntax and punctuation, entailed a pattern complex enough to baffle its early readers; later revisions introduced a further measure of narrative complexity, with the larger presence of the poet-persona suggesting the necessary limitations of Browning's own poem.

The circular motion of *Sordello* comes to rest in the questions of Book 6, and the narrative structure itself makes these questions more real, less abstract. *Sordello* is Browning's attempt to work out his own doctrine of the "man and the moment," the poet and the poet's circumstances. Browning asks what makes a poet like Sordello able or unable to seize the opportunities of his time. In Book 6 of *Sordello* we see that poetry and aspiration, like poetry and action, should be inseparable. But neither the poet-persona nor Sordello shows us how aspiration turns into poetry as action. In the sequence of questions—"But does our knowledge reach / No farther?" "Must life be ever just escaped, which should / Have been enjoyed?"—the poet-persona suggests that for Sordello aspiration is at odds with action and with the necessary limitations of earthly poetry. The narrator asks:

> Never may some soul see All
> —The Great Before and After, and the Small
> Now, yet be saved by this the simplest lore,
> And take the single course prescribed before
> As the king-bird with ages on his plumes
> Travels to die in his ancestral glooms?
>
> (*Sord.*, 6.579–84)

Here again we come up against the paradox of the limited prophet; true poets, by implication, see both the historical and spiritual before and after, and they act in the "Small Now."

The narrative circularity of *Sordello,* then, is the circularity of apocalypse deferred. The complete vision of time and eternity is not to be. The poem builds almost to a climax in Book 6, but the climax is deliberately undercut. The narrator asks the meaning of Sordello's end. Then instead of answering his own question he interrupts to "befriend / And speak for" the troubadour. Instead of showing us the poet triumphant in death, he reminds us of Sordello's lack of love for "all conceived by man." And he leaves unanswered his question, "What has Sordello found?" (6.603). The circularity of *Sordello* suggests that poetic empowerment may be all compacted in a moment, but unless the poetic or prophetic vision is also worked out through time it destroys the visionary. The poem *Sordello* does not seek to enact the visionary moment; it circles that possibility. The repetitions of narrative structure in *Sordello* explore the troubadour's entanglement in a complex web of circumstance. The circular motion of the narrative structure is thus both explanatory and deliberately baffling. We are not to see Sordello triumph or to find his failure caught up in the narrator's success. Whatever motion is possible comes only in the "proportioning" of the soul to the world of circumstance.

Though the poet seems to present the story of *The Ring and the Book* more straightforwardly than he does the story of *Sordello,* Browning's magnum opus is yet another experiment in pattern. Browning focuses not so much upon an unfolding story of murder, trial, and execution as upon the motives and social forces that underlie these actions. The exploration of motives is, in turn, not a structure of suspense and revelation (though individual monologues may move toward revelations); instead, to an important degree, Browning develops a character's motives and psychology by situating him or her in a social and political context. In the first book Browning invents a hypothetical conversation with Romans unsympathetic to his researches who thank him for the story "long and strong, / A pretty piece of narrative enough" (1.442–43). Just this "pretty" narrative is what Browning is at pains to make clear at the beginning of *The Ring and the Book*. As Loucks and Altick point out, Browning determinedly avoids what we usually call suspense (L and A, 76). His murder story may be taken to have two parts: the story of Pompilia's marriage, misery, rescue, and murder; and the narrative forming the "present" of *The Ring and the Book* in which Pompilia dies and Guido is tortured, tried, condemned by the Pope, and executed. Yet even this "present" narrative is not like the consequential plot of, say, *The Heart of Midlothian* in which we follow Jeanie Deans's dilemma and moral resolve, her painful journey and eventual reward. Guido's execution, rather, is a foregone conclusion. It is more accurate to see the story of his trial as a narrative thread for linking the monologues than it is to see each monologue as furthering the narrative the way a chapter in a traditional novel might. The resolution of the murder story, Guido's admission of guilt and his subsequent execution, is overshadowed by a complex patterning that requires its own sort of completion.

As we have seen, a contextualist view lends itself more easily to patterned than to consequential plotting. Indeed, the only three monologues of *The Ring and the Book* that function primarily in retelling the story are the early triad, Books 2–4. These accounts expand the presentation of the murder story we have met briefly in Book 1. They also in some measure prepare us for the trial proper which begins in Guido's first monologue. Half-Rome and The Other Half-Rome are characterized briefly but tellingly; in these early accounts, however, their personal biases are not important for themselves but only as they alter our judgments of the narratives these speakers present. Though we remark their individuality, such as it is, and their representativeness of public opinion, we find them less clearly delineated even in their speech than the principal actors in the story or even than that actor in his own drawing room comedy, Tertium Quid. Compare the beginning of The Other Half-Rome's monologue with Caponsacchi's first words:

> Another day that finds her living yet,
> Little Pompilia, with the patient brow
> And lamentable smile on those poor lips,
> And, under the white hospital-array,
> A flower-like body, to frighten at a bruise
> (RB, 3.1–5)

> Answer you, Sirs? Do I understand aright?
> Have patience? In this sudden smoke from hell,—
> So things disguise themselves,—I cannot see
> My own hand held thus broad before my face
> And know it again. Answer you? Then that means
> Tell over twice what I, the first time, told
> Six months ago:
> (RB, 6.1–7)

With Tertium Quid matters are more complicated than with Half-Rome and The Other Half-Rome, for to an important extent Browning characterizes this aristocratic partisan of Guido by his social situation. Tertium Quid's monologue does present yet another narrative of the murder, but more significantly it fills in the social picture by delineating the corrupt world of the aristocracy and clergy that Caponsacchi narrowly escapes.

No more than the recounting of the murder does the narrative of the trial provide an organizational principle through which we can account for the poem's unity. In his close analysis of *The Ring and the*

Book, Bruce McElderry insists that every book, except that of Pompilia, is used to build up interest in the murder trial so that it forms an "undisputed climax"[32]; such an interpretation, however, places a misleading emphasis upon suspense and the unfolding of consequential plot as the thread leading us through each book and from book to book. In fact, Browning's connections between books are of a different order. As Pompilia's monologue reminds us, we are concerned with understanding a number of personal views, biases, and moral positions and with the pattern of values they form. The Pope's monologue, furthermore, is the climax of a hierarchy of value rather than the climax of an action; the Pope is literally and thematically beyond the faulty and inadequate justice of the trial. Guido's second monologue, of course, is quite compelling, and his final climactic appeal certainly provides a dramatic resolution to his monologue; yet even this moment of intensity does not resolve conflicts among characters. In *The Ring and the Book,* the individual monologues do not primarily establish interaction of characters (though of course we see many connections), but rather they lead us to relate each character to a larger design. Consequently, however disproportionate we may find the length of the lawyers' monologues, we do not conceive them as an interruption in the revelation of personal motives any more than we feel Pompilia's monologue interrupts the narrative of the trial. As Pompilia's speech fills in an important part of a moral picture, so the social satire of the lawyers' monologues provides this picture's indispensable background.

The most useful discussions of the design of *The Ring and the Book* are those that interpret the poem through architectonic metaphors. Isobel Armstrong, for example, takes the poem as a "spiral of repetition" and discovery.[33] Along with two other models Loucks and Altick also describe the poem's structure as a spiral, this time an inward and elliptical spiral at the center of which is a "hard core of truth" (L and A, 79–80). These descriptions have in common with the preceding analysis of *Sordello* an emphasis on pattern rather than sequence. As Loucks and Altick remark, *The Ring and the Book*, "while it lacks the sort of unity that is supplied by a continuous development of plot and the presence of a central, controlling intelligence, has an adequately solid and symmetrical structure imposed on it by its philosophical preoccupations" (L and A, 75). According to Loucks and Altick's scheme, the poem consists of a ring (Books 1 and 12) enclosing three symmetrical triads and Guido's climactic monologue. The first two monologuists of each triad are speakers who "represent extreme opposites" in point of view and line of argument, yet who have some kind of affinity. These triads have an apex in the third speaker who has either social or moral authority over the first two (L and A, 37–81). Boyd Litzinger adds that these groups may also be seen as thesis-antithesis triads of rumor (2–4), testimony (5–7), and judgment (8–10).[34]

In all these views, *The Ring and the Book* is a symmetrical architectonic structure with one "extra" column, perhaps, on its right side in the form of Guido's final monologue. These approaches articulate a sense of the connections in Browning's massive poem. They suggest that in reading *The Ring and the Book* we fill in connections and relationships among details instead of following an action and working out a conflict towards a resolution. The Pope's and Guido's monologues do exhaust the possibilities for moral judgment and the knowledge it requires, and the last book knots the slender thread of narrative in Guido's execution. With the reiteration of historical and social context in the juxtapositions of Book 12 and with the reappearance of the poet-persona (with his imagistic connections to the Pope), the pattern of *The Ring and the Book* is complete. We experience its resolution by stepping back with the poet in Book 12 to consider the whole, but this resolution does not create the same kind of satisfaction we feel upon seeing Effie Deans retire to a convent and Jeanie and Reuben "live beloved and die lamented" in *The Heart of Midlothian.* In this respect *The Ring and the Book* is indeed simultaneous. We experience the murder and trial in their proper emotional, moral, and social contexts by creating for ourselves a completed pattern of relationships.

In both *The Ring and the Book* and *Sordello,* resolution is achieved through completion of pattern rather than through the peripetia and denouement common in consequential plots. In *Sordello* Browning works toward unity through repetition of various tableaux and through juxtaposition of Sordello's private history, the Ghibellines' public history, and the poet-persona's perspective. Narrative transitions and ellipses allow us to move from one element of the historical context to another and to return more than once to the same scene in order fully to understand its significance. In *The Ring and the Book,* the persona's role is less obvious than in *Sordello,* and yet again we are asked to complete a pattern and to consider the Roman murder story in several different contexts.

There is pattern, then, in *The Ring and the Book* as there is in *Sordello,* and despite the poet's greater effort to write that "whoso runs may read" even *The Ring and the Book* remains a disconcerting poem. Its affirmations—of good judgment, human love, and noble action—emerge in a context of skepticism, of the chaos of history that neither begins nor ends with the Pope or the poet-persona. The disconcerting power of this chaotic history is primarily due to Browning's narrative experiment in *The Ring and the Book.* As the historical situation moves closer to his own, from *Sordello,* to the Renaissance monologues, to the Pope's proleptical vision of Voltaire and his successors, the poet for all his belief in progress can only fitfully enact a progression in morality or in art. *The Ring and the Book* presents a succession of moments bounded on one side by Euripides' reading of the Pope's time and on the other by the readings first of Browning's contemporaries and then of their posterity. It is no wonder then that reviewers of Browning's "epic" often remarked his poem as particularly modern. Subsequent generations of readers have become accustomed to call *The Ring and the Book* Victorian and to turn to the still more circular and more resolutely experimental patterns of *Sordello* as the epitome of Browning's modernity.

PATTERN IN THE LONGER MONOLOGUES

The sense of resolution by completion of a pattern may well make us a bit uneasy if we allow the narrative connections to lead us to expect the kind of resolution common to a consequential plot. Equally unsettling is the pattern of some of the longer dramatic monologues in which Browning stretches and experiments with the possibilities of the lyric much as he experiments with narrative in *Sordello* and *The Ring and the Book*. In "Bishop Blougram's Apology," in several of the *Dramatis Personae* monologues, and in the late "Prince Hohenstiel-Schwangau," Browning makes of the poem a sort of Chinese box. The major speech is set into a frame that sometimes gives us a glimpse of attenuated narrative or places the speech in a larger pattern. Although the framing of the monologue may provide a definition of contour and a sense of closure, the longer monologues depend equally on interpolated dialogue for movement from emotion to emotion or from argument to argument.

The introduction and epilogue construction is more common to Browning's longer monologues than to the relatively short ones. One senses Browning reaching for this kind of symmetry in the absence of the more controlled intensity of a poem like "Andrea del Sarto" where dramatic situation and emotional tension are begun and resolved in the movement from "But do not let us quarrel any more" to "Go my love." In fact, the more prolix the monologuist, the more argumentative or casuistic he or she is, the more difficult it usually is for the poet to conclude. The problem of closure becomes increasingly more difficult as we move from "Andrea del Sarto" to "Fra Lippo Lippi" to "Bishop Blougram's Apology." "Andrea del Sarto" is a progressive revelation of Andrea's character, saving the worst (his behavior as a son) for last. At the same time it is a progression of questions and answers beginning with, "You turn your face, but does it bring your heart?" Most importantly, the poem carefully delineates one half of a colloquy as Andrea responds to Lucrezia's impatient presence: the poem amply fulfills the painter's promise that "all shall happen" as Lucrezia wishes.[35] "Fra Lippo Lippi" pushes further toward the boundaries of lyric than "Andrea del Sarto." Lippi's monologue is more prolix (fifty percent longer) and more argumentative than Andrea's, and his confrontation with the police is less important for the direction his monologue takes than is Andrea's quarrel with Lucrezia. The closure in "Lippi," consequently, depends more heavily on repetition and on an elaborate and subtle paralleling of situations than on the resolution of a colloquy. At the end of the poem, Lippi's projected painting echoes the monk's situation at the beginning of the poem. He will appear "mazed, motionless, and moonstruck" in his own painting and be "caught up with my monk's things by mistake," just as he appeared at the monologue's beginning caught, monk's robes and all, by the watchmen's torches. Beginning with the admiration of "sportive ladies," Lippi ends by describing "The Adoration of the Virgin."[36] Although Andrea del Sarto's monologue ends both with strong closure and a sense of finality, Lippi's conclusion is characteristically a "beginning," the coming dawn. Lippi's painting stands as a summation of his character and his art; his goodbye to the watchmen concludes his relationship with his interlocutors.

The endings of Browning's longer monologues are not always so satisfying as the endings of "Fra Lippo Lippi" or "Andrea del Sarto." The epilogues concluding monologues such as "Bishop Blougram's Apology" or "Mr. Sludge, the Medium" may give us a glimpse of action as the poem moves toward narration along the outer boundary of the lyric. The introduction and epilogue construction, however, often carries the burden of comment and interpretation that is provided indirectly and with more intensity in a monologue such as "Andrea del Sarto." Mr. Sludge's revelation of his real feelings about Horsefall at the end of his monologue, the introduction and conclusion to "Caliban Upon Setebos," and the epilogue to "Bishop Blougram" play upon the discrepancy between speech and thought; and in Blougram's and Sludge's cases the epilogue creates for us in miniature a story that extends an argument into an action. These attenuated narratives, nonetheless, are subordinated to pattern.

The epilogue to "Bishop Blougram," for instance, is in some measure balanced by the poem's introduction. The monologue begins with some initial throat clearing. The Bishop introduces himself in his ecclesiastical role by discussing Pugin's Gothic revival "stucco-twiddlings"; this said he turns to the conversation at hand, "Now, we'll talk. / So, you despise me, Mr. Gigadibs" (12–13). After all the Bishop's talk comes the poet's chance to clear his own throat; for at line 970 is a decisive break after which we find more than forty lines of commentary. An unidentified narrator gives us a god's eye view of Blougram's motives and a glimpse, too, of the bishop's effect. Gigadibs, we are told, has started precipitately for Australia. The ending of "Blougram," even more than the ending of "Mr. Sludge," may feel a bit abrupt, even forced, for the monologue does not prepare us for the weight of this final commentary. The lyric, strained to breaking by the bishop's prolix casuistry, becomes, for a moment, a narrative. In contrast to the complex closure of "Andrea del Sarto," depending on the recorded and symbolic passage of time and on the resolution of dramatic situation and emotional tension, the ending of "Bishop Blougram" relies upon the exhaustion of argument and the symmetry of tectonic patterning.

The element of formal pattern is also essential to "A Death in the Desert," but here the pattern is the quite complicated series of a speech contained in a narrative contained in what is probably a speech (or at least a commentary). This kind of Chinese-box effect looks back to the interpolated speeches in *Sordello* and forward to the spatial and temporal distortions of "Prince Hohenstiel-Schwangau." The pattern of "A Death in the Desert" is Browning's attempt to set up a kind of mock critical apparatus to a fictional hagiography—an attempt in poetry perhaps to beat Strauss at his own game. The poem begins with the speaker extracting from a chest and reading an old parchment written by one Pamphylax, an eye-witness to St. John's last days. Pamphylax narrates the story of John's death and gives us, at some length, John's last words. John's words are interrupted by the original speaker who provides us with Theotypas's "glossa" on man's soul. Finally Pamphylax narrates John's death; then the original narrator quotes a commentary on a commentary (presumably by Cerinthus whose doubts about Christ's divinity are omitted), and he concludes that " 't was Cerinthus that is lost." What we have, then, is a partly narrative monologue, or, from another perspective, a monologue interpolated in a narrative (interpolated in a "monologue").

The culmination of these experiments in pattern

is Browning's diffuse and confusing monologue, "Prince Hohenstiel-Schwangau." Though it lacks the earlier poem's effective imagery and historical particularity, "Hohenstiel-Schwangau" could be placed beside *Sordello* as a problematic experiment. Clyde de L. Ryals sees "Hohenstiel-Schwangau" as a formal experiment in which Browning tries to make of the dramatic monologue "a form which would present different points of view, not sequentially but almost simultaneously, within one poem." Ryals argues that this experimental urge rose after *The Ring and the Book* when Browning discovered himself still "at the mercy of a sequential structure."[37] This attempt at simultaneity, however, is also the effort of *Sordello* and even "A Death in the Desert" (and in a different way of *The Ring and the Book*). Against a background of nineteenth-century French and Italian history in "Hohenstiel-Schwangau" we see the Prince musing in the Residenz in Paris (we presume, having caught the allusion to Napoleon III), imagining himself in exile at a house in Leicester Square where he reconstructs his past life for a young woman of the streets. Within this inner box, he concocts what Ryals calls an "internal dialogue" between two allegorical figures, the "Head Servant" and "Sagacity." If this summary sounds confusing, the confusion is no less than Browning's intention. We must contend in "Hohenstiel-Schwangau" with the Chinese-box method of "A Death in the Desert," but here the fit of these interpolations is far from clear. And here we again meet the method of *Sordello*. We begin with a tableau that we cannot explain, and only at the end of the poem can we conclude that the opening scene is just the Prince's imagining. In the interstices between the layers of the Prince's monologue we seek the ironic juxtapositions by which to judge his statements, and our problem is compounded by the fact that the Prince is a self-conscious monologuist. For the sake of self-revelation, not to obtain a particular object like many Browning monologuists, the Prince constructs the whole elaborate situation. He soliloquizes and then comments upon the soliloquy; and just here is the trap. The Prince himself concludes that his previous words, all words, deflect the truth; but even in this reflection, we see him still caught in a "ghostly dialogue" that effectively hinders him from making a reasoned judgment and embarking on a course of action. He can only conclude, "Double or quits! The letter goes! Or stays?" (2155). We judge the Prince only when we can finally place these ghostly dialogues in their proper context. We must also place the whole monologue in its historical context. Even more than *Sordello* (which explains things, if obliquely), "Prince Hohenstiel-Schwangau" is historically allusive. In order to appreciate the ironies of the Prince's conclusion, we must penetrate his thin disguise and bring to bear on his moment a knowledge of Napoleon III and the Franco-German War. With this understanding we reconstruct the pattern of "Prince Hohenstiel-Schwangau" and explain for ourselves the position and significance of the opening scenes.

Browning's emphasis on a moment in context in these historical poems is largely achieved through various patternings that attenuate the linear aspects of narrative and emphasize circularity and repetition or juxtaposition. Given the nature of these patterns and the reduction of narrative tension in these works, the poet's problem is clearly one of maintaining his readers' engagement. This is particularly true in the long monologues. To develop a kind of movement within the monologues, Browning often turns to interpolated dialogue.[38] In *Sordello* and "Prince Hohenstiel-Schwangau," interpolated quotations form a pattern within a pattern, and what in *Sordello* is a confusion of voices becomes in the late poem an empty device.

Yet Browning's approach to the difficulties of the long monologue is often a productive one. In *The Ring and the Book,* Browning also uses dialogue within a monologue to explore a character's motives. Guido, for example, recounts a fairly complex dialogue with an imaginary "fellow" on the subject of worldly success (5.190). As a means of motivating the course of Guido's speech, moreover, Browning has the count ask the judges' questions for them (5.640). The speech within a speech method is even more prominent in the Pope's monologue as the pontiff calls up Euripides, presents various modern versions of earlier beliefs, and finally concludes in an internal debate with the spirit of culture (10.1663–1783, 1927–46, 2020–2101). Euripides' speech involves, once again, quotation within quotation. Unlike the progress of "Hohenstiel-Schwangau," however, the movement of Euripides' argument is clear:

> "The inward work and worth
> Of any mind, what other mind may judge
> Save God who only knows the thing He made,
> The veritable service He exacts?
> It is the outward product men appraise.
> Behold an engine hoists a tower aloft:
> 'I looked that it should move the mountain too!'
> Or else 'Had just a turret toppled down,
> Success enough!'—may say the Machinist
> Who knows what less or more result might be:
> But we, who see that done we cannot do,
> 'A feat beyond man's force,' we men must say.
> (*RB,* 10.1663–74)

The quotations within the monologues of *The Ring and the Book* lighten somewhat the heavy load of extended speech. They may serve as verbal projections of internal conflicts, as presentation of opposing points of view, or as a rhetorical strategy for keeping the poem moving by motivating shifts in argument or subjects of concern.

As these examples suggest, the longer the poem the more pressing the need for elaborate patterning and for such techniques as interpolated dialogue, ellipses, or formal introductions and epilogues. Though they evidence less formal patterning than the extended monologues, even the shorter historical monologues reveal Browning's contextual approach to history and his fascination with the impact of historical time on the individual consciousness. As I shall argue in chapter 5, Browning invites his readers to judge his monologuists according to the adequacy or inadequacy of their views of history. Beyond these particular historical judgments, we can see that the nature of temporality and of history is very often the subject of the monologuists' reflections. In the monologues time and history assume a thematic as well as a structural importance.

To a great extent, Browning's speakers are tested against the end of human time—against death or the more pernicious death-in-life of stasis. Though Browning's poetic forms emphasize pattern over sequential narration, thematically Browning is concerned with the necessity of change. Browning repeatedly opposes change to stale perfectionism and to inaction; human time and history are necessarily incomplete and imperfect, and the struggle with incompletion and imperfection involves both the historian-poet and the historical individual. In such poems as "The Statue and the Bust" and "A Grammarian's Funeral," Browning portrays deferred action as a form of death. To the narrative of "The Statue and the Bust" Browning appends a first-person epilogue pointing his moral: "the sin I impute to each frustrate ghost / Is—the unlit lamp and the ungirt loin" (246–47). "A Grammarian's Funeral" provides a more ambiguous version of stasis. Like the would-be lovers in "The Statue and the Bust," the grammarian has come to a full stop, "famous, calm, and dead." Unlike the would-be lovers, he has at least done something in his struggle with ancient learning. But the grammarian's attitudes toward temporality and toward his own mortality are problematic. The grammarian has declared, "'What's time. Leave Now for dogs and apes! / Man has Forever'" (83–84). In neglecting the "Now" and in striving to "image the whole," to image perfection first, the grammarian limits his appreciation of and participation in this world. Though the grammarian opposes earthly imperfection to heavenly perfection and lives, one might think, rightly in the expectation of heavenly completion, in fact the grammarian defers an active life in this world. Browning's ironies suggest that the grammarian's deferrals would make heaven itself nothing more than cold grammatical completion—missing the vital spark of poetry. The failures of the lovers in "The Statue and the Bust" and the ambiguous triumph of the grammarian suggest an important temporal dialectic in Browning's work.

Browning's experimentation with narrative and his fascination with history, his reflection and his monologuists' reflections on temporality evidence what Paul Ricoeur has identified as the most serious question such meditations can pose: the extent to which reflection on time and narrative "may aid us in thinking about eternity and death at the same time."[39] Not to recapitulate Ricoeur's complex argument, it is enough to suggest here that Browning's reflections on narrative and temporality engender in his poems a dialectic similar to that Ricoeur identifies as important in his hermeneutics of narrative. Ricoeur draws his meditation from (1) Augustine's (and the Christian tradition's) tendency to regard time with reference to an eternity where everything is simultaneously present and (2) from Heidegger's reflection on the ideal of "finitude sealed by being-towards-death."[40] Ricoeur's own reflections pose this dialectic as a way of questioning history and the work of art and as a way of reflecting on human understanding of temporality. Ricoeur's work suggests that the very act of telling a story, the form of narrative, is constituted in this tension between the singular finitude of death and the idea of a simultaneous eternity.

Browning's poems, I would argue, are most interesting as they are constituted in a similar dialectic, as they bring together his reflections on historicity and finitude with his Christian conviction of the reality of eternity as completion. Browning's monologuists often display a tension between the attempt to seize the present in the face of death and a reliance on completion in eternity. Those monologuists (and those poems) that have the most vitality are those for whom this dialectical tension is maintained.

Three monologues treating explicitly theological matters will serve to illustrate the importance of this historicity / eternity dialectic. In "Bishop Blougram's Apology," the monologuist has a good deal of vitality—the ability to speak at length—yet he is too firmly enmeshed in his finitude to maintain the dialectic of historicity and eternity. As I shall suggest in discussing Browning's ironic treatment of Blougram, the Bishop uses his place in history too easily as a justification for skepticism. Blougram's finitude and his historical moment may indeed promote skepticism, but Blougram's avowal of his own finitude and limitation approaches complacency. Blougram's famous simile of the "tire-room" reveals his nature as well as any part of his argument. He imagines himself an "unbelieving" Pope touched by God and likens the possibility to the actor who plays death only to meet "Death himself" in the "tire-room" afterward. That he chooses the metaphor of acting Death not only raises the question of how far Blougram is a sham; it also shows us how far he identifies his clerical office with finitude, with being (or acting) toward death rather than eternity.

Browning's Cleon is equally obsessed with finitude and even less equipped to reflect on eternity than Blougram. His response to such reflection is despair: "life's inadequate to joy, / As the soul sees joy." Cleon concludes that praise of the "natural man" is more reasonable than praise of "conscious" or self-conscious man; but ironically even the "natural" man who would seize pleasures in the face of death is forced to acknowledge "our bounded physical recipiency." Seizing the pleasures of the day is in Cleon's experience as inadequate as the attempt to imagine some unlimited "future state revealed to us by Zeus" (325). Both Cleon and Blougram are unable to experience the dialectic of historicity and eternity in a creative way: Blougram's complacency with finitude and Cleon's despair are equally damaging.

Browning's Karshish, in contrast, contemplates eternity with a native wonder scarcely tempered by his medical training. It is just because Karshish is actively torn between his physician's knowledge of human finitude and his ability to imagine Lazarus's experience of eternity that the physician is a far more appealing figure than Lazarus himself. Lazarus, indeed, seems almost inhuman, for he has experienced eternity in the midst of life. Browning suggests through Karshish's epistle that the most fully human reflection on time entails both the experiencing of finitude and the imagining of eternity. Significantly, for the poet, as for his monologuists, the rewarding result of this temporal dialectic is the compulsion to realize it as a story: Karshish declares, "An itch I had, a sting to write, a tang!" (67)

These reflections on finitude and eternity then are thematically central to many of Browning's monologues. As Browning places his historical characters in their particular historical contexts, we see that the finite time of history—and the individual finitude of death—requires continual struggle rather than complacency, activity rather than perfectionism, and the ability to imagine the completion of eternity.

The ways in which Browning's monologuists situate themselves in time provide keys to their characters as well as an explicit theme for their reflections. Their meditations on history, I shall suggest, furnish much material for Browning's irony. But even aside from their explicit reflections on history, Browning's characters may be understood by their characteristic approaches to time. In Fra Lippo Lippi's monologue, for example, everything has great immediacy. Fittingly, the monologue ends at dawn. Browning subtly reveals Lippi's nature in the painter's reiterated, "Now." Lippi's "Now" is a mere turn of phrase, but it indicates his thorough appreciation of the moment. Andrea del Sarto, in contrast, sacrifices the present for the future; he defers action and aspiration. Andrea's evening reflections are shot through with references to what might be done "tomorrow." In these and other monologues, the language of time, the temporal setting, and historical circumstances are specified as indications of, even determinants of, character. Not only does each monologuist reveal his character in his attitude toward and reflections on time, each monologuist speaking to an auditor or an ostensible auditor records himself in the public time of history. The very act of speaking or the sting to write would seem to impel the monologuist to try to think beyond the span of his own life and its end in his own death. He must consider himself, or at least the reader must consider him, in light of a history that goes beyond individual mortality and yet cannot compass the perfection of eternity. The dialectic of historical finitude and eternity is thus essential both to structure and to theme in Browning's historical poetry.

Structurally, the long monologues unite the thematic concerns of the shorter monologues with narrative devices that emphasize simultaneity. Browning's interpolated dialogues and quotations within quotations become part of the elaborate patterning of the longer monologues. Like the ellipses in *Sordello,* these quotations may re-create naturalistic dialogue, or they may contribute to a complex modification of chronology. In the longer monologues, Browning relies on symmetrical patterning of quotation or of introduction and epilogue to arrive at a balanced completed form. The Chinese boxes of "A Death in the Desert" exhibit in small the rejection of simple chronology that grounds the more difficult patterns of *Sordello* or *The Ring and the Book*. In these two long poems the poet comes face to face with the tension between the "successive" and the "simultaneous," between consequential plot and the lyric or image-like composition. In *Sordello* we begin to understand Browning's tableaux by colligation of particulars and by moving back and forth in time; we experience the completion of *The Ring and the Book* as a symmetrical pattern. Like the contextualist history, these works give us moments in patterned juxtaposition. They record the poet's struggle to find a formal equivalent for his contextual apprehension of history.

PATTERN, HISTORY, AND SPATIAL FORM

Browning's contextualist approach to narrative bears a striking resemblance to modern experiments with form, and the metaphors I have chosen to describe his poems parallel, in some respects, the critical language of "spatial form." This analysis of Browning's experiments with pattern suggests yet another view of spatial form, and, in turn, a reconsideration of spatial form will allow me in concluding to suggest a new way of understanding Browning's importance for modern poetry.

Two recent approaches to the question of spatial form are important bases for any discussion of simultaneity and repetition or of sequentiality and pattern in literature. In "Spatial Form in Modern Literature"

(1945), Joseph Frank initiated the critical discussion of spatial form as unique to modernism, and thus Frank's definition and recent reassertion of his position are relevant to a discussion that seeks to connect Browning's work to modern poetry.[41] More recently, W. J. T. Mitchell has taken a broader and more systematic view of spatiality in the arts. At least partially in response to Frank, Mitchell reminds us of what would otherwise be the commonplace conclusion that "spatial form is no casual metaphor but an essential feature of the interpretation and experience of literature."[42] He proposes a new or renewed critical project: the discrimination among different kinds of spatial forms in literature and their relationships to spatiality in other arts. As Mitchell observes, one cannot discriminate among such forms by falling back on a space-versus-time antithesis. Rather, he suggests that "continuity and sequentiality are spatial images based in the scheme of the unbroken line or surface; the experience of simultaneity or discontinuity is simply based in different kinds of spatial images from those involved in continuous, sequential experiences of time."[43]

I cannot attempt here the systematic discussion of spatiality that Mitchell advocates, but I have suggested that Browning is much concerned with the relationships between sequential and simultaneous spatial images. Such spatial images, of course, are equally important in histories and in fictions. Both in the shaping of his narratives and in the choice of images to describe those narratives, Browning makes use of the patterns and images common to contextualist histories. Browning's experiments with form, as I have suggested, arose out of the tension he and Carlyle articulated in a similar way—the tension between the successive and the simultaneous, the linear and the solid. Or as Carlyle put it, the threading of a "chainlet" through the "every-living, ever-working Chaos of Being." As we have seen, Browning attempts to capture the solidity and interconnectedness of history, metaphorically in the images his longer works propose of themselves, and formally in juxtaposition, repetition, ellipsis, interpolated dialogues, and symmetrical epilogues and conclusions. These images and these formal choices cause us to experience *Sordello* and *The Ring and the Book* as patterned rather than consequential plots.

To describe Browning's formal experiments it is important to distinguish among different types of patterns and to place Browning's work in the context of poetic as well as historical tradition. When we consider Browning's experiments with pattern we find a likely precedent for modernist spatial forms. Certainly there are precedents other than Browning's works for patterned forms of poetic organization—Chaucer's framing tale, Spenser's *Shepheardes Calender*, even Herbert's *The Temple;* but Browning's framed "stories" are not tales in the conventional sense, and his longer poems have more fully developed narratives than Spenser's *Calender* or Herbert's lyrics. A closer parallel might be Meredith's *Modern Love,* though Meredith simply omits a number of the connecting links in a consequential narrative.

Perhaps the most interesting parallels among nineteenth-century English poems to Browning's experimental forms are the conflation of persona and character in Byron's *Childe Harold* and the manipulation of time in *The Prelude*. Although Byron's Harold might offer an interesting comparison to Browning's poet-personae, *The Prelude* is still more interesting than Byron's poem for its treatment of narrative time.

The closest affinities between Wordsworth's and Browning's poems are not between *The Prelude* and *The Ring and the Book,* but between Wordsworth's poem and *Sordello* (published ten years before *The Prelude*). Both *The Prelude* and *Sordello* experiment with complex temporal relations. In the opening of *The Prelude*,

CHAPTER FOUR 153

the time we assume to be the present becomes the past, and the poem continues to follow the temporal sequence of memory and meditation. *The Prelude* proceeds by a process of overlap, repetition, and "rebound,"[44] and in this it resembles the treatment of time in *Sordello*. The overall movement of Wordsworth's poem, as Geoffrey Hartman argues, is a recovery that is not simply a return to an original condition but a development; the temporal complexities of recollection are subsumed in the process by which we follow the growth of the poet's mind.[45] *The Prelude* thus lends itself to interpretation through spatial metaphors, and the poem itself presents several concrete images of its form.

In his more general discussion of spatial form, W. J. T. Mitchell takes *The Prelude* as a case in point. He sees it as a work that dramatizes the establishment, elaboration, and revision of its "dominant image patterns, including the sense of space and spatial form." Viewing the question of spatial form as the "interpretive dialectic between image and verbal expression," Mitchell sees in *The Prelude* images both of organic shape and of the "natural-supernatural structure of Gothic architecture." Thus *The Prelude* is modeled on the "winding, serpentine path or river" in its "backtracking and groping forward"; it is modeled ideally on the "antechapel" to the cathedral; it is obsessed with the image of ruins; and, finally, it is a process of replacement of images by transcendent anti-images which in turn "summon up new images borrowed from the sensible world." Much is to be learned, Mitchell suggests, by examining the correlation between these images of form with the "temporal, narrative, or rhetorical features" of *The Prelude*.[46]

Like *The Prelude*, *Sordello* presents several images of its own form, though these are less explicitly developed and of another kind than those in *The Prelude*. Particularly important in *Sordello* are images of the poem as drama (spectacle or diorama), the poem as circle, and the poem as the "armor" of whole perception. Thanks to the mediation of the poet-persona, the reader of *Sordello* has the sense of being asked to regard a spectacle. This sense is strengthened as the poet brings, or brings back before us tableau after tableau connected elliptically by juxtaposition rather than sequentially or discursively. These images themselves suggest the differences between the repetitions of *Sordello* and those in *The Prelude*. In both poems we stand with the poet overlooking the poem's space. In *The Prelude* our view is a landscape, with or without its ruins, through which runs the stream of memory; in *Sordello* the spectacle before us is a theatrical tableau. The world often appears to Sordello as tableau, and Sordello himself often appears to the reader as the central figure in a spectacle. The form of *Sordello* thus suggests the image of the palimpsest rather than the serpentine, the layered history rather than the naturally meandering river. The changing scenes and juxtaposed circles of *Sordello* consequently come as close to the patterning of *The Cantos* as to *The Prelude*.

The images of their own form in *The Prelude* and *Sordello* suggest differing approaches to time. Wordsworth's images predominantly suggest the passage of time as a natural and organic process; the tableau or the palimpsest of *Sordello* arises from an understanding of time as predominantly human and historical. In *Sordello*, as in *The Ring and the Book* and some of Browning's monologues, historical time is imaged as theatrical time, and the theatrical spectacle, as I have argued, is broken by frequent parabasis. A parabasis like the poet's appearance in Book 3 of *Sordello* focuses our attention on theatrical spectacle instead of on a dramatic succession of events. The theatrical metaphors of *Sordello* or *The Ring and the Book* consequently underscore the poem's complex patterning. Ironically Browning's writing for the theater is less effective than the poems that image themselves as theatrical tableaux. Browning had difficulty compressing dramatic action into the represented time on stage; he is more at ease in using theatrical metaphors to represent psychological time or as a means of understanding historical time. Although in *The Prelude* one finds history subsumed in memory, in *Sordello* the historical individual is subsumed in the wider context of a theatrical tableau.

From the perspective of Mitchell's definition of spatial form, we can see that both *Sordello* and *The Prelude* offer interesting images for their own forms; each poem suggests its own geometry. These images of form, however, need not indicate that the two forms are the same; nor do they imply the kind of spatial form Joseph Frank attributes to modern literature. The geometries of *The Prelude* and *Sordello,* though both involve repetition, differ significantly. Although the repetitions of *The Prelude* follow the stream of memory, as the image of the river itself suggests *The Prelude* retains the linearity of sequential narration. The more radical discontinuities of *Sordello,* on the other hand, are resolved in a more radically tectonic pattern than Wordsworth's cathedral architecture.[47] Sequential narration is subordinated at almost every turn to the disjunctive force of ellipsis and repetition. This ascendancy of pattern plot or of juxtaposition over consequential plot is the mark of many experimental novels, and is equally evident in the complexities of *The Cantos* and *Paterson.* To connect Browning's narrative experiments with these modernist works, however, is both to suggest and to call into question "spatial form" as Joseph Frank defines it.

In his theory of spatial form, Frank describes many modernist texts as requiring "synchronic" processes of understanding. In these texts, both prose and poetry, lyric principles have been substituted for narrative ones, Frank claims, and the "units of meaning" in these texts must be "apprehended reflexively in an instant of time." Thus, the reader must place "internal references" in patterns in order to understand the text; and these patterns, as Frank's examples indicate, are frequently ironic.[48] Frank's insights, I believe, might easily be applied to Browning's work, for surely the ellipses and circularity of *Sordello* are as spatial as the layerings Frank describes in the fair scene of *Madame Bovary*.

One wonders, however, if Frank would enroll Browning in the ranks of the modern creators of spatial form, for he contends that "spatial form" expresses a "negative response to history." Frank values just this negative response, and declares only fools or fanatics would claim "there are no good grounds for refusing to worship before the Moloch of 'history' in the old starry-eyed nineteenth-century fashion, with its built-in theological postulates."[49] In the modernists, particularly Pound and Eliot, Frank is "concerned to disengage this latent ahistoricity contained in what seemed a skeptical and self-conscious historical imagination. Certainly the latter was there, but it was striving to transform itself into myth."[50]

The premises underlying Frank's view of spatial form do not always lead to a Frankean condemnation of history. In "Mimesis and Time in Modern Literature," Nathan Scott shares Frank's analysis but condemns the modernists (Joyce and Woolf, not Eliot and Williams) for wishing to escape time altogether. Such "mythography," Scott argues, is "cryptognosticism."[51] Whether this definition of spatial form proceeds from the acceptance or the rejection of history, it leads us back to the critical dualisms that we began by trying to escape.

The dualisms Frank finds useful are indeed complex, but I think he makes parallel two groups of categories that need not necessarily be parallel. In Frank's view there is a necessary affinity among linear time, consequential plot, and history; and another affinity among cyclical time (space as Frank defines it), spatial form, and a rejection of history in favor of myth. Now obviously this pairing assumes that history is linear and that nonlinear form is therefore ahistorical. Browning's narrative experiments, however, disrupt these parallels and call into question Frank's assumptions.

Browning, to be sure, had what the twentieth-century critic might construe as a healthy skepticism about historical knowledge and some healthy distrust of traditional religious dogma, yet even Browning's most skeptical reader must admit that he, like many another "starry-eyed Moloch worshipper," lived with a fair number of "built-in theological postulates." The poet also created works that look much like modern "spatial forms." But these poems are neither mythical nor ahistorical, except in the sense that all history is rhetorically ordered. We have already seen that "myth" and "history" make a dubious dualism and that for Browning history subsumes the changing forms of myth. The opposition of history and linearity to myth and spatial form, I think, works no better. As Frank Kermode observes in response to Joseph Frank, "One cannot distinguish historical from other forms of discourse simply on the basis of the historian's normal preference for sequentiality; that is a rhetorical decision, and to take a different course would hardly make history ahistoric or convert it into 'myth'."[52] As my discussion of contextualist history suggests, a historian or poet may in fact make his rhetorical decision for nonsequential discourse in order to form a narrative that satisfies his historical conception.

Yet another critique of the parallel opposition between history and myth, linearity and repetition is possible in light of Paul Ricoeur's analysis of "narrative Time." Ricoeur argues that the "temporal dialectic" is one that elicits "a configuration from a succession." He sees the historian's "colligatory terms" (e.g. "the Renaissance") not as atemporal but as more deeply temporal than episodic succession. Following Kermode, Ricoeur takes the "sense of an ending" as one of the ways human action is established within time and within memory (both in time "stretching-along" and in time as repetition).[53] Exploring the congruences of a phenomenology of time and a theory of narrative, Ricoeur would, like Kermode, reject an opposition between history/linear succession/narrative and myth/repetition/spatial form. Ricoeur sees Proust's *Le Temps retrouvé,* for example, not as mythical or ahistorical spatial form, but as close to the "kind of repetition suggested by Heidegger's analysis of historicality." In a work such as Proust's memory is "no longer the narrative of external adventures stretching along episodic time." Rather, it is a "spiral movement" through anecdotes and episodes, and the "end of the story is what equates the present with the past, the actual with the potential. The hero *is* who he *was.*"[54] This description, it seems to me, is equally applicable to Browning's hero Sordello. Following Ricoeur's lead, we might conclude that Browning's narrative experiments are not ahistorical; rather they provide a basis for a critique of the notion that historicality is reducible to simple succession.

I have discussed this debate in some detail because I think it leads to two important conclusions. First, it suggests that modernist poets owe much to the narrative experiments that grew out of Browning's understanding of history. Second, Frank's rejection of any history that is not strictly linear, his distrust of any history except Carlyle's "chainlets," brings us back to Dilthey's worry that Burckhardt was ahistorical; this similarity suggests, further, that the debate over spatial form is in some respects a controversy over the importance and the proper conception of history. Involving the problems of historical knowledge, relativism, the relation of history and narrative, the spatial form controversy touches the same questions with which Browning struggled as he resuscitated the past in *Sordello, The Ring and the Book,* and the historical monologues.

CHAPTER FIVE
HISTORICAL PERSPECTIVE AND IRONY IN SOME DRAMATIC MONOLOGUES

I HAVE SUGGESTED THAT IN BROWNING'S POETRY HISTORY is opaque, resistant to simple forms of chronology, defeating the poet's claims to unlimited vision. Browning presents the historical individual as necessarily situated in a web of circumstances, and like the contextualist historian the poet must explore this web of interconnections. Browning develops his poet-personae and his narrative experiments as strategies for confronting the 'solidity' of action in time and the complexities of historical motivations and constraints. Browning's monologues in their way also explore the solidity of the past, often by representing the monologuist as self-conscious about the passage of time. More fundamental than the thematic importance of time in the monologues is Browning's development of the monologue form as a vehicle of his historical view. The complexities provided in the long poems by Browning's manipulation of poet-personae and by his narrative experiments are provided in the historical monologues by the careful manipulation of perspectives. Browning's contextualism and his insistence on the limitations of the historian's or the poet's knowledge imply that history involves difficult judgments that can be reached only through the interplay of or contradictions in various points of view. In *Sordello* and *The Ring and the Book,* the multiplicity of perspectives is suggested in narrative dislocations and layerings, in the self-consciousness of the poet-personae, or, in *The Ring and the Book,* in the multiplication of speakers. In the historical monologues, Browning's poet-persona has become invisible, but we still ask where the poet stands in relation to his characters and where we stand with him. In the monologues Browning takes the traditional dimensions of the lyric, stretches them to imply a narrative, and establishes juxtapositions of perspectives that guide the reader's understanding and judgment.

The inevitable correlative of Browning's historical contextualism, the natural accompaniment of his perspectivism, is historical irony. As Robert Langbaum has argued, the dramatic monologue is "an excellent instrument for projecting an historical point of view" (*PE,* 96). Browning's sense of the past as opaque and of the historian's limitations in seeing through it results in a focus on the importance of historical point of view itself. Calling the dramatic monologue the "genre of historicism," J. Hillis Miller persuasively argues that Browning like the historicist attempts to "inventory all the diverse forms which human life has taken or could take.... If these perspectives contradict one another, so much the better, for that opaque, ambiguous, multiple thing, reality, exceeds any one pair of eyes."[1] These contradictory perspectives generate sometimes solvable, sometimes unresolvable questions as Browning or his characters question history and themselves, or as the reader questions the poem. To read the monologues we must ask where Browning's ironies begin and end and how far Browning's historical speakers are ironists themselves. There are, I shall suggest, both stable and unstable ironies in Browning's monologues, both local ironies and, more generally, an ironic way of looking at the world.

The full complexity of the monologues becomes clear in the context of Browning's historical understanding and its implications for an ironic world view. In order to appreciate the monologues, then, it will be useful to begin with and to return to the question of irony. We need, first, to explore the mode of irony Browning adopts and its relationship to historical perspectivism, and, second, to understand how the poet manipulates perspectives and thus establishes ironies within particular poems.

HISTORY AS IRONIC DRAMA

Browning's use of the monologue form springs from a dialectical understanding of temporality and a contextualist way of conceptualizing the historical field. Setting events in their contexts, Browning, like Burckhardt, invites self-consciousness about one's standpoint or premises for judgment. As he shows us characters collapsing under or thriving upon the tension between historical finitude and infinity, Browning explores historical ironies of situation and also ironies within character. These ironies arise from precisely that aspect of contextualism Hayden White identifies in Burckhardt's work, the skepticism for which, Burckhardt said, religion is the only "amelioration," the skepticism that is necessary because historical beginnings and endings are all unknown.

The dramatic monologue is the ideal form for a contextualist historical view that emphasizes the play of perspectives, insists on isolating a moment and tracing its context, and calls for a self-consciously limited or even disappearing historian. The monologue, as Browning develops it, allows him to attempt precisely what Burckhardt advocates in *Force and Freedom*—the judgment of historical figures from their own premises. And it enables a shifting of perspective on various familiar historical periods as Browning selects a historical or fictional character who was or would have been a figure of secondary or tangential importance in his day. Thus through Karshish Browning's readers see Lazarus; through Cleon, Paul; through Andrea del Sarto, Michelangelo. By shifting our perspective and filtering our vision through a historically secondary figure, Browning gives us a feel for history as a densely textured fabric of interconnected individuals and events. Browning's monologuists, with all their flaws, complexities, and historical concreteness, are conceived in the mode of much subsequent poetry—the mode of irony, and Browning's ironies are often dependent upon this density of historical detail. History itself, in Browning's texts, can be understood as ironic drama. The dramatic dimension of the monologue, the distance between poet and speaker, speaker and audience, and the historical basis of this distance are the constitutive elements of Browning's ironic mode.

Many critics have noted that Browning's training in the theater was useful to him in developing the dramatic monologue. But one can also say that the theater served Browning as a workshop of irony. In *Irony and the Ironic* D. C. Muecke argues that the theater and irony naturally go together and that any irony has its theatrical aspect. Muecke, like Kenneth Burke whom he follows, connects drama, dialectic, peripety, and irony.[2] As I have already suggested, Browning's historical poetry—and his historical characters—are most interesting as they are fully caught up in a temporal dialectic of aspiration and finitude, change and changeless stasis. There is or should be, Browning implies, no revelation except progressive revelation, no heaven except ceaseless striving. In his stage plays Browning began to work out the terms of this often ironic dialectic, in part by investigating the necessary historical limitations of his characters. We have already seen the historical irony in *Strafford* where the better man espouses the worse cause. By the time of *Luria,* Browning's understanding of political expediency became such that he was forced to confess he sympathized as much with Luria's enemies as with his "golden-hearted" hero. Heroic tragedy became ironic stalemate. In *A Soul's Tragedy,* politics is presented as a form of theater, and all action is ironized, to such an extent that Browning himself characterized the play as "all sneering and disillusion." Browning suggests that when political action is reduced to theater and nobility becomes an act, human beings are lulled into self-delusion; delineating this process, the playwright or poet develops an irony in which characters betray themselves. Even those who do not inadvertently betray flaws and failures may be caught in situational ironies. For Strafford, King Charles, or Djabal success in some measure must be failure. Beneath the surface of Browning's dramas is a sense of theatricality as imposture and of dramatic situations as inherently ironic.

Although many of Browning's monologues are not, thematically, so negative as *A Soul's Tragedy,* the dramatic monologue is in its form an invitation to irony. The monologue precludes the kind of peripety, the kind of closure that dramas often have. Browning's monologuists do not change, do not reach points of self-understanding or newly comprehend their circumstances. Foolish, ignorant, or wise, they can only become more so. Resolution, closure, comes rather in the mind of the reader, who in the course of the monologues comes more clearly to recognize Browning's speakers for what they are. In fact, the ironies of the monologues point up one of the problems of Browning's plays—his weak handling of action, peripety, and resolution. The plays are afflicted with a kind of stasis that is no problem in a patterned closet drama like *Pippa Passes* or in the monologues, but that impedes the action and weakens the interest of the dramas. Browning's stage plays are not formally daring enough to accommodate the ironies they suggest. In the historical monologues and in *Sordello* and *The Ring and the Book,* Browning's formal choices accord better with his emphasis on irony and perspectivism. It seems too simple in this respect to argue as Clyde Ryals does that Browning began and ended as a romantic ironist but in his middle period (which includes most of the monologues) retreated from the ambiguities and tensions of irony.[3]

Ryals himself argues that the irony of fate is suggested in Browning's recurrent use of theatrical metaphors and metaphors of puppetry. A close reading of Browning's historical monologues suggests that although the theatrical metaphor itself appears infrequently, pretense, role-playing and imposture—the theatrical side of human relationships—are central. Besides an obvious imposter like Mr. Sludge, one finds the pretense of piety in the Bishop of St. Praxed's and, I shall argue, the pretense of simplicity in the Duke of Ferrara. A different kind of theatricality operates in "The Epistle of Karshish" where I will suggest the speaker himself is an ironist. Even in "Fra Lippo Lippi," one of the least ironic of Browning's monologues, Lippi dramatizes himself; his description of his next painting, that "something in Sant' Ambrogio's," is a small theatrical scene. One of Browning's most difficult monologues, "Bishop Blougram's Apology," involves theater and irony in all these senses. As I shall suggest in detail, "Blougram" is complicated by imposture and by ironic feigning. Not coincidentally, Blougram's most striking metaphor is the metaphor of the "tire room"; the line between acting and reality, imposture and identity, disappears. Like his creator Blougram recognizes the ironic potential of drama.

The ironies in such monologues as "Bishop Blougram's Apology" suggest that a distinction like

Clyde Ryals's between Browning's great monologues of his middle period and his earlier and later work is too simple. Ryals argues that the earlier and later work is more radically experimental and more fundamentally ironic than the monologues; he views the ironies of the monologues as essentially local ironies pointing to fixed meanings.[4] It is surely true that Browning's local ironies do have such fixed meanings, but if we examine the monologues in the context of Browning's historical poetry and his understanding of history, we can see that many of the monologues are in their own ways experimental, ironic, and challenging to their readers.

It is possible to argue that Browning is fundamentally an ironist without arguing that all of his poems are equally ironic and without holding them to a single standard of ironic complexity or, as Ryals does, to a standard of romantic irony. As my reading of Browning's narrative experimentation has suggested, Browning's vision of human existence in time is essentially dialectical. It is this dialectic that Ryals properly associates with Browning's irony. Browning's philosophical or romantic irony, Ryals argues, involves a "dialectic of order and change, love and power, the conditioned and the free, the finite and the infinite."[5] This dialectic is not less central to the historical monologues than to *Sordello* or *The Ring and the Book;* in all these poems Browning's ironic dialectic is fundamentally a historical one. Despite the stability of the local ironies of the monologues, many of these poems suggest a deeply ironic—though not gloomy—understanding of human history. Anne Mellor has described as typical of the romantic ironist a vision much like that I have characterized as historicist: the world is an "abundant chaos" in which "no far goal of time" determines the progression of events. She describes the elements of romantic irony in a way that makes clear how deeply touched Browning was by this strain of nineteenth-century thought. Romantic irony, in Mellor's view, is characterized by a "philosophical conception of the universe as becoming, as an infinitely abundant chaos; a literary structure that reflects both this chaos or process of becoming and the systems that men impose on it; and a language that draws attention to its own limitations."[6] Mellor suggests that a romantic ironist like Carlyle was not able always to remain amid the chaos, to ironize his own desire for order or system, to retain the radical formal experimentalism required by a thoroughgoing ironic orientation to the world. No more, I think, need we see Browning as altogether and everywhere an ironist. Nonetheless I will suggest in the next chapter that Browning's fascination with the prosaic is part of his self-consciousness about the limitations of poetic vision and poetic language. In the dramatic monologues, moreover, Browning's perspectivism is a natural corollary to the notion that causality is complex and that all individuals, including ourselves, are in some way limited by their times.

Browning would concur with the historicists that values are manifested temporally and that these manifestations are constantly changing. This understanding of history and morality is of the sort Muecke finds characteristic of general or "the morals of the universe" sort of irony. Muecke associates general irony with the development of an "open ideology" in the nineteenth century. This ideology, as Muecke defines it, involves a number of assumptions similar to those I have shown to be Browning's own: the sense of continual change, of dynamic history, and specifically the sense that "it might just as well have happened the other way round."[7] Among the contradictions and situations that Muecke lists as "ready-made containers" of irony are topics and figures with which Browning is often concerned. Contradictions that may be taken as ironic, Muecke says, often arise in speculation on such topics as free will and determinism, society and the individual, art and life; and in situations involving dualities of God and man, audience and play, puppetmaster and puppet, artist and work of art, past and present.[8] These contradictions are as significant in Browning's monologues as in his long poems.

In the historical monologues, then, Browning is ever the ironist; an examination of the play of perspectives in the historical monologues suggests not only the crucial role of historical detail for our understanding of Browning's characters but also the varying degrees to which they are ironically treated. In Browning's poems irony may be a metaphysical and aesthetic position or a strategy for eliciting our understanding of and pleasure in his characters.

READING BROWNING'S MONOLOGUES

To understand the general irony that complicates many of Browning's historical monologues, it is essential first to see how the monologue form itself is a vehicle of Browning's perspectivism and then to see how the local ironies of the monologues are dependent upon historical judgment. The perspectivism of the monologues is established in the relationship among three agents: the dramatized speaker, the implied author, and the reader.[9] Something like this triangular paradigm is described by Robert Langbaum when he says of the monologue that "there is at work in it a consciousness, whether intellectual or historical, beyond what the speaker can lay claim to. This consciousness is the mark of the poet's projection into the poem; and is also the pole which attracts our projection since we find it in the counterpart of our own consciousness" (*PE*, 94). In reading monologues we are invited, as Langbaum hints, to understand both the speaker's own perspective and another "consciousness" as well.

How does this understanding come about? Langbaum's own solution has provided the basis for so many subsequent readings of the monologues that it should be briefly reconsidered; for Langbaum does not emphasize the discrepancies between the speaker's consciousness and a wider view of an implied author so much as the relationship between the speaker and the reader. This emphasis leads Langbaum to his model for reading a monologue: as readers, he says, we experience tension between sympathy with and judgment of the speaker, and we suspend judgment as we "sympathize in order to read the poem" (*PE,* 92). For Langbaum, the lyric form of a dramatic monologue works against moral judgment because characterization in these poems is "self-expressive" or "self-justifying" rather than "teleological" or "moral" (*PE,* 200–202). As Ralph Rader points out, however, the nature of characterization and judgment in monologues becomes clearer if we also examine the relationship of the poet (or implied author) to the speaker.

In "The Dramatic Monologue and Related Lyric Forms," Rader distinguishes four kinds of poems conventionally labeled monologues—expressive lyrics, mask lyrics, dramatic lyrics, and dramatic monologues. Whereas Langbaum contends that as readers we suspend judgment in poems as different as Tennyson's "Tithonus" and "My Last Duchess," Rader argues that we react differently to the two poems; for "Tithonus" is a mask lyric in which the "lyric actor" and the poet are quite close, but "My Last Duchess" is a dramatic monologue in which the "lyric actor" appears to us very much as "an 'other' natural person would."[10] Seen in this light, as an "other" natural person, the duke of "My Last Duchess" has a character both moral and determinate. Our understanding of him develops as we seek to reconcile the implied author's perspective with the duke's point of view. The duke in some sense "expresses" himself and is thus (in

Langbaum's formulation) characterized lyrically; at the same time, the duke's very words raise moral questions or create for us a sense of the duke's *ethos* or moral bent.[11] As Langbaum suggests, the resolution of "My Last Duchess" is, indeed, a lyric resolution; we do feel that we understand what Langbaum calls the completeness that "resides within the speaker." But this kind of resolution need not be "morally indeterminate" and antithetical to a characterization involving *ethos* (*PE,* 202). Rather, in the intricate interplay of perspectives, the characterization of the duke might best be described by the Aristotelian understanding of *ethos* as a "state of character" or moral bent that "comes about as a result of habit."[12] The poem's completion, consequently, is our complete view, not of an emotion, but of the duke's *ethos.* In contrast to "My Last Duchess," the mask lyric "Tithonus," as Rader suggests, establishes a correlative of the poet's private emotion; and like many mask lyrics "Tithonus" does not enter the realm of judgment at all. Unlike "Tithonus," Browning's monologues, especially the historical monologues, frequently present character in its various senses: the duke is, like Tithonus, the agent or actor who speaks; he is also "quite a character," that is, a bundle of personal peculiarities; and he has character (or *ethos*). In other words we might say that in "Tithonus" we are not called upon to judge, but in "My Last Duchess" judgment and sympathy are integral parts of a single reading process—the process in which we comprehend the gap between the speaker's and the poet's perspectives.

Rader's divisions among kinds of first-person poems enable us to appreciate the variety of works that have conventionally been called dramatic monologues. A close analysis of the poet-speaker-reader paradigm will make clear the nature of judgment in a number of the poems Rader designates dramatic monologues, a category that includes nearly all of

Browning's historical monologues. In reconsidering the question of judgment we should certainly bear in mind Langbaum's view that in reading "My Last Duchess," for example, "condemnation is not our principal response" (*PE*, 82). Langbaum's emphasis on sympathy serves as a warning that, after all, we are not reading didactic poetry and, more importantly, that judgment can be not simple moralistic condemnation but a very complicated thing indeed.

To investigate the complexities of judgment in the historical poems we may begin with Langbaum's and Rader's interest in what Langbaum calls "our consciousness of a consciousness beyond the speaker's." Another careful reader of Browning's monologues, Philip Drew, also points to this sense that we readers have a more complete view than that of the speaker: "Even in 'Fra Lippo Lippi', in which, since there is very little sense of Browning extending ironically beyond the speaker, our identification is almost complete and hence Langbaum's way of reading a dramatic monologue is more or less applicable, there is nevertheless, the sense that Browning's *historical* grasp is wider than Lippi's, that *he* realizes as Lippi could not, how pertinent to the arts of succeeding ages were the monk's comments on his own painting."[13]

Langbaum himself investigates this discrepancy in the poet's and the speaker's perspectives; and though he concludes that one suspends judgment in encountering this discrepancy, he rightly suggests an analogy between the question of perspective in the monologues and questions of historical perspective. Of the historical poems he concludes, "Since the past is understood in the same way that we understand the speaker of a dramatic monologue, the dramatic monologue is an excellent instrument for projecting an historical point of view. For the modern sense of the past involves, on the one hand, sympathy for the past, a willingness to understand it in its own terms as different from the present; and on the other hand it involves a critical awareness of our own modernity" (*PE,* 96). Perhaps, then, the question of judgment might be better phrased in terms of historical understanding. Whatever the semantics of the situation, however, I think in turning our attention to the relationship of perspectives in Browning's monologues we shall see that coming to understand these poems frequently does involve judgment. But judgment is not simply black and white, a labeling of moral qualities; in the process of reading the historical monologues we come to see the individual's relation to his circumstances, to understand how he handles his limitations, and, finally, to appreciate how these limitations and circumstances relate to our own.

I have characterized Browning's contextualism as an effort to explore the individual's complex connections with his circumstances. In his narrative experiments, we have seen Browning attempt the difficult task implicit in his poetic theory: the task of seeing and interpreting the web of historical interconnection. This effort is made difficult, moreover, by the necessary limitations of the historical individual and of the historian or poet himself or herself. The Pope in *The Ring and the Book* and John in "A Death in the Desert" see that the welter of the world must be "made pass / A spectrum into mind, the narrow eye." The necessity of interpreting history brings us to the paradoxical situation in which the individual is enmeshed in circumstances and yet is able, in some cases, to judge those circumstances. Given this situation, questions about historical causation and about values and historical judgment present themselves. In Browning's work such questions are raised in much the same way they presented themselves to Friedrich Meinecke in his formulation and defense of the historical tradition.

As I have already noted, Rankean historiography posed an opposition between the subjectivity of historical individuals and objectively existing patterns or values. In exploring the questions of value relativity to which this opposition gave rise, Meinecke focuses specifically on notions of causation and value. I have already alluded to Meinecke's discussion in "Historicism and Its Problems" of Ranke's "artistic-intuitive" approach to history; Meinecke prefaces this discussion with the argument that Ranke's "scientific" approach eschews "any unequivocal and general causal explanation" of historical phenomena. Consequently, the historicist becomes aware of interaction of mechanistic (economic, etc.), biological (influence in gradual formation of structures), and individual-personal causality. Outside the realm of mechanistic causality, what Meinecke calls "cultural" or "spiritual" values arise, and we can understand these values only in appreciating their place in this dense web of causality. The historical view associated with Ranke, Meinecke says,

> bore a kind of inborn aversion lest any one of these causes be overpowered and extinguished by the other. In explaining individual phenomena and assembling them in larger sequences and structures it preferred to be guided more by indefinable finesse than by an explicit and principled position. It regarded artistic intuition and the artistic-intuitive shaping of events not only as beautiful, but more or less superfluous, embellishment of an historical substance discovered purely causally, but as an essential and indispensable technique in view of the only partially, never completely, decipherable manner in which the three imprints interpenetrate.[14]

Meinecke recognizes that this intuitional way of establishing value might give rise to relativism: by considering "cultural contributions in terms of their own premises" do we arrive at a position in which all values are purely subjective and all judgment forever suspended? Meinecke in this context makes claims for

Ernst Troeltsch's view of values in *Historismus* in which Troeltsch declares, "Value-relativity is not relativism, anarchy, accident, arbitrariness. It signifies rather a fusion of the factual and normative, which is ever moving and newly created and cannot, therefore, be determined universally and timelessly."[15] Or, as Meinecke concludes, "Value-relativity, in other words, is nothing other than individuality in the historical sense. It is the unique and intrinsically valuable imprint of an unknown absolute."[16]

This view of values in history as a fusion of the factual and the normative, as emerging, that is, from the "partially" decipherable web of causality and motive is strikingly like Langbaum's analysis of "relativism" in *The Ring and the Book*. Langbaum believes that for Browning truth is not indefinite but is "relative—psychologically, to the nature of the judge and person being judged; historically, to the amount of disequilibrium in any given age between truth and the institutions by which truth is understood" (*PE*, 122). We should, then, expect to find judgments emerging along with values in the juxtaposition of perspectives in the monologues. To establish the interplay of the speaker, his circumstances, and a modern historical view, Browning must create for us a sense of his speaker's milieu; he must examine cultural contributions in terms of their own premises.

HISTORICAL MILIEU IN THE MONOLOGUES

For establishing historical perspectives in the dramatic monologues, Browning's choice of detail is especially important. It is scarcely possible to underestimate the effect of Browning's eye for the revealing detail. In historical particulars we see both what is important to the speaker and what the poet finds essential to our understanding of the speaker; details resonate in the poem to the speaker's advantage or disadvantage. In historical allusions Browning tells us about a character and his age, and by a process of accretion we come to see the speaker's historical premises. A primary pleasure in reading the monologues, of course, is the delight of discovering a richly textured picture of the past forming in an almost off-handed way. Ruskin's praise for "The Bishop Orders His Tomb" reflects this pleasure. "I know of no other piece of modern English, prose or poetry," Ruskin wrote, "in which there is so much told, as in these lines, of the Renaissance spirit,—its worldliness, inconsistency, pride, hypocrisy, ignorance of itself, love of art, of luxury, and of good Latin."[17] We sense, too, Ruskin's fascination with finding in Browning's monologue a history that at least partially matches his own conception of the Renaissance.

In reading Browning's monologues we often create a historical context by assimilating details that are either descriptive in themselves or that evoke a context through allusion or through association with general historical conceptions. We might take "Fra Lippo Lippi" as an example of this context-through-particulars method. In Lippi's talk the details slip in, tumble over each other, and bring us to appreciate the depth and breadth of Florentine culture and the acuteness of the painter's eye. We know through the painter's rapid sketch how Florence looks—"yonder river's line, / The mountain round it and the sky above" ("Lippi," 288–89)—how the poor live, and how the rich. Lippi frequently enumerates:

> I did renounce the world, its pride and greed,
> Palace, farm, villa, shop and banking-house,
> Trash, such as these poor devils of Medici
> Have given their hearts to—
>
> ("Lippi," 99–101)

We know in detail about how life goes in the cloister and the church. The prior's pious theories of art and his theological confusions are punctuated by references to his "niece"; we see the monks themselves and the church-goers in their variety. More significant are the painters we must recognize and reckon with. Giotto, Fra Angelico, and Lorenzo (Monaco) are the predecessors against whom Lippi directs his realist's rebellion. Though Browning's dates have since been proven wrong (*Handbook,* 195), it is important that we see in Guidi, or Hulking Tom, the Masaccio who painted the famous frescoes in the Branaci chapel of the Carmine. Part of our understanding of Lippi, though we may enjoy him without this knowledge, is in seeing him as the necessary link between the painters of souls and the artists of the High Renaissance. We grasp an additional dimension of the monologue when we supply a knowledge of Lippi's paintings of John the Baptist, Jerome, and the "something of Sant' Ambrogio's" or the *Coronation of the Virgin*. We bring to "Fra Lippo Lippi" a knowledge of Renaissance painting and perhaps of the variousness and even the contradictions of the period, and we find these notions are made concrete either through allusion or through inclusion of particulars. Browning appeals in this sense to external verification. We understand his poem because we feel he has caught the life of the Renaissance. But of course though this verification is essential, it need not be minutely correct in terms of art historical scholarship. It is enough that Browning enables us to see Lippi in historical perspective.

The creation of historical context through allusion is much more straightforward in "Lippi" and most of the other monologues than in *Sordello* or *Prince Hohenstiel-Schwangau*. Although it is necessary that we see Sordello or the Prince caught in the crossed threads of historical circumstance, in these works a historical context can only be established if we bring a good deal of previous knowledge to our reading. These poems work as much by allusion as by inclusion.

The narrative complexity of both poems adds to our difficulty. In *Sordello* we understand why Browning debated the addition of notes, for his allusions to the byways of Italian history send the reader begging for an annotated index. The difficulties of *Hohenstiel-Schwangau* arise primarily through the layering of speakers and through the modern reader's possibly shaky grasp of the history of the Second Empire. The Victorian reader undoubtedly had an easier time with Browning's allusions, but enough difficulties remained that the *Edinburgh Review* called the poem a "eulogism on the Second Empire" while another review regarded it as a "scandalous attack" (*Handbook*, 321). On such a controversial subject, of course, opinion was divided; and given the complexity of the Prince as Browning presents him, it is no wonder opinions differed.

In other monologues, as in "Fra Lippo Lippi" or "The Bishop Orders His Tomb," Browning's own judgment of the speaker in his context is clearer, and, whatever our prepossessions, we find the selection of a speaker's context subtly guiding our judgment of him. The monologues on historical subjects, of course, do not always provide such a rich texture of historical allusion and detail. Our judgment of "Pictor Ignotus, Florence 15—" depends upon our bringing to the poem only a general notion of the greatness of Renaissance art. Because we know about the achievements of the sixteenth-century masters and because from our modern perspective we recognize, as the painter himself does not, that the endurance of this art is important, we can answer his rhetorical questions affirmatively. As in "Fra Lippo Lippi," but this time to the painter's disadvantage, we are called upon to approve the earthy element in the Renaissance character when the painter asks,

> O youth, men praise so,—holds their praise its worth?

Blown harshly, keeps the trump its golden cry?
Tastes sweet the water with such specks of earth?
("Pictor Ignotus," 70–72)

Although we know enough generally to assess the anonymous painter's failure to measure up to the achievement of "that youth," we do not feel the impact of his failure as strongly as we do the fatal choice of Andrea del Sarto. Andrea's gray decline has great immediacy because of the poem's imagistic complexity and because we recognize a specific once-living painter. The density of historical particulars also goes far to make the painter's failure real to us. Andrea seems truly to breathe the same air as Michelangelo. In "Andrea" and in the other historical monologues, Browning experiments with allusion to and inclusion of historical details—names, dates, places, incidents—and Browning's monologuists, in establishing this historical context, reveal themselves as having more or less accurate understandings of their circumstances.

Historical material in the monologues, then, can constitute an appeal to verification and give us pleasure by calling upon or by corresponding to our historical views; in a more complex way it often serves as premises for our judgment. Browning forces us to consider the speaker's relationship to his historical circumstances and the speaker's consciousness of this relationship. Often, in fact, our positive attitude toward a speaker varies in proportion to the breadth of his own historical conception and his conscious sensitivity to his place. Paradoxically, we see the "best" of Browning's monologuists asserting permanent values in their own times by becoming conscious of their own historical limitations. These speakers, like the poet himself, might be said to overcome perspective through perspective.

The view of human nature we discover in the monologues is not a simple one. Virtually all the speakers in Browning's historical monologues are living examples of the paradox of history as Browning seems to see it: they are what their circumstances make them, but they are also what they make of their circumstances. They are different in every age, and yet, if they would act morally, understand spiritually, or paint with genius, they must achieve such contact with transcendent values as is possible in their times. Because Browning presents us with multiple historical perspectives, we may find his view closer to the unspoken assumptions of our own historicity than we do the visions of his predecessors. Just as Browning could arrive less easily than Coleridge at a fusion of the subjective and objective poet, so he could not dismiss what Wordsworth called the "obstacles" of history from the province of poetry. To a greater degree than his predecessors, Browning chose to explore the difficult territory that Wordsworth wished to leave to the historian or biographer and that Shelley relegated not to poetry but to "story."[18] The consequence of Browning's view, as we have seen, is that perspective becomes essential in the historical or poetic enterprise. We are no longer convinced in the monologues as we are in "Tintern Abbey," for example, that the "mind of the creator" is the "image of all other minds."[19] The poet's mind gives rise to the image of, say, the Duke of Ferrara's mind only through an intricate process of refraction. The prism for this refraction, like the Wordsworthian obstacles of the biographer or historian, is the background of historical specificity itself.

JUXTAPOSED PERSPECTIVES AND JUDGMENT

To understand, then, how we read monologues and to describe the pleasure they give us, we must consider the process of forming judgments through juxtaposed perspectives. In "Fra Lippo Lippi," "The

Bishop Orders His Tomb," "My Last Duchess," and "Cleon," our judgment varies with the speaker's consciousness of his relationship to his circumstances. In the play of the speaker's, the poet's, and the reader's perspectives, Browning shows us how much of what a character is and does comes from the proclivities of his time.

In reading "Fra Lippo Lippi," we see Lippi partially overcoming the prior's constricted notions of art in order to paint things as he sees them. By making Lippi both the unabashed sensual man and a monk, Browning risks our thinking Lippi an immoral hypocrite like the prior; but the poet constantly disarms our criticism not only through the painter's frankness but in sketching for us early in the poem the social conditions that led Lippi to be dedicated to the monastery while still a child. Similarly, Lippi's satiric portrait of the prior shows us the corruptions within the institution and indicates that the monk himself disapproves of these conditions. Against this background we see Lippi as sensualist by nature (and by the nature of his age) and as a monk by circumstance; in his painting Lippi both loses and wins in a contest with his circumstances. Like his art, Lippi partakes of and transcends his historical milieu.

The perspectives of speaker, poet, and reader in "Fra Lippo Lippi" quickly converge, for Lippi sees himself as we and the poet see him. He is aware from the beginning of the contradictions of his situation and in his nature, and he is only as "hypocritical" as he has to be to avoid antagonizing the law or his patrons. So Lippi modifies his indictment of the prior's view of art while confessing that he is excusing himself:

> —That is—you'll not mistake an idle word
> Spoke in a huff by a poor monk, God wot,
> Tasting the air this spicy night which turns
> The unaccustomed head like Chianti wine!
> Oh, the church knows! don't misreport me, now!

> It's natural a poor monk out of bounds
> Should have his apt word to excuse himself:
> ("Lippi," 336–42)

Our sympathy is engaged by Lippi's admission that he has been caught in an unpromising situation and that he is excusing himself. We see his mild retraction, "don't misreport me," as a necessary concession, and we excuse his improper behavior as a monk because we feel his social circumstances have placed him in this awkward position. His heart, furthermore, is in the right place; he paints, for example, a Christ in the murderer's church of asylum "whose sad face on the cross sees only this / After the passion of a thousand years" ("Lippi," 156–57). In his most important aspect, as a painter, Lippi resolutely transcends his milieu. He paints when possible not according to convention but according to the conviction of his own vision. Lippi, in other words, has an accurate view of himself, his personal circumstances, and his historical situation, and we, like the poet, share this view. Speaker, poet, and reader are almost at one in their perspectives.

Perspectives diverge much more considerably in "My Last Duchess" and "The Bishop Orders His Tomb" than in "Fra Lippo Lippi." In both these poems we are again given a great deal of circumstantial and historical detail, and again we see Browning's speakers as in some measure inevitably limited by their circumstances. But neither the duke nor the bishop rises above the limitations of his age or is aware except fleetingly that more than one view may be taken toward his behavior. We do see both these speakers as representative of their age and of their class or office. We delight that Browning has created a habit of mind different from our own and is concerned with a set of particular circumstances we recognize as essential to the Renaissance. We do not expect the bishop's character to be that of the minister of a dissenting chapel, and in this regard, as Robert Langbaum puts it, our judgment is "mainly historicized, because the bishop's sins are not extraordinary but the universally human venalities couched, significantly for the historian, in the predilections of the Italian Renaissance" (*PE*, 97). We do not condemn the bishop for being a child of his age, but we do, I think, judge him for not at least being more aware of the inconsistencies of his situation. As readers we enter the bishop's perspective just enough to see the attractiveness of the things he finds compelling.[20] We understand the appeal of the lapis lazuli "Bedded in store of rotten fig-leaves soft"—even the sibilants and liquids of Browning's lines reinforce this impression. But our perspective is so immediately in tune with the wider view of the implied author that any empathetic identification with the bishop is subject to constant revision. The same lapis lazuli is also "big as a Jew's head cut off at the nape." The juxtaposition of perspectives consistently and carefully directs our judgment so that the reader who is aware of these juxtapositions can easily characterize the bishop in terms of his "human venalities."

It is not the case with the bishop that our moral judgments may "differ as they do about the past itself" (*PE*, 97), except in the sense that some readers may find the bishop's plight more comic than others do: to understand the bishop at all we must judge him to be a man inordinately subject to "human venalities." In the first five lines of the poem, Browning establishes for us the inconsistencies we will follow throughout the bishop's speech:

> Vanity, saith the preacher, vanity!
> Draw round my bed: is Anselm keeping back?
> Nephews—sons mine ... ah, God, I know not!
> Well—
> She, men would have to be your mother once,
> Old Gandolf envied me, so fair she was!

The first two lines bring no particular surprises. A cleric on his death-bed might well appreciate the

CHAPTER FIVE 183

force of the pronouncement from Ecclesiastes. We expect then (on first reading, that is) that the bishop will be delivering an admonition to the priests or other persons surrounding him. But immediately we are called upon to see the bishop in an unexpected perspective: "Nephews—sons mine . . . ah, God, I know not!" Here we have the bishop even now keeping up social appearances, "Nephews"; then admitting he has sons; and then, no sooner than he calls them sons, wishing it back and turning away from considering the vanity of past indulgences, "ah, God, I know not!" Next the bishop admits and refuses to admit that their mother was his mistress by calling her, "She, men would have to be your mother once." Again, the bishop deflects the admission and this time couches it in terms of a public opinion. In the next breath, of course, we know that certainly there was a mistress who was mother of these sons, and the bishop's pleasure in the woman and in Gandolf's envy echoes jarringly against his "vanity, vanity." In savoring these juxtapositions, we share the poet's larger perspective and quickly learn that the bishop has built his life on unacknowledged or only partially acknowledged contradictions. Already, by the third line, we are asked to make connections the bishop himself does not make; through a perspective both historical and moral we see the bishop caught in the inconsistencies of his age. The bishop himself lacks the ability to see his life in either historical or moral perspective. He sees himself rather as the sculpture of his own tomb, so thoroughly does he divorce the aesthetic from the moral and spiritual dimensions of life. Even his inevitable reckoning with death is a confrontation with ugliness, as he imagines, "Gritstone, a-crumble! Clammy squares which sweat / As if the corpse they keep were oozing through" ("The Bishop," 116–17). Unlike the bishop we arrive through an intricate play of irony at a multidimensional understanding of the speaker's character and of his age: in the bishop's case we at once appreciate his aesthetic sense and judge its limitations.

In the duke of "My Last Duchess" we confront an aestheticism of a different and darker stripe. We become acquainted with a man who is like the bishop in being unable to see his own life in a moral perspective. The duke, however, is not internally divided by the inconsistencies of his age[21]; on the contrary, his pride of place, his unstooping reverence for himself as the bearer of a nine-hundred-years-old name reveal a chilling consistency. His wife, fittingly, is "my duchess," an object like the duchess-to-be whom he calls the count's "fair daughter's self." Our ability to see the duke's deficiencies, of course, depends upon our having a perspective different from his, and in this juxtaposition of views our judgments allow us to construct an ironic characterization. Just what the poet's and reader's perspectives are in "My Last Duchess" is worth examining in light of Langbaum's contention that we suspend judgment in reading this monologue. As Langbaum says, we are captivated by the duke's extraordinary combination of villainy with taste. This combination "pleases us the way it would the historian, since it impresses upon us the difference of the past from the present" and, Langbaum says, it provides a kind of historicizing of judgment. Langbaum concludes that since the duke's crime is too "egregious for historical generalization," the poem requires a kind of psychologizing sympathy: "More important, therefore, for the suspension of moral judgment is our psychologizing attitude—our willingness to take up the duke's view of events purely for the sake of understanding him, the more outrageous his view the more illuminating for us the psychological revelation" (*PE*, 97).

Langbaum justly claims that we "take up the duke's view." How we enter the duke's view, nevertheless, is meticulously controlled by the poet. Ralph

Rader, Laurence Perrine, and Victor Vogt have convincingly argued against Langbaum's view that the duke's speech is an almost gratuitous self-revelation and an indiscretion on the duke's part.[22] I think an examination of the play of perspectives in our experience of "My Last Duchess" supports their reading of the duke's speech as a warning to the envoy. We discover easily enough that the duke, very much like Guido in *The Ring and the Book,* views the world from an autocratic perspective; all values for him, even aesthetic values, are reduced to questions of place and station. Unlike the bishop, the polymorphous aesthete, the duke collects art and wives as befitting his social position. Other beauties—sunset, cherry blossoms—having no status-value, have no value for him at all. Far from stepping into the duke's shoes in a sympathetic suspension of judgment, we come to understand that the duke's failing is just this lack of ability to put himself in any shoes other than his own; in making this assessment we are aware, as Rader says, before "any analytic reflection" that the duke "is held within and sustained by the poet's creative consciousness."[23]

Our knowledge of the duke forms in the interplay of the poet's perspective and the duke's, and our sense of the distance between these perspectives is created through the dissonances of the duke's own words. The first two lines of the poem need not alert us to this dissonance at first though they inevitably do so on repeated readings or when the conditional "as if alive" is repeated. At first glance the duke merely means he possesses a lifelike portrait (though the woman is the "last" duchess), but the second description of the painting repeats the conditional and says, in effect, she is dead:

> I gave commands
> Then all smiles stopped together. There she stands
> As if alive.
> ("My Last Duchess," 46–47)

In the circumlocution the duke walks around the moral issue, though obviously he is not going to admit to the envoy that he is a wife murderer. The second conditional has the effect of calling on us to decipher and reconstruct it in much the same way we reconstruct the bishop's "She, men would have to be your mother." As we read on, the dissonances of "My Last Duchess" increase. We come to understand the duke from a broader perspective than his own. We see the first clear incongruity when we realize that the duchess's "spot of joy" and the "depth and passion" of her "earnest glance" are anathema to the duke. But surely we feel an earnest glance is close to an honest glance and no cause for offense, and surely the simply beautiful things the duchess loves are cause enough for gladness. The duke's reactions seem disproportionate when seen from any point of view other than his own.[24] Our perspective further diverges from the duke's as he calls the breaker of the bough of cherries an "officious fool" and his duchess "such an one." From line 30 onward our tentative judgment of the duke is confirmed and reconfirmed: we perceive clearly how egocentric is his vision in his "disgust" at the duchess ranking his "gift of a nine-hundred-years-old name / With anybody's gift."

By the end of the poem we see not only that the duke means more than he says but also that what he says means more than he knows. The duke's disclaimers should alert us that he is warning the envoy. His "how shall I say," "I know not how," and his "Even had you skill / In speech—(which I have not)" are obviously clues to his calculations. His manipulation of understatement should recall the success of orators from Cicero to Shakespeare's Antony who declares, "For I have neither wit, nor words, nor worth, / Action, nor utterance, nor the power of speech, / To stir men's blood." A different interpretation of the duke's disclaimers is possible, but I think not wholly convincing. Herbert Tucker, for example, sees the duke's disclaimers as an "expression of private struggle" and as evidence of the duke's inability to interpret the duchess.[25] In my view the duke is marked not so much by ongoing private struggle as by his largely successful efforts to eradicate contradiction within himself and opposition from his duchess. Though Tucker's reading is generally provocative, I think we need not abandon the notion that the duke is warning the envoy. The duke, as Tucker says, cannot understand the duchess, but he is at no loss to describe his own response to the duchess's opposition. The duke has words enough, at least, to say, "'Just this / Or that in you disgusts me.'" Like Antony's audience, presumably like the envoy, we get the duke's point.

But of course we get a number of other points besides. As we come to regard the duke from juxtaposed perspectives we see that he would lessen as well as "lesson" his wife, that the count's daughter will indeed be an "object"; and finally the duke's reference to the Neptune sculpture not only provides a fitting rhetorical closure but stands as a total exposure of the duke's character. In examining the poem's conclusion, Rader emphasizes the rhetorical aspect of the duke's last remark and concludes, "Thus the bronze figure of Neptune pointed to by the duke at the end of his speech to the envoy, so often made to bear general meanings of all sorts, has, I suggest, only literal dramatic meaning; by pointing to this (perhaps characteristic) item of his collection the duke is understood by the reader as implicitly denying to the envoy that he has stooped to threaten him." The duke says in effect, "'Of course we've been talking really about art all this time, have we not?'"[26] Although I agree that the duke's gesture has an immediate rhetorical purpose, it seems a limited number of "general meanings" may also be assigned to Neptune. We see the bronze, in other words, from the duke's perspective *and* from the poet's. Just as the cherry blossoms look different to us (and the poet) and to the duke, so we also see the sculpture in two ways at once. Neptune does not gratuitously *tame* a sea-horse here. Nor is it gratuitous that the duke's last word is "me." As Tucker puts it, the duke's reference to Neptune shows him reaching "for godlike, repressive power over protean circumstances he would like to forget."[27]

Because of the juxtaposition of perspectives, the way we understand Neptune is quite different from the way we grasp, for example, the significance of the bird in Hardy's "Darkling Thrush." In Hardy's poem all details describing the bird corroborate the speaker's response to it; insofar as we see the bird, we see it as the speaker does, though of course our attention is focused on and through the speaker's emotions. We may attach numerous meanings to Hardy's thrush, but these meanings are in no way antithetical to the speaker's understanding of the bird. In "My Last Duchess" the bronze Neptune is seen by the speaker, but like the poet we are aware that the speaker's understanding of it in important ways falls short of our understanding of the sculpture.

Furthermore, if we credit the poem's historical referent, we may attach a specific irony to this Neptune from Innsbruck. Louis S. Friedland makes a case for this Duke of Ferrara as Alfonso II and his prospective bride as the daughter of Ferdinand, Count of Tyrol.[28] For the reader who has unearthed this reference, the duke's Neptune may seem a first step in the control of Tyrolean beauty: his next acquisition from across the Alps will be human. Equally telling is the fact that Alfonso II imprisoned Tasso: judging from this reference we may see the duke as a man who would, at any extreme, dominate the creative force of art.[29] More essential, of course, than these particular referents is our coming to share and to confirm the poet's larger perspective; we judge the duke's deficiencies in terms of values he does not perceive at the same time that we savor the ironies arising from our view of his ignorance.

Like the bishop and the duke and unlike Fra Lippo Lippi, Browning's late Greek philosopher Cleon is caught in a web of circumstance and convention he is unable to transcend. In "Cleon," Browning most clearly poses the problem of whether a man can rise above his circumstances when the very virtues of his culture block him from some kinds of understanding. Our judgments of Lippi and of the bishop are complicated by our conviction that the Renaissance was an age of sensuality and of internal contradictions. Browning in effect leads us to make allowances for differences in epochs and cultures. But do we see Cleon as a hapless victim of his built-in historical perspective or as necessarily limited by the views of his culture despite his thirst for a different kind of knowledge? Cleon himself possesses a fairly sophisticated historical view. As we have seen, he rejects a view of the past as an unsurpassable golden age and advocates a multiple perspective view of history. Cleon's view contrasts markedly with that of Empedocles in Arnold's "Empedocles on Etna" to which Browning's "Cleon" may be a reply.[30] Unlike Cleon, Empedocles looks back and speaking for his age (and Arnold's?) declares:

> And we shall fly for refuge to past times,
> Their soul of unworn youth, their breath of
>   greatness;
> And the reality will pluck us back.[31]

Despite his unwillingness to fly to the past for refuge and despite his theory of history, Browning's philosopher is able to see only those possibilities in his historical situation that spring from the refinement of Greek culture (a culture somewhat like the voice of "culture" in the Pope's monologue of *The Ring and the Book*). As

Herbert Tucker points out, Cleon is uncomfortable with "barbarian beginnings." Cleon imagines that a god descended and

> showed simultaneously
> What, in its nature, never can be shown,
> Piecemeal or in succession;—showed, I say,
> The worth both absolute and relative
> Of all his children from the birth of time.
> ("Cleon," 117–21)

Like his longing for "some future state . . . unlimited in capability for joy," this hope for the timeless view Cleon finds only a dream; and Cleon sees in Paul only a "mere barbarian Jew." Cleon's longing for timelessness in itself reduces future possibilities. As Tucker concisely puts it, Cleon "denies not just the future according to Paul, but even the future as offered on venerable pagan grounds. . . . He rejects the living word in both Christian and pagan senses because what he would purge from the word is its staying power, the elusive life of poetic figuration."[32] As Tucker notes we need not expect Cleon to 'convert' in order to see his deficiencies. Does Browning imply, then, that we should not expect Cleon to transcend his own cultural and intellectual milieu?

We have several indications that Cleon's emphasis on multiple perspective and his impulses toward growth are countered by personal pride and a clinging to personal prejudice. Cleon's pride, unlike the duke's, is based upon accomplishment, but we may well question whether Cleon is indeed a "better flower" though smaller than Homer. As in so many other monologues, our perspective on the speaker is unlike his view of himself. Browning gives us a standpoint for regarding Cleon by beginning the poem with an epigraph from Acts 17. Browning quotes the sermon from the Areopagus in which Paul chides the Athenians for superstition. Paul admonishes these Stoics and Epicureans, to whom he seemed "a setter forth of strange gods," that they should seek the Lord: "For in him we live, and move, and have our being; as certain also of your own poets have said, For we are also his offspring" (Acts 17:28). Paul goes on to warn his hearers that although once men lived in ignorance, "the times of this ignorance God winked at; but now commandeth all men every where to repent" (Acts 17:30). Paul's warning should, I think, be set beside Cleon's boast that:

> I have written three books on the soul,
> Proving absurd all written hitherto,
> And putting us to ignorance again.
> ("Cleon," 57–59)

Cleon comes close to being one of those "certain poets," but in determinedly maintaining his ignorance he reasons himself into a corner. He is as much a prisoner of thought as Arnold's Empedocles. And he is as condescending toward Paul and Protus, too, as the duke is toward his social inferiors:

> Thou wrongest our philosophy, O king,
> In stooping to inquire of such an one,
> As if his answer could impose at all!
> ("Cleon," 346–48)

Cleon, even more than Sordello, allows himself to be overcome by his circumstances; he is caught in a web of personal situational irony ("my sense of joy / Grows more acute . . . while every day my hairs fall"), and, from the point of view of the poet and his readers who recognize Paul's significance, Cleon is caught too in a historical irony.

In Cleon, and in Lippi, the bishop, and the duke, we come to understand speakers who are to varying degrees aware of the limitations of their natures and of their own ages. As we read the monologues we form judgments by placing their limited perspectives in the wider consciousness of the poet's view, which we eventually come to share (though again the poet's historical view may differ from a twentieth-century perspective). In addition to providing historical detail, a number of Browning's monologuists place themselves in explicitly historical perspectives. The Pope, John, Cleon, Andrea del Sarto, and Fra Lippo Lippi furnish us with the historical perspective through which they should be judged. And those speakers who best perceive their situations in this way overcome perspective through perspective. Cleon gives us half a context—he sees the workings of history and places himself against the background of Greece's great age, but, as we have seen, Cleon misses the important half of the historical view—the future. Other Browning monologuists fare better. These speakers can steadily view themselves from what Langbaum calls a general perspective. In distinguishing the soliloquy from the dramatic monologue, Langbaum notes that the soliloquist in self-analysis and internal debate views himself from "a general perspective which corresponds to the audience's perspective; the monologuist directs his attention outward and consequently, there is a disequilibrium in what the speaker reveals and what he understands about himself" (*PE*, 146). Langbaum's distinction may be more useful for discussing perspective in monologues than for dividing monologues from soliloquies. As we have noted, both St. John in "A Death in the Desert" and the Pope in *The Ring and the Book* see themselves from a general historical perspective. John views the world as continual change; for him value is indeed in the individual unique imprint of an absolute:

> Since all things suffer change save God the Truth,
> Man apprehends Him newly at each stage
> Whereat earth's ladder drops, its service done;
> And nothing shall prove twice what once was
>   proved.
>   ("Death in the Desert," 431–34)

The Pope too looks to the world of the next century, and, though we may cavil at his embracing eighteenth-century skepticism as medicinal doubt, we commend the breadth of perspective that underlies his astuteness as a moral judge.

Browning's two painters, Lippi and Andrea del Sarto, create in an equally specific way the contexts in which they are to be judged as artists and as men. In contrast to Lippi, John, or the Pope, Andrea del Sarto, like Cleon, creates a context that betrays his failure. His preoccupation with Leonardo, Michelangelo, and Raphael belies his protestation of independence:

I, painting from myself and to myself,
Know what I do, am unmoved by men's blame
Or their praise either.
("Andrea," 92–94)

A hundred lines later, however, we find Andrea quoting Michelangelo's early praise of him. This internal contradiction motivates Andrea's attempts at rationalization; in conceiving himself in the context of the history of great art he also perceives, from moment to moment, his deficiencies. Andrea asks the world, as the poet asks us, to judge him against Renaissance greatness; he creates a perspective for us but cannot look for long at himself in this context. The poet, the reader, and Andrea share a common perspective from moment to moment, but then the speaker turns away and leaves us pondering the discrepancy between the grand scale on which he would be judged and the pettiness of his rationalization. We thread a labyrinth of contrast. In a striking series of vacillations, Andrea complains to Lucrezia:

> Had the mouth there urged,
> "God and the glory! never care for gain
> The present by the future, what is that?
> Live for fame, side by side with Agnolo!
> Raphael is waiting: up to God, all three!"
> I might have done it for you. So it seems:
> Perhaps not. All is as God over-rules.
> Beside, incentives come from the soul's self;
> The rest avail not.
> ("Andrea," 127–35)

Andrea would judge the "present by the future" and cannot; but the poet asks his readers in observing Andrea's contradictions to do just that. As we follow Andrea's shifting thought our judgment is constantly modified. In Andrea's failure of will, in his half-realization that his excuses are weak, we feel a certain pathos. By the end of the poem, though, Andrea's bald pleading and his admission that he has wronged Francis and his parents prepare us to see him almost transform the future in order to make the present more bearable. Like the bishop who would keep his senses in eternity, Andrea makes heaven after his own image:

> In heaven, perhaps, new chances, one more chance—
> Four great walls in the New Jerusalem,
> Meted on each side by the angel's reed,
> For Leonard, Rafael, Agnolo and me
> To cover—the three first without a wife,
> While I have mine! So—still they overcome
> Because there's still Lucrezia,—as I choose.
> Again the Cousin's whistle! Go, my Love.
> ("Andrea," 260–67)

Andrea cannot sustain even this dream of heaven, and he is aware of its crumbling. Although he turns away from judging himself by the future, we continue to do so, and as a result we feel that we see his half-conscious inconsistencies from a perspective broader than his own.

Our sense of a character judging himself in light of a future that includes us is even stronger in "Fra Lippo Lippi" than in "Andrea del Sarto." Lippi lives in confidence that his is the rising tide of art, and his prognostication is confirmed from our later point of view. Even if we are aware of Browning's confusion over the dates of Masaccio ("Guidi"), we can share Lippi's view of the future and his judgment of himself by it. He declares confidently:

> —why, I see as certainly
> As that the morning-star's about to shine

> What will hap some day. We've a youngster here
> Comes to our convent, studies what I do,
> Slouches and stares and lets no atom drop
> . . . .
>   he'll paint apace,
> I hope so—though I never live so long,
> I know what's sure to follow.
>
> ("Lippi," 271–80)

Lippi defends his theory of art as seeing, lending our minds out, and he wishes to be allowed to paint all things truly:

> How much more,
> If I drew higher things with the same truth!
> That were to take the Prior's pulpit-place,
> Interpret God to all of you! Oh, oh,
> It makes me mad to see what men shall do
> And we in our graves!
>
> ("Lippi," 308–13)

With Lippi's prescience we concur. Our sense of the history of art confirms his judgment; and we even share his way of seeing the faces and places that appear in the poem. Their meaning for and effect on him are their meaning for us. Our perspective and the poet's match Lippi's but for two things: first, we come later still than any future Lippi can foresee, and so our historical perspective, though in harmony with his, is somewhat broader; and second, taking Lippi's views as true for art generally, we take Browning's poem itself as a confirmation of Lippi's way of seeing. Our broader historical perspective, however, establishes a yet higher degree of ironic complexity in our reading of Lippi than in his understanding of himself. The general contours of a reading of Lippi's character are clear, but the particular cast of our understanding depends greatly on our confidence in historical and aesthetic progress. Whether he realizes it or not, Lippi may be interpreting God well enough in his own way; a thoroughgoing historical perspectivism is likely to temper confidence that future art shall do it better.

The measure of Lippi's character may be not that he predicts the future, but that he is poised before it both with confidence and with an awareness of limitation.

It is the paradoxical nature of this balancing between past and future that forces us to see a certain irony in Browning's treatment of even his most admirable monologuists—Lippi, St. John, or the Pope. All three of these monologuists encompass the future only so far as mortals may. The poet is historically beyond them, as we are beyond him. St. John expresses a willingness to continue his ministry despite his readiness for death, but he dies when the work of the next age is yet to be done. And the writer of the postscript, the "one" who comes after John, has ironically missed the purport of John's words, for he expects the millenium imminently. In "A Death in the Desert" we can know nothing that is not provisional, subject to change in time. The only escape from this flux is through faith and ultimately through a faithful death or through the false sense of certainty exhibited by the writer of the postscript. Browning's St. John and his Pope Innocent share equally a conviction of the importance of Christian revelation, yet neither is free of his time. Both are precursors to ages of doubt, though neither doubts some form of revelation will be possible in time to come. As each of them explores the nature of historical limitation each is largely spared the poet's local irony. It is only in the wider sense of being, like the poet himself, caught in the necessary ignorance before the future that these monologuists are treated ironically. Although they can still speak they can have only a temporary place on which to stand. Neither the Pope in *The Ring and the Book* nor John in "A Death in the Desert" is given the last word. And even Lippi ends by scuttling off, claiming ambiguously "so all's saved for me" and facing a "grey beginning."

Browning's more limited speakers, Cleon or Andrea del Sarto, for example, are treated more iron-

CHAPTER FIVE 197

ically still. Whereas Lippi, the Pope, and St. John rise through an understanding of their historical situations to a view of themselves and their vital concerns that we can in large measure share, Cleon and Andrea del Sarto are caught in half-awareness. Because their perspectives are considerably more limited than ours, we may join the poet in regarding these speakers in a doubly ironic light.

In examining these monologues—and they are in the main monologues about time and art—I have suggested that Browning carefully juxtaposes historical perspectives and invites his readers to understand and to judge his monologuists in historical context. But judgment, as I began by suggesting, is more complex than moral condemnation, and the juxtaposition of perspectives may result in a balance so delicate that the reader need not feel any moral or historical superiority to the speaker. "A Tocatta of Galuppi's" is perhaps the best example of this balance. We need not make up our minds about whether the speaker in "Galuppi" is unusually limited.[33] In fact it would appear that the speaker both is and is not limited by his historical perspective, by his scientific and mathematical leanings, by his delight in lovely women, by the common human fate that he shares even with the light Venetians.

Galuppi's music provides the thread that connects the monologuist, a nineteenth-century Englishman, with the past of eighteenth-century Venice. The focus of the monologue is equally on the monologuist and on the past he imagines, at first in clichés and then in sensuous detail. It is only through the speaker's imagination upon hearing the toccata that the reader sees Galuppi, hears Galuppi's music, or imagines Galuppi's audience. Thus the monologuist is one of two audiences for the cold ironies of Galuppi's music. The Venetians turn from praising the tocatta, to kisses and to death. The music tells them, so the monologuist imagines, that their lives and loves are vain. The speaker hears a message in the tocatta for himself as well. He imagines Galuppi's music warning him that for all his science and his belief in immortality, he is as mortal as the dead Venetian pleasure-seekers. The message of Galuppi's music may be ironic, but the monologuist who hears it is neither an ironist nor a victim of irony. The speaker wants the heart to scold either Galuppi or the men and the women who were Galuppi's audience.

The speaker in "A Tocatta of Galuppi's" is left feeling "chilly and grown old" just as the Bishop of St. Praxed's, Cleon, and Andrea del Sarto are. But as readers we have no perch in the aery dome of St. Praxed's from which to regard the limitations of the speaker, for the speaker seems well aware of the complexities of his historical position. His imagination of Galuppi's musical message shows clearly that the speaker sees the possible contradictions between his scientific world view and his belief in immortality. The message the speaker imagines in the music makes equally clear that he recognizes his evocation of the past may be nostalgic or sensual indulgence. The speaker does not acquiesce finally to Galuppi's skepticism or to his own clichéd imaginings; he acquiesces unwillingly to the passage of time. The reader can only feel superior to the monologuist to the extent that he or she can feel superior to the force of time.

The monologuist of "A Tocatta of Galuppi's" greets the tension between past and present and the contest between sensuous delight and death with a sympathetic sigh; and the poet balances the speaker's moment of grave contemplation against the energy of his words. It is hard indeed to read only grave resignation into "Galuppi's" troachaic fourteener triplets. In "Galuppi," Browning creates an equipoise between past and present, between the possibilities and limitations of art or love. For many of Browning's other monologuists, however, history is more limiting and more cruel than it is for the speaker of "Galuppi." Their historical situations invite the reader to see through local and specific ironies and to become caught up in the endless and ironic dialectic of history.

IRONIC SPEECHES AND IRONIC SPEAKERS

As this exploration of historical detail and juxtaposed perspectives in the monologues suggests, Browning's dramatic speakers are treated with varying degrees of irony. In some of the historical monologues, one feels an easy fit between the reader's and the poet's perspectives—the ironies of, say, the Bishop of St. Praxed's situation are established clearly, and our understandings of his position vary only as we find his monologue more or less comic. The Bishop's hypocrisy, like Andrea del Sarto's failure, is understandable through the interpretation of stable ironies. In other monologues a more general irony operates, and it is more difficult, consequently, to find a fit between the poet's perspective and our own. Indeed the monologuist may be ironic at his listener's expense, and the degree of the poet's irony may be hard to measure. The scope of these local and general ironies is fairly represented by three different treatments of Christian belief: "An Epistle of Karshish," "Cleon," and "Bishop Blougram's Apology."

As paired poems both "Karshish" and "Cleon" offer a number of local ironies and exploit a number of the ready-made containers for what Muecke calls general irony. Wayne Booth's model of stable irony is particularly helpful in describing how we read these monologues. Booth analyzes the reading of stable irony in terms of the metaphor of building. In stable irony we have two edifices, one clearly superior to and above the other. The lower edifice is built of the contradictions and incongruities that, when put together, form unacceptable conclusions or inconsistent characters. When, as readers of an ironic work, we become aware of these inconsistencies and find them unacceptable, we reconstruct them according to some other scheme, and in doing so we accept the author's invitation to come "dwell" with him in his superior edifice. In the lower dwelling remain the victims of irony (the characters who remain trapped in their inconsistencies) and readers who cannot make the leap to the room with an ironic view.[34] In discovering inconsistencies and incongruities we may find contradictions within the speaker or between his view and our own context. Such contradictions are a source of stable or local ironies in our historical judgment of the Bishop of St. Praxed's or the Duke of Ferrara; Cleon and Karshish, too, must be understood through the reconstruction of contradictions.

In "Karshish," for example, we find inconsistencies both within the speaker and between his view and our own historical context. Karshish himself cannot make mind and heart agree about Lazarus's story. He exclaims, "The very God! think, Abib; dost thou think?" while he calls Lazarus a madman; and, though Karshish can be an ironist himself, he is unaware of these contradictions. In seeing how medicine, magic, and spiritual intuition make for internal conflict, we rise to the ironic view of Karshish. The physician's story is also ironic in contrast to the understanding of history the poet expects us to share with him. As is consistent with his connections to the teacher-sage-physician he shared with Abib, Karshish presents Lazarus as a case study and his cure as a potent spell. When we discover at line 108 that the "case" is what we regard as the most dramatic of Christ's miracles (whether or not we are committed to a belief in miracles), we enter the ironic point of view by setting the physician's point of view against the traditional Christian view. In Karshish's attributing the earthquake at the Crucifixion to the prefiguration of his own sage's death, we see a similar discrepancy. Karshish in fact describes himself as an ironist—the classic ingenu ironist—who has "feigned / To be an ignoramus in our art according to some preconceived design" and who has heard the "land's practitioners" "prattle fantastically" ("Karshish," 236–41). He also views ironically the skeptics who expected Christ to stop the earthquake; but, as David Shaw puts it, we see Karshish "being ironical at the skeptics' expense, while Browning is being ironical at his."[35] In achieving a complete picture of Karshish's character, we reconstruct consistencies from contradiction. We reconcile his enthusiasm and his pose of calm detachment, and we come to understand his explanations of events, which contradict our own explanations, as manifesting the limitations of his character and his time.

Like "An Epistle of Karshish," "Cleon" is ironic in its juxtaposition of historical points of view. We again see the ironic contrast within a personality in the clash between Cleon's intuitions and his reasoning from the premises of Greek culture. Though the process of reconstruction involves similar elements, we reach different judgments of the two characters. Karshish's blind spots seem not so much culpable ignorance as an inability to give full expression to his instinctive belief. In Cleon, on the other hand, we have a general ironist of the Muecke variety—Cleon senses his own life as ironic, but he can find no solution to the infinite negativity that follows from his premise that God either does not care or is an absentee landlord. When we discover Cleon's historical mistake, his refusal to recognize Paul, we construct the ironic building and move in; and, if we are willing to share a Christian context at all, we reject at the same time the premises that make absolute Cleon's negativity.

To this point, we can interpret the historical and individual ironies in "Cleon" and "Karshish" in similar ways, though we arrive at reconstructions of quite different men. "Cleon," however, offers more difficulties of interpretation than "An Epistle of Karshish." In "Cleon" we must ask ourselves the question Booth so often repeats, "Where do we stop?" How much of Cleon's monologue, how many of his arguments, must we ironically reconstruct? Booth points to varying degrees of uncertainty in different aspects of interpreting monologues. We know with certainty about the total character of a speaker, but, Booth says, "We are not quite so sure about whether the author would share our precise tone in describing him." Because the monologue form denies us the larger context that directs our judgment in novels there will be room for critical debate about the "intended moral placement, if any."[36] Furthermore, we are often even less certain how a monologue like "Cleon" reflects the author's world view.

In noting the difficulties of reading ironically poems such as "Cleon" or "Bishop Blougram's Apology," we must reconsider those judgments I have been calling essential to our experience of dramatic monologues. A certain number of "precise judgments," as Booth calls them, are surely necessary to understand the local ironies in the monologues and to establish in this process a picture of the speaker's total character. We do judge Cleon's egoism and his cultural chauvinism as a mistaken pride when we see that these characteristics allow him to dismiss his positive intuitions as dreams and to remain oblivious to Paul's importance or to any growth at all. In this we take a first step toward moral placement. To interpret Cleon's character completely and to understand how the monologue reflects the author's view, we have to establish how far Browning's irony goes. In assessing the irony of "Cleon," Park Honan concludes that the speaker's "vanity, his blinding pride, his self-centered smugness and limited intellectuality are all illustrated in his reaction to an event directly different from our own reaction to it."[37] Most readers of "Cleon" will agree with most of this judgment and will feel they dwell with the poet in the house of irony. This assessment, however, need not cast doubt upon all of Cleon's intellectual activities. If we see from his misjudgment of Paul that Cleon is also mistaken in being one-sidedly rationalistic, we need not necessarily conclude that all Cleon's historical notions are unsound. I have already argued that Cleon's belief in viewing the past from multiple perspectives stands in contrast to his inability to change perspectives and that this contrast serves our total picture of Cleon's character by strengthening the final irony. Our total view of Cleon, the tone of our judgment, depends upon how we assess his intellectuality and particularly his historical views. If we feel Browning shares Cleon's disbelief in "golden ages" and his belief that all eras are worth consideration, we will feel the irony of Cleon's life not in his intellectuality or mistaken notions, but in his inability to see the limits of intellect itself. The tone of negative judgment toward Cleon, then, might be mitigated while the irony increased if we regard Cleon as the man of all men and women who (but for his pride) should know how mistakes in historical judgment can be made. If we take the philosopher's historical notions seriously and feel that Browning's irony does not undermine them, we see it is ironic that Cleon should struggle so consciously with historical questions and still be mistaken about what is important in his own age. Our ironic perspective is further widened as we come to realize that in different circumstances a man of Cleon's impulses would have seen Paul differently. For Cleon, in other words, "it could have happened the other way round," and in recognizing this possibility we see that there, but for the grace of our historical perspective, go we.

We place Cleon morally and understand the tone

of Browning's own judgment by seeing the irony of Cleon's historical position, and we must judge the degree to which we feel Cleon's notions should be regarded ironically. A similar but more challenging problem arises in the interpretation of "Bishop Blougram's Apology." With "Bishop Blougram" the reader no longer finds a firm place to stand, a stable structure to construct. Blougram, even more than Cleon, is caught in the play of a general irony, made particularly acute by the fact that Blougram appears to be a thoroughgoing ironist and relativist himself. Blougram is both victim and master of ironies, for he is above all a player of roles. The difficulties in understanding Blougram are especially obvious in the contrast between Blougram and that other limited cleric, the Bishop of St. Praxed's. The depth and certainty of our understanding of these worldly clerics varies in proportion to our ability to see how their perspectives differ from the poet's. In reading "Bishop Blougram" as in "Cleon," we must ask ourselves where to stop; that is, how ironically Browning treats Blougram. In Blougram's case we have fewer indications of the bishop's real beliefs and of Browning's attitude toward him than we do in "The Bishop Orders His Tomb." It is difficult in fact to make of Blougram a consistent character, to reconcile his inconsistencies into a single ironic reading. Blougram, of course, is hardly Browning's only inconsistent character; the Bishop of St. Praxed's has some remarkable inconsistencies of his own. But in "The Bishop Orders His Tomb" one can with some certainty organize the bishop's inconsistencies around a number of clearly defined motives—his desire for a fitting tomb, his rivalry with Gandolf, his lingering concern for public opinion, and his love for the aesthetic and sensual pleasures of this life. Blougram's motives are a good deal less clear than the Renaissance bishop's, and his inconsistencies consequently remain enigmatic. Perhaps this is why, despite its imbalances,

"Bishop Blougram's Apology" continues to attract critical attention. It tantalizes and invites us to achieve a consistent reading at the same time that it baffles.

Such fascination has given rise to any number of radically contradictory interpretations of the poem based on evidence internal to the poem itself, and it has led to an even greater variety of interpretations based on possible historical referents or 'models' for the characters of Blougram and Gigadibs. On the basis of Browning's own comments and of the historical allusions within the poem itself, critics have generally agreed that Blougram is a fictional version of Cardinal Wiseman. But who is Gigadibs? According to various detailed historical reconstructions he has been identified with R. H. Horne, with Rev. Francis Mahony ("Father Prout"), and with none other than Thomas Carlyle.[38] The question of interpretation in "Blougram," then, is not only a question of where the irony stops, but also a question of where one draws the line between too little and too much historical referentiality. Despite the weight of detail involved in the identification of Gigadibs, I would argue that the poem is not entirely a roman à clef and that the character of Gigadibs is too strongly mediated by the bishop's own view clearly to be identified with a single individual. Gigadibs appears much less concretely than Lucrezia does in "Andrea del Sarto." We know certainly that Lucrezia has asked Andrea to paint for her "cousin"; that she desires money for his gambling debts and perhaps also for a new ruff; that she must be entreated to pause with the painter for an hour; that she has insisted on returning to Italy from the French court; that she is listening to Andrea's talk only while she awaits the "cousin's" whistle. We even and perhaps most tellingly learn that, in entering the room, Andrea's "serpentining beauty" has smeared his painting by "carelessly passing" with her "robes afloat" ("Andrea del Sarto," 75). We can say with certainty much less of importance about Gigadibs than about Lucrezia. We know only that Gigadibs has made some sort of agreement with the bishop as to the course of their talk, that he writes "statedly" for *Blackwood's,* sometimes in a Dickensian manner, that he has drunk wine and played with cutlery, and finally that he has started suddenly for Australia. As for Gigadibs's opinions about the bishop and his questions about religion, we know only what the bishop imputes to him. The focus of the monologue, in consequence, is doubly difficult. Although we may find Blougram enigmatic, we must also admit the difficulties of distinguishing between Gigadibs's opinions and Blougram's conjectures about what Gigadibs "will say" or "would reply."

To make matters yet more difficult, Blougram, like Cleon, is himself an ironist. In the epilogue to the "Apology," Browning tells us Blougram "believed, say half he spoke." But deciphering the bishop's irony toward Gigadibs is just as difficult as evaluating Browning's toward the bishop. Blougram from time to time is openly sarcastic. He challenges Gigadibs:

Present your own perfection, your ideal,
Your pattern, man for a minute—oh, make haste,
Is it Napoleon you would have us grow?
("Blougram," 434–36)

He speaks sarcastically too of the "dear middle-age these noodles praise." We may find it ironic that in comparing himself to Shakespeare the bishop does what he sarcastically challenges Gigadibs to do. But we are given few clues as to which of the arguments the bishop offers reflect his own belief.

Not only does Blougram's irony raise difficult inconsistencies, but further complications are also introduced as the poem raises the old theological debate about the relationship between the man and the office.[39] The distinction between the possibly sinful man and the sacramental power of his priestly office was instituted by the Catholic Church (and with less sacramental emphasis was implicitly retained by many Protestant churches as well) in order to separate the force of the sacraments from the sins of the man who might perform them. Blougram is quite aware of the distinction between man and office, but his arguments demonstrate how such a doctrine can become another "ready-made container" of irony. The doctrine itself focuses our attention on the disparity between the individual priest and the priestly ideal. The separation of the man from the office was never intended as a justification for the sins of the man, but only as a justification for the efficacy of the sacraments as channels of grace. In the bishop's arguments, however, this distinction is indeed a "dangerous edge of things"; its original significance is in danger of being lost. The bishop's words lead one to ask whether his sacred office can be merely a role. The bishop comes as close to justifying himself, "a man who is a man and nothing more," as he does to justifying his office. He first introduces what is almost a parody of the distinction by suggesting that Gigadibs despises him as a man while respecting his office—not his priestly office but his "place," or "*status, entourage,* worldly circumstance" (26). Blougram goes on to mention the more orthodox distinction in a way that suggests he has a shaky grasp on how it applies to himself. He describes his clerical clothing and concludes:

>   now folk kneel
> And kiss my hand—of course the Church's hand.
> Thus I am made, thus life is best for me,
> And thus that it should be I have procured;
> And thus it could not be another way,
> I venture to imagine.
>   ("Blougram," 335–40)

Here we see in Blougram, as Susan Hardy Aiken suggests, a sham hero made by his clothes and by clerical hand-kissing.[40] Like Cleon's situation, the bishop's situation is deeply ironic. He may distinguish man and office, justifying the man in the process: "Thus it could not be another way." And yet Blougram is at least as death-haunted as Cleon, for in the end the Church's hand like the Church's clothes revert to the Church, and Blougram will be left like an actor undressed, a player when the play or the game is ended. In this light Blougram's famous analogy of Popes and actors is clearly a perversion of the separation between man and office and a recognition of its ironic consequences:

> It's like those eerie stories nurses tell,
> Of how some actor on a stage played Death,
> With pasteboard crown, sham orb and tinselled dart,
> And called himself the monarch of the world;
> Then, going to the tire-room afterward,
> Because the play was done, to shift himself,
> Got touched upon the sleeve familiarly,
> The moment he had shut the closet door,
> By Death himself. Thus God might touch a Pope
> At unawares, ask what his baubles mean,
> And whose part he presumed to play just now.
> ("Blougram," 66–76)

By his own analogy the bishop himself proves to be the dangerous edge of things, the body in whom man and office of necessity come together. Eventually play, player, and Blougram will be one.

Metaphorically, Blougram and the player are difficult to distinguish by the end of the poem. In his double-edged comparison of himself with Shakespeare, Blougram seizes the moment to ask rhetorically a question that we cannot answer as he would wish:

> Why then should I who play that personage,
> The very Pandulph Shakespeare's fancy made,
> Be told that had the poet chanced to start
> From where I stand now (some degree like mine
> Being just the goal he ran his race to reach)

> He would have run the whole race back, forsooth,
> And left being Pandulph, to begin write plays?
> 								("Blougram," 521–26)

As he plays his part and constructs his similes Blougram lessens himself bit by bit.

Blougram's analogies give rise to yet another ironic reversal. In Blougram's imaginary sea voyage, we see both sides of Catholicism, the ascetic and the worldly. Of course, "worldly circumstance" so dominates Blougram's thought that its ascetic antithesis only appears as if by accident. Ironically, Blougram associates asceticism with Gigadibs and with skepticism. So the bishop imagines Gigadibs fitting up his cabin with "slabbed marble, what a bath it makes" and with a painting of the ascetic St. Jerome.[41] When these furnishings don't fit, Blougram says, Gigadibs will travel in "naked boards" and "mortified" mutter about Blougram's own outfit. Finally, Blougram abandons the premises he attributes to Gigadibs and argues for instinctive faith:

> Trust you an instinct silenced long ago
> That will break silence and enjoin you love
> What mortifed philosophy is hoarse,
> And all in vain, with bidding you despise?
> 								("Blougram," 630–33)

Figuratively speaking, Jerome is mortified, Gigadibs is mortified, skeptical philosophy is mortified, but the bishop is comfortable and reduces the pinch of evil to a pinch of snuff to set his complacency tingling.

But is this all? Neither the bishop's worldliness nor his image of humble asceticism and blind faith is particularly appealing (see lines 705–9); yet the bishop would seem to have a valid objection to philosophical complacency. Total submission to papal authority beats

> acquitting God with grace
> As some folk do. He's tried—no case is proved,
> Philosophy is lenient—he may go!
> ("Blougram," 710–12)

Moreover, the Bishop's central argument on Christian ground (lines 599–712) is in relatively more simple and direct language than his beginning arguments.[42] For all his self-justification, Blougram appears to have some self-knowledge, too. The bishop clearly sees that he may be taken for a fool if he believes dogmatically or for a knave if his belief is hypocritical. Furthermore, he has a measure of that general historical perspective Browning usually commends. The bishop sees his plight or, rather, Gigadibs's accusations as the curse of his time:

> It's through my coming in the tail of time,
> Nicking the minute with a happy tact.
> Had I been born three hundred years ago
> They'd say, "What's strange? Blougram of course believes;"
> And, seventy years since, 'disbelieves of course.'
> ("Blougram," 412–16)

Blougram further implies that Gigadibs is like those who would expect Blougram's belief to correspond to the temper of his time because their own beliefs are purely conventional. Gigadibs, Blougram argues, is an unthinking and fashionable skeptic, and were the fashion different his beliefs would change. Blougram asks Gigadibs, coming in the middle ages, the time of belief,

> How should you feel, I ask, in such an age,
> How act? As other people felt and did;
> With soul more blank than this decanter's knob
> ("Blougram," 688–90)

Here we may feel a congruence of our perspectives with Blougram's and not ironic distancing.

The Bishop's self-knowledge, however, is also

double-edged. Self-knowledge is only a hair's breadth from self-justification. In the bishop's comparison of himself with Shakespeare, self-knowledge and self-praise are coupled:

> Spare my self-knowledge—there's no fooling me!
> If I prefer remaining my poor self,
> I say so not in self-dispraise but praise.
> If I'm a Shakespeare, let the well alone;
> Why should I try to be what now I am?
> If I'm no Shakespeare, as too probable,—
> His power and consciousness and self-delight
> And all we want in common, shall I find—
> Trying for ever?
> ("Blougram," 494–502)

Even in his final turn on Gigadibs, the tension between self-knowledge and self-defense is evident. The bishop lists those "exceptional / And privileged great natures that dwarf mine" (935–39). And he admits such men "Carry the fire, all things grow warm to them / Their drugget's worth my purple, they beat me" (941–42). We cannot help but agree with the bishop that his is no privileged great nature; at the same time the great poet, statesman, or artist, like the great painters in "Andrea del Sarto," provides a context in which we judge the bishop. It is significant, however, that in his list of great natures Blougram can come up with no better a religious model than "a zealot with a mad ideal in reach" (936). This detail points in fact to the heart of Blougram's predicament—his absolutism.

Like Cleon, Blougram sees his life as immutably what it is: "And thus I have procured." His view of religion itself is equally absolute. He began his argument by justifying the religion he "happened to be born in" as the "most pronounced moreover, fixed, precise / And absolute form of faith in the whole world" (305–7). Blougram cannot, it seems, muster the absolute vocational commitment that his view of religion requires; the man cannot come up to the absolute demands of the office. But unlike Lippi, Blougram has no other vocation by which to justify himself.

In some measure, then, we can construct a consistent reading of the bishop's character by noting the ironic consequences of his absolutism and of the distinction between the man and his office. The bishop's limitations may even be balanced by his self-knowledge, by his historical perspective, and by the sheer delight and virtuosity of his argument. Still, I would argue, the bishop eludes us; we cannot be sure about the "intended moral placement" in "Bishop Blougram's Apology." The inconclusiveness of the bishop's position and the fact that Gigadibs is given no room for reply within the bishop's speech necessitate the epilogue.

The epilogue, in turn, creates more difficulties than it resolves, and finally it robs us of the kind of closure that is so satisfying in "The Bishop Orders His Tomb." In "The Bishop" we clearly stand with the poet somewhere above St. Praxed's "aery dome" and savor the contradictions of which we are sure the bishop is unaware. His final reversal, his conquest of Gandolf in the reassertion, "as still he envied me, so fair she was," is the bishop's character encapsulated and our ironic understanding of him completed. In "Bishop Blougram" we must be told something of what the bishop thinks in addition to what he says; it is as if the poet must step in to provide a perspective for us that the bishop's words themselves do not create. The implied author tells us directly of the bishop, "He said true things, but called them by wrong names." It is difficult to decide, finally, which things the bishop called by wrong names, to determine how much he knows of himself, and to say exactly how compromised he is by ignoring certain "hell-deep instincts." Ultimately, it is even impossible to say that the bishop has 'converted' Gigadibs. Gigadibs does have an attack of healthy vehemence, but we are only told that the poet *hopes* he is ploughing and studying the gospel. For all we know, Gigadibs is simply cultivating *son jardin* and meditating his mortified philosophy. The final shift of focus from Blougram toward Gigadibs, moreover, weakens the poem's closure and, in effect, opens the ending. We are left with the shadowy figure of Gigadibs and the still enigmatic and more powerful presence of Bishop Blougram.

Blougram's absolutism hinders him from fully participating in the dialectical tension of aspiration and finitude; it bars him from turning his skepticism, his ability to see ironies, and his historical relativism into enthusiasm; his love of luxury prohibits him from the only refuge of the skeptic—the unencumbered leap of faith. If Cleon is, as I have suggested, the contextualist historian gone bad, Blougram is the historical ironist or relativist gone bad. Cleon's aestheticism, his capitulation to his circumstances, trap him in the cruelly ironic position of the aging epicure. Blougram's absolutism bars him from voyages of spirit he can metaphorically envision. Stationary, he can only cut away the ground on which he stands. Browning gives due measure both to Cleon's historical contextualism and to Blougram's irony and skepticism: in these monologues as in the minds of these monologuists, reality is various and multiple; the present no less than the past is ambiguous. But the poet's ironies suggest something more.

The dramatic monologue is in Browning's hands a formal strategy for the presentation of a contextualist understanding of history; but in the monologues, Browning also explores the possible limitations of contextualism—aestheticism and sheer relativism. The monologues attempt the double, even paradoxical, task of historicizing our judgment and yet asserting permanent values. Reading the monologues therefore is sometimes a process of reconstructing stable ironies and sometimes the perplexing endeavor of establishing where Browning's ironies stop. The historical complexities of even Browning's local ironies suggest that the process of understanding history is always a struggle with necessarily limited perspectives. Only God can be the perfect poet, the historian to whom all ironies are clear. For the mortal poet the past remains opaque. The best one can do is to counter one perspective with another. As we read the monologues, Browning forces us continually to readjust perspectives. We shift the prism of history until its values have "passed the spectrum into mind, the narrow eye," and we may discover that the eye need not be so narrow after all.

CHAPTER SIX
THE AMBIGUOUS PRESENT AND THE LANGUAGE OF POETRY

IT IS NOT ONLY BROWNING'S IRONIES THAT CONVEY THE complexities of his historical understanding and raise sometimes perplexing interpretive questions. Browning's style has been, if anything, more problematic than his ironies, for it challenged the aesthetic premises of his contemporaries. Even Swinburne, an avowed admirer of Browning's art, exclaimed, "Never surely did any wretched inoffensive dialect of human speech endure such unnatural tortures as those time after time inflicted with diabolical versatility of violence in our patient mother-tongue by the inventive and unsparing author of *Sordello*."[1] The unsparing author of *Sordello* developed his deliberately experimental style from the premise that the ideal poet should combine subjective and objective tendencies or provide "insight" and "outsight," too. In pursuing "objects for men's outer sight," Browning turned to history and, in general, to the matter of fact as the ground for his aesthetic. On the basis of this aesthetic of inclusiveness Browning sought to establish his own position in the English poetic tradition.

I shall argue here that Browning inherited questions about the importance and nature of the lyric that were already marked in romantic poetry[2] and that he inherited an aesthetic in which the lyric was—and has continued to be—the dominant poetic form. Browning's fascination with history, in complex ways, ran counter to this emphasis on lyric, and from the critic's perspective is inseparable from his experiments with genre and with language. Although the poems of the major English romantic poets exceeded the categories of the current aesthetic, by the 1830s the notion of the musical lyric had become a measure of poetry; and according to this standard Browning's readers found his language harsh, dissonant, even barbarous.[3] Browning's own metaphors for his subject matter and for the poetic process can be accounted for in the context of this nineteenth-century criticism. Browning's figures for his art make clear that his poetry is a deliberate struggle with resistant matter, with the "mud," the "clayey field" of historical reality. In his later poetry, Browning became increasingly explicit in his own defense, and in the *Parleyings with Certain People of Importance in Their Day,* especially in the "Parleying with Gerard de Lairesse," Browning satirized what he conceived as the excesses of the sublime style. A systematic consideration of Browning's style in the context of romantic aesthetics, of Browning's figures for the poetic process, and of Browning's stylistic satire will make clear how the style of colloquial speech became the norm in his historical poetry. Against this style we can understand Browning's characters; we can see more clearly the limitations of the numerous monologuists who are self-conscious poetizers; and we can interpret Browning's historical ironies.

The view that Browning's style is deliberately experimental is not entirely new. Walter Bagehot attributed Browning's "grotesqueness" to his realism.[4] Saintsbury credited Browning with deliberation, not ineptness, when he proved that the poet could choose to be "as smooth as smooth."[5] Earlier critics, too, were not slow to recognize the unconventionality of Browning's style; nor, for the most part, were they slow to deplore it. One critic, describing *Sordello* in the *Dublin Review* of May 1840, regretted that Browning's "harsh" and "knotty" poetry did not contribute to the stores of "philosophic insight and harmonious thought." He speculated disapprovingly, "All this makes us fear that the defects, which we had previously fancied were ascribable to immaturity, are the result of some obstinate system which has now obtained too strong a control over the writer, ever to let him stand up a free man, to discourse of noble and regenerating themes in a mode worthy of such, or of the sublime and responsible avocation of a poet."[6] To reviewers with such hopes of the sublime, Browning replies in the "Parleying with Christopher Smart," "learn earth first ere presume / To teach heaven legislation" (255–56).

Learning "earth first" was, for Browning, inextricable from the attempt to understand history, and the multitudinousness of "earth" or of history frustrates any unmediated attempt at the sublime, any reaching for a unified melodic expression of a pure emotion. As Browning understood it, history exceeds any single perspective; historical change challenges any one manifestation of values; historical interconnections compel the poet toward narrative even as they complicate any single narrative thread; and historical ironies are generated by the necessary limitations of finite creatures facing the future. The matter of fact has a density that seems at once to challenge and to run counter to the lyric impulse.

As he took up the matter of history and conceived history in these terms, Browning made an effort to accommodate poetic language to new demands. His knotty and complex style, especially in his blank verse, is an attempt to incorporate and transform the prosaic and is a measure of his distrust of the elevated style. Browning's style, which often dismayed Victorian critics, is both an index to and a consequence of his understanding of history. It is important to recognize, however, that both Browning's historical and his nonhistorical poetry are characterized by metrical versatility and a colloquial and forceful diction. The early lyrics and romances have a dramatic freshness and metrical complexity that one finds also in *Sordello* and the early dramatic monologues. The lyrics, especially, are formally experimental with striking variations in poetic line and stanzaic pattern. *Sordello* and the monologues, in contrast, are often less experimental as to line—they are predominantly iambic pentameter—but they are innovative in their own ways. *Sordello* and "My Last Duchess" exhibit Browning's mastery of the pentameter couplet, and the blank verse monologues from the first show Browning experimenting with subtle variations in diction. It is conceivable that had he never written on historical subjects, Browning's style would have been much the same. It is more likely, though, that Browning's understanding of history was crucial for his differentiation from his predecessors.

In taking up the resistant matter of history Browning embraces the very elements of his materials that romantic poets and critics often called prosaic. Browning's stylistic standard is not a standard of purification but of inclusiveness. This inclusiveness relates equally to language and to subject matter, and it arises in the dialectic of finite and infinite, stasis and change, fact and imagination that Browning repeatedly returns to. These tensions are central both to Browning's understanding of history and to his aesthetic sense.

POETRY OF OBSTACLES: BROWNING AND THE ROMANTICS

Browning's obstinate system so disappointed the Dublin reviewer and other Victorian critics because it both modifies and exploits romantic theories of poetry. As the Dublin reviewer sensed, poetry for Browning is an art of obstacles and struggle, not a spontaneous and natural achievement of lofty harmony. By including history and seeking a style commensurate with what he sees as the difficulties of history, Browning makes poetry itself the ground of struggle. He challenges or modifies the assumptions of such critics as Shelley, Hazlitt, Carlyle, and Wordsworth by insisting that poetry give evidence of the difficulty of its making.

Risking the complaint that his work is harsh or barbarous, Browning deliberately encounters the obstacles that Wordsworth defines as foreign to the poet. In the preface to *Lyrical Ballads* Wordsworth asserts that between the poet and the "image of things" there is no impediment. Poetry, Wordsworth says, "is the image of man and nature. The obstacles which stand in the way of the fidelity of the Biographer and Historian, and of their consequent utility, are incalculably greater than those which are to be encountered by the Poet who has an adequate notion of the dignity of his art."[7] Though some of the historian's particulars are dear to him, Wordsworth would have poetry transcend those things that Browning is at pains to include in his poems. Wordsworth's ideal poet binds together human society "in spite of differences of soil and climate, of language and manners, of laws and customs, in spite of things silently gone out of mind and things violently destroyed."[8]

Browning's poetry of obstacles is equally far from Shelley's conception of poetry. Despite his admiration for his predecessor, Browning often dedicates himself to what Shelley would have called, not poetry, but story. For in Shelley's sense, a story is the "partial" evocation of a "definite period of time, and a certain combination of events which can never again recur." In comparing poem and story, Shelley makes a distinction similar to Wordsworth's distinction between poetry and history. Shelley defines a poem as "the image of life expressed in its eternal truth," and he declares:

> There is this difference between a story and a poem, that a story is a catalogue of detached facts, which have no other bond of connexion than time, place, circumstance, cause and effect; the other is the creation of actions according to the unchangeable forms of human nature, as existing in the mind of the creator, which is itself the image of all other minds. The one is partial, and applies only to a definite period of time, and a certain combination of events which can never again recur; the other is universal, and contains within itself the germ of a relation to whatever motives or actions have place in the possible varieties of human nature.

Shelley concludes that particular facts may obstruct poetry, for the "story of particular facts is as a mirror which obscures and distorts that which should be beautiful: Poetry is a mirror which makes beautiful that which is distorted." Shelley believes that even portions of prose compositions may be poetical; when Plato and Thucydides are poetic they rise above particulars. Paraphrasing Bacon, Shelley cautions, "Epitomes have been called the moths of just history; they eat out the poetry of it."[9]

In Shelley's view true poetry should avoid the impediments of story; to Wordsworth the poem is the force that binds together the "vast empire of human society" transcending time and place. Like Wordsworth and Shelley, William Hazlitt also believes that true poetry transcends impediments, and he lists in still another way the obstacles a poet had best avoid. Writing "On the Prose Styles of Poets," Hazlitt concludes that when the poet takes up prose matter he must fail, because "in prose-subjects, and dry matters of fact and close reasoning, the natural stimulus that at other times warms and rouses, deserts him altogether. . . . Nor does he collect his strength to strike fire from the flint by the sharpness of collision, by the eagerness of his blows."[10] For Hazlitt, poetry is not struggle but the product of natural stimulus.

Yet another version of these distinctions is found in Thomas Carlyle's early advice to Browning that he should try his hand at prose. Characteristically, Carlyle cautions Browning that (prosaic) "diagrams" must precede (poetic) "cartoons": "Not that I deny you poetic faculty; far, very far from that. But unless poetic faculty mean a higher power of common understanding, I know not what it means. One must first make a *true* intellectual representation of a thing, before any poetic interest that is true will supervene."[11] Some fifteen years later, Carlyle forgives Browning his verse, for he perceives "it has grown to be your dialect, it comes more naturally than prose." Though Carlyle eventually conceded poetry to Browning, calling it "fine dancing, if to the music only of drums," yet he remains troubled by what he perceives as Browning's obscurity. He harks back to his "private notion of what is poetry"—a notion of verbal and spiritual music.[12] As Carlyle told an audience (including Browning) in May 1840, "If your delineation be authentically *musical,* musical not in word only, but in heart and substance, in all the thoughts and utterances of it, in the whole conception of it, then it will be poetical; if not, not."[13]

Carlyle, Hazlitt, Shelley, and Wordsworth, for all their differences, share a belief that poetry should be without impediments. For them, "diagrams," "prose-subjects," "stories," historical and biographical fact form the ground above which true poetry rises. Against this understanding of the poetic, Browning develops his own. The essence of Browning's aesthetic is most succinctly displayed in a fugitive poem, "Deaf and Dumb," written in 1862 to accompany a painting by Thomas Woolner:

> Only the prism's obstruction shows aright
> The secret of a sunbeam, breaks its light
> Into the jewelled bow from blankest white;
> So may a glory from defect arise.[14]

Here we have Browning's favorite metaphor—the prism and the pure white light—and his doctrine of imperfection brought together to defend "obstruction" in art. Here, too, Browning chooses for poetry the metaphor that eighteenth- and nineteenth-century tradition had chosen for science.[15] For Keats the prism is an emblem of poetry's undoing, an image of philosophy unweaving the rainbow of art. For Browning the prism is essential to art; only obstruction makes poetry possible.

The poetry of obstacles frequently provoked critics to call Browning's work prosaic. In achieving prosaic strength, the poet accepted and in his own way extended two tenets of romantic poetry: Wordsworth's rejection of artificial poetic diction and defense of poetry as in no way differing from the language of good prose; and the refusal to equate poetry with verse.

When he redefined the division between poetry and prose Wordsworth was forced to defend his "prosaisms" and prose generally, whereas Shelley on the contrary countered the possible ascendency of the prosaic by insisting, like Carlyle, on the importance of music. The difficulty of characterizing any work as prosaic, and the approach to poetry that makes Browning's experiments possible, is most clearly put in Wordsworth's note to the the 1802 Preface. In Wordsworth's additions we see a challenge to the conventional decorum of prose styles with prose subjects, and poetic diction with poetic subjects. Wordsworth explains,

> I here use the word 'Poetry' (though against my own judgment) as opposed to the word Prose, and synonymous with metrical composition. But much confusion has been introduced into criticism by this contra-

distinction of Poetry and Prose, instead of the more philosophical one of Poetry and Matter of Fact, or Science. The only strict antithesis to prose is metre; nor is this, in truth, a *strict* antithesis; because lines and passages of metre so naturally occur in writing prose that it would be scarcely possible to avoid them even were it desireable.[16]

In this note, as well as in the body of the Preface, Wordsworth's enlargement of the poet's province in matter and manner, and his case for a new poetic diction, turn upon a defense of prose. The lines that critics call "prosaisms," Wordsworth says, have a fit place in verse. These lines "metrically arranged" and "according to the strict laws of metre" need in no respect differ from the language of "good prose." Similarly, "some of the most interesting parts of the best poems will be found to be strictly the language of prose, when prose is well written."[17]

In thus defending prose as perfectly appropriate to poetry, Wordsworth takes prose to mean language arising naturally from its subject. In this respect he differs from Hazlitt who sees proper figures and metaphors in prose as the language achieved in a struggle with resistant matter. To put it simply, for Wordsworth prose style and poetic subjects do not necessarily exclude each other, but prose subjects or "matters of fact" are inappropriate to poetry. One feels, consequently, that the real prosaic for Wordsworth is not the *language* of prose so much as the matter of fact that he opposes to poetry. The language of prose becomes the litmus paper for the false in poetry. Thus, prose and the prosaic become two distinguishable categories. The word *prosaic* acquires negative connotation and comes eventually to stand for "dry matters of fact and close reasoning" or for unmusical language.[18]

In establishing his own kind of poetry, Browning pursues still further than Wordsworth the possibilities of "prosaisms" in syntax and diction, and he does not insist so strongly as Wordsworth that these prosaisms be ordered "according to the strict laws of meter." In fact, Browning loosens the strictness of metrical regularity and refuses, especially in his blank verse, to make harmony his first priority.

Whatever their predispositions, Browning's readers have frequently found his work "unpoetic," and their discussions of his style often use the metaphorical vocabulary common to earlier discussion of prose. Saintsbury, for example, concludes that Browning's blank verse is technically defensible but "nearer prose in some ways than any verse we have." Though Saintsbury praises Browning's lyric poems, he refuses to discuss "the propriety of presenting long trains of this verse, upholstered in a diction prosaic enough, for the most part, to bring Wordsworth himself to a sense of the peril of his theory."[19] Curiously, Browning's verse is in fact closer to Hazlitt's description of Edmund Burke's *prose* than to any romantic description of poetic style, including Wordsworth's. In Burke's prose Hazlitt perceives a collision with obstacles that poetry should sedulously avoid. Of Burke, Hazlitt says:

> The principle which guides his pen is truth, not beauty—not pleasure, but power. He has no choice, no selection of subject to flatter the reader's idle taste, or assist his own fancy: he must take what comes, and make the most of it. He works the most striking effects out of the most unpromising materials, by the mere activity of his mind. . . . The nature of his task precludes continual beauty, but it does not preclude continual ingenuity, force, originality. He had to treat of political questions, mixed modes, abstract ideas, and his fancy (or poetry, if you will) was engrafted on these artificially, and as it might sometimes be thought, violently, instead of growing naturally out of them, as it would spring of its own accord from individual objects and feelings. There is a resistance in the *matter* to the illustration applied to it.[20]

Power rather than beauty, violent grafting rather than natural growth, struggle of mind with matter rather than a natural harmony of subject and song—as Hazlitt distinguishes these qualities of Burke's prose, he poses the antithetical categories in which Browning's poetry was judged.[21] No less for Browning than for Burke, writing required struggle with the obstacles of resistant matter.

THE POETRY OF CLAYEY SOIL

Browning never constructed a systematic exposition in prose of his poetic theory, yet in the stylistic exhibition of the "Parleying with Gerard de Lairesse" and in the metaphors he and his readers repeatedly chose to describe his poetry, we can see that he consciously experimented with a new poetic idiom. Metaphorically, Browning defends a poetry that walks instead of soars, that reaches whatever "ultimates" it can without overreaching itself to create from fancy a vision of the sublime. Browning's metaphorical self-defense is at once a justification for his stylistic choices and for his dedication to the matter of fact or history. He conceives of inspiration won through struggle rather than granted in an unbidden burst of song.

In one of the most interesting reviews of Browning's *Men and Women*, George Eliot establishes the context of metaphor in which Browning and his critics debated the nature of poetry. Eliot admires Browning's clear sight, his originality, and his revelations of character, and she attributes his "obscurity" not to obscurity in the poems but to "superficiality" and "drowsy passivity" in the reader. To a reader expecting "conventional phrases and the sing-song of verse" Browning will, indeed, be difficult, for he "has no soothing strains, no chants, no lullabys." Though Eliot prefers originality to conventional harmony, yet like

Wordsworth she holds a "sublime" notion of the office of poetry, and she finds this sublimity incompatible with the struggle she senses in Browning's verse. Browning's greatest deficiency, Eliot says, is his "want of music":

> We have said that he is never prosaic; and it is remarkable that in his blank verse, though it is often colloquial, we are never shocked by the sense of a sudden lapse into prose.... But we must also say that though Browning never founders helplessly on the plain, he rarely soars above a certain tableland—a footing between the level of prose and the topmost heights of poetry. He does not take possession of our souls and set them aglow as the greatest poets—the greatest artists do. We admire his power, we are not subdued by it. Language with him does not seem spontaneously to link itself into song, as sounds link themselves to a melody in the mind of the creative musician; he rather seems by his commanding powers to compel language into verse. He has *chosen* verse as his medium; but of our greatest poets we feel that they had no choice: Verse chose them. Still we are grateful that Browning chose this medium; we would rather have "Fra Lippo Lippi" than an essay on Realism in Art; we would rather have "The Statue and the Bust" than an three-volume novel with the same moral; we would rather have "Holy Cross-Day" than "Strictures on the Society for the Emancipation of the Jews."[22]

For Eliot, then, Browning's poetry rarely soars; it is not spontaneous song but a struggle with language, and it may appropriately be compared to such prose forms as the novel and the essay.

The alternative to soaring is walking poetry. Not surprisingly, Hazlitt uses the pedestrian metaphor for the unspontaneous Burke; and Browning uses a similar figure in precisely the same way. Both Hazlitt and Browning describe pedestrian language that ascends but does not soar. In *The Plain Speaker,* Hazlitt says Burke's style is "airy, flighty, adventurous":

but it never loses sight of the subject; nay, is always in contact with, and derives its increased or varying impulse from it. It may be said to pass yawning gulfs 'on the unsteadfast footing of a spear'; still it has an actual resting-place and tangible support under it—it is not suspended on nothing. It differs from poetry, as I conceive, like the chamois from the eagle: it climbs to an almost equal height, touches upon a cloud, overlooks a precipice, is picturesque, sublime—but all the while, instead of soaring through the air, it stands upon a rocky cliff, clambers up by abrupt and intricate ways, and browzes on the roughest bark; or crops the tenderest flower.

Encountering resistance in his matter, Burke like prose writers generally "always mingles clay with his gold" and has "a journey to go some time through dirty roads, and at others through untrodden and difficult ways."[23]

In his own comments on poetry, Browning takes up precisely this vision of the climber of Alps to describe how his poetry should be read, and he insists, too, that the poet deliberately goes afoot. Both in metaphor and in style we find in Browning the sense of resistant matter that Hazlitt describes as the challenge of writing prose. In a letter replying to John Ruskin's comments on *Men and Women,* Browning remarks:

> We don't read poetry the same way, by the same law; it is too clear. I cannot begin writing poetry till my imaginary reader has conceded licences to me which you demur at altogether. I *know* that I don't make out my conception by my language, all poetry being a putting the infinite within the finite. You would have me paint it all plain out, which can't be; but by various artifices I try to make shift with touches and bits of outlines which *succeed* if they bear the conception from me to you. You ought, I think, to keep pace with the thought tripping from ledge to ledge of my 'glaciers,' as you call them; not stand poking your alpenstock into the holes, and demonstrating that no foot could have

stood there;—suppose it sprang over there? In *prose* you may criticise so—because that is the absolute representation of portions of truth, what chronicling is to history—but in asking for more *ultimates* you must accept less *mediates*.[24]

Although for Browning the walking metaphor is often a criticism of false soaring in poetry, here he chides Ruskin for taking a too pedestrian view of writing; and his notion that poetry is to prose as chronicling is to history is reminiscent of Shelley's calling epitomes the "moths of just history." I think it fair to call Browning's poetry a conscious struggle with resistant matter, but not a deliberate cultivation of the pedestrian or prosaic in the sense that chronicles or "epitomes" can be considered prosaic. Browning keeps the goal of ascent but changes the means of ascent from soaring to climbing. His poet, like Fra Lippo Lippi, would "go a double step," left foot and right foot, body and soul.

Browning again uses the walking metaphor in the "Parleying with Francis Furini." He puts a "sermon" directed to the "evolutionists" in the painter's mouth and has him ask:

> How far can knowledge any ray project
> On what comes after me—the universe?
> Well, my attempt to make the cloud disperse
> Begins—not from above but underneath:
> I climb, you soar,—who soars soon loses breath
> And sinks, who climbs keeps one foot firm on fact
> Ere hazarding the next step: soul's first act
> (Call consciousness the soul—some name we need)
> Getting itself aware, through stuff decreed
> Thereto (so call the body)—who has stept
> So far, there let him stand, become adept
> In body ere he shift his station thence
> One single hair's breadth.
>   ("Furini," 363–75)[25]

And Furini suggests a symbol for the convergence of finite and infinite when he concludes:

> Was such the symbol's meaning,—old, uncouth—
> That circle of the serpent, tail in mouth?
> Only by looking low, ere looking high,
> Comes penetration of the mystery.
>
> ("Furini," 544–47)

The poet, like the painter Furini, does not soar into thin air, but climbs, carrying his own weight with him. He more closely resembles the chamois than the eagle.

In Browning's view the poet who climbs and leaps crevices may well go "dirty roads" and mingle "clay with his gold" as Hazlitt says Burke does. Indeed, it seems one could scarcely read or write walking poetry in the nineteenth century without muddying his feet. In describing *Sordello,* for example, George Henry Lewes remarks that Browning's poem requires such labor as "walking on a new-ploughed field of damp clayey soil would be skating compared to it."[26] Browning's own metaphors for his art take up in similar terms Elizabeth Barrett's early declaration that "we want new forms." Referring to the fable of a husbandman bequeathing to his sons a mysterious treasure, the soil itself, she writes to Browning:

> Why should we go back to the antique moulds . . . classical moulds, as they are so improperly called? . . . Let us all aspire rather to *Life*—& let the dead bury their dead. If we have but courage to face these conventions, to touch this low ground, we shall take strength from it instead of losing it; & of that, I am intimately persuaded. For there is poetry *everywhere* . . . the "treasure (see the old fable) lies all over the field."[27]

In defending *The Ring and the Book* against Julia Wedgwood's moral strictures, Browning uses the same metaphor to describe his poem's business as the explanation of fact. He touches the "low ground" of the market rubbish detailed in the poem's first book, and he calls his matter "this chance lump taken as a sample of the soil."[28] Browning presents the process of shaping the "lump" into poetry through a central metaphor of *The Ring and the Book*. Whereas Hazlitt says the poet shines "without the effort to dig for jewels in the mine of truth," Browning sees the poetic process in just the opposite way:

> From the book, yes; thence bit by bit I dug
> The lingot truth, that memorable day,
> Assayed and knew my piecemeal gain was gold—
> Yes; but from something else surpassing that,
> Something of mine which, mixed up with the mass,
> Made it bear hammer and be firm to file.
> Fancy with fact is just one fact the more.
>
> (*RB*, 1.453–59)

Poetry, then is not the natural and unbidden burst of song but the thing made on the poet's forge. The earth-bound poet puts strength before beauty; as Browning says in the "Epilogue" to *Pacchiarotto*, he makes his vintage from nettles or "grape of the ground," not from fairy cowslips. Or, as he advises in "Reverie," one should "Try the clod ere test the star!"[29] In the struggle for poetry, the artist participates in the larger struggle with formlessness that constitutes life for the best of men who strive to convert even air into "a solid he may grasp and use" ("A Death in the Desert," 585).

It would be misleading, however, to suggest that Browning's aesthetic, his defense of the poetry of clayey soil, is always so unambiguously presented as it is in such poems as "Reverie." I shall argue, indeed, that the "Parleying with Gerard de Lairesse" represents a subtle and satirical approach to "walking poetry" and the false sublime. More deeply ambiguous is Browning's other poem which is directly indebted to Gerard de Lairesse, "Childe Roland to the Dark Tower Came." As Clarice Short has argued, in "Childe Roland" Browning's dramatic speaker is not a mounted knight but a pedestrian.[30] The ground he traverses is unusually muddy, even in Browning's work. He turns out of the "dusty thoroughfare" and into the "darkening path" to the tower, slogging his way through soil that looks "kneaded up with blood" (75). Across the river the land is no better. Some beast has trampled the "dank / Soil to a plash," and all that remains between the speaker and the dark tower is a plain of "marsh," "bog, clay and rubble, sand and stark black dearth" (150). The marshy rubble is broken by clumps of moss or "substances like boils" (153). Just as the whole of the poem is a nightmarish transformation of Browning's emphasis on struggle, so the land of "Childe Roland" is a ghastly transformation of the "earth," "clods," and "soil" Browning's poems often celebrate.

In the striking stanza of "Childe Roland" that I have been quoting, Browning rhymes "earth" with "mirth" and "dearth"; the range of the rhyme can be taken to represent the range of Browning's aesthetic. "Earth" and "mirth"—or at least earth and the plenitude of the actual—are frequently coupled in Browning's poems. In "Childe Roland," however, earth is characterized by scarcity; dearth is coupled with death. Like *King Lear,* the play that furnished Browning his title, "Childe Roland" "smells of mortality."[31]

Whereas the earth of "Childe Roland" is more than characteristically muddy, the poem's style is more than characteristically knotty, harsh, and difficult. The speaker's words are not part of any specifiable occasion; he has no interlocutor except, briefly, the hoary cripple, and his audience generally is undefined. As the speaker recounts his struggle through marsh, mud, and imprisoning battlefield, the language itself is tortured. Browning's nightmare poem culminates in the very stylistic excess of which his critics complained. Consider, for example, stanza twelve, a descriptive passage thoroughly the reverse of Wordsworth's ideal of common experience presented in common but purified language.

> If there pushed any ragged thistle-stalk
>   Above its mates, the head was chopped; the bents
> Were jealous else. What made those holes and rents
> In the dock's harsh swarth leaves, bruised as to baulk
> All hope of greenness? 't is a brute must walk
>   Pashing their life out, with a brute's intents.
>   ("Childe Roland," 67–72)

Acoustically, this passage expresses the speaker's horror at the violence he either perceives in or attributes to his surroundings. At the same time, it could have furnished Swinburne with a perfect exhibition of the versatile violence Browning exerted upon our mother tongue. Nothing could be less musical. Instead of music, "Childe Roland" ends with the speaker entrapped, "inside the den." And the den becomes "din": "noise was everywhere." Noise, neither language nor music, increases "like a bell" until it becomes a deathknell for the speaker himself and can only be answered by the speaker's challenge, the enigmatic sounds of his slughorn.

"Childe Roland," then, can be read as a nightmare of language, ending in a den / din, a deathknell, and a challenge to which there is no recorded response. Equally, it is a nightmare of a man afloat in time and faced with imminent extinction. The speaker is cut loose from all social and historical context. Even if, as David Erdman suggests, the poem represents Browning's reactions to industrialism and to the demise of the French Republic, these historical realities are transformed beyond recognition, and it is time itself that the speaker confronts. The past provides the speaker no comfort; he calls it up only to reject it as worse than the present. (Does "Childe Roland" comment obliquely on Victorian medievalism?[32]) The future for the speaker seems equally ominous; Browning's imagery, as Erdman astutely puts it, is "quasi-apocalyptic." This apocalypse bears with it no redemption that we know of. Here is "teleology without a telos" and with a vengeance. When the historical individual is divorced from a social context he confronts a tower "blind as a fool's heart." His quest has taken him away from the world of human interconnectedness and of love.

Like Donne's poem that he reworks, Browning begins his poem with death, but "Childe Roland" never reaches the affirmation of "A Valediction Forbidding Mourning." Browning's questor is left with a vision of his dead companions not redeemed but resurrected as the "living frame / For one more picture!" (200–201). In our last view of him, we see the speaker poised before the turret. In this scenario, as in the poem as a whole, the questor is frozen into art. Alone, he is undaunted, and his challenge, if it calls forth anything, must, one feels, call forth his own death. The speaker of "Childe Roland" has, like Sordello, moved quite "out of time and this world." For him there is no coming back. The historical dialectic of finite and infinite has been left behind, and the poem's harsh, earthy language is reduced to a riddling allusion.

It is no wonder that "Childe Roland" has been so fascinating to Browning's readers. Not only does it have the gripping inevitability of ballads, myths, and fairy tales. It also deals in the central terms and tropes of Browning's aesthetic. It is an enigmatic suggestion of what happens when individuals and poets take leave of the historical world, as in death they must. These same terms and tropes are more explicitly treated in the daylight and discursive world of the "Parleying with Gerard de Lairesse."

WALKING POETRY AND THE FALSE SUBLIME: "GERARD DE LAIRESSE"

Browning's quarrel with the romantic ideal of natural lyricism and with Victorian critics who prized melody above all else was not a difference of aesthetic theory only but also a matter of poetic practice. It is likely that Browning's defense of earth-bound poetry grew out of his experiments with style and his fascination with history; it is important consequently to examine both the metaphorical and the stylistic character of his pronouncements on poetry. Browning's most complex treatment of poetic subject matter and poetic style comes in the late "Parleying with Gerard de Lairesse" (1887). The *Parleyings* have recently received substantial critical attention, but with little concern for the poet's subtle manipulation of tone. In two of the best studies of "Gerard de Lairesse," Philip Drew and Clyde Ryals note the poem's satiric element. Ryals remarks that Browning's "walk" through Greek history "includes glances at Arnold, Tennyson, Swinburne, and Morris, and perhaps, in the Prometheus episode, at Shelley, in each vignette mimicking their style in the treatment of Greek subjects."[33] As Ryals's observation suggests, when we examine this penultimate parleying we find a stylistic satire and also a parody of the romantic sublime. As he satirizes the sublime style, Browning reverses his common practice. Rather than historicizing the mythic (situating mythic material in a detailed historical context), Browning mythologizes the historic.

In "Gerard de Lairesse" Browning again takes up the poem as earth metaphor to contrast himself with the idealizing painter. While Lairesse glances along through clouds of Greek fancy over the "Dutch veritable earth," the poet paces among men:

> Awake, nor want the wings of dream,—who tramp
> Earth's common surface, rough, smooth, dry or
>   damp.
>
> ("Lairesse," 112–13)

So the speaker describes himself in the poem's first section. The parleying falls into three parts and a coda, and its progression of styles serves as proof by example of Browning's thesis.

In the first part, sections 1–7, Browning has Lairesse correctly see the importance of the present:

> But—oh, your piece of sober sound advice
> That artists should descry abundant worth
> In trivial commonplace, nor groan at dearth
> If fortune bade the painter's craft be plied
> In vulgar town or country!
> ("Lairesse," 52–56)

Browning here echoes the real Lairesse's advice in *The Art of Painting in All Its Branches* where Lairesse admonishes the artist to "represent the true nature and state of things."[34] In Browning's view, however, the now blind painter explores "Holland turned Dreamland" and ignores the "true wonders" that are seen by those who like the poet are "ignobly common-sensed." Browning asks Lairesse why all "inglorious tarriers-at-home" like himself miss the wonders Lairesse imagines, and he suggests that Lairesse's blindness, his "sealed sense," freed the painter's mind from the "obstruction" of the senses. But as we might expect from Browning, such soaring over obstacles is not appropriate for modern artists and audiences. Not only does the painter miss the true wonder of common things, but he is mistakenly "bent on banishing ... All except beauty from its mustered tribe / Of objects" ("Lairesse," 97–98). Implicitly, Browning maintains that the poet's true province includes the ugly as well as the beautiful. Or as he earlier phrased it in connection with *The Ring and the Book:*

> The business has been, as I specify, to explain *fact*—and the fact is what you see and, worse, are to see.... Before I die, I hope to purely invent something,—here my pride was concerned to invent nothing: the minutest circumstance that denotes character is *true:* the black so much—the white, no more. You

are quite justified perhaps in saying "Let all that black alone"—but, touching it at all, so much of it must be.[35]

In Browning's view a desire for pure states—whether pure beauty or pure goodness—is antithetical to art.

The desire for pure beauty leads Lairesse to a false conception of the classic. Browning argues that though the classical writers did pour "rich life" on "dead ground," Lairesse does not recognize that in ancient times,

> The reason was, fancy composed the strife
> 'Twixt sense and soul: for sense, my De Lairesse,
> Cannot content itself with outward things,
> Mere beauty: soul must needs know whence there springs—
> How, when and why—what sense but loves, nor lists
> To know at all.
> ("Lairesse," 138–43)

For the Greeks themselves, then, poetry arose from the link fancy provided between soul and sense, heaven and earth. For modern men, Browning insists, these same connections no longer exist, and fancy or "poetizing" must take a different place. And "mere" beauty, too, outward beauty, must be subordinated to unseen fact. Somehow fact, Browning says,

> Has got to—say, not so much push aside
> Fancy, as to declare its place supplied
> By fact unseen but no less fact the same,
> Which mind bids sense accept.
> ("Lairesse," 150–53)

Poetry is not the creation of the beautiful through fancy—a process of facile poetizing; rather, the poet must turn his attention to the "daily and undignified" and see the soul in it. One who views the past as superior to the present, as Lairesse does, forgoes the "strife / Through the ambiguous Present to the goal / Of some all-reconciling Future" ("Lairesse," 369–70). Seeing fancifully, Browning says, would only be worthwhile if he could at the same time

> ... lose no gain, no hard fast wide-awake
> Having and holding nature for the sake
> Of nature only.
> ("Lairesse," 122–24)

Yet Browning is not content with simple argument in "Gerard de Lairesse." In the second and third sections of the poem he explores, through examples, the implications for poetic language of his theory of art. In the second part, 8–12, he would beat Lairesse at his own game, out-poetize and out-classicize the painter. The poet volunteers to create a version of "the Walk" Lairesse described in *The Art of Painting*. Suddenly, his style shifts radically. Its high and hollow sound matches the vacuousness of its version of mythology. Not all of Browning's readers, however, caught the note of satire in "the Walk" or were sensitive to his parody of the sublime. The *Athenaeum* reviewer observed, for example, "The 'parleying' that will, we think, best please the mere exoteric reader is the one with Gerard de Lairesse. . . . In it are descriptive passages of extraordinary excellence—passages which Mr. Browning alone, perhaps, could have written."[36]

Browning's "extraordinary excellence," I would suggest, has here a satiric thrust. He gives us verse paragraphs tracing, mythologically, the course of a day, from Zeus and Prometheus, to Artemis, to Lyda and a Satyr, to Darius and Alexander, until finally at evening the spirit of antiquity is reduced to a voiceless ghost who "scarce strives with deprecating hands" ("Lairesse," 362). The section begins:

> Thunders on thunders, doubling and redoubling
> Doom o'er the mountain, while a sharp white fire
> Now shone, now sheard its rusty herbage, troubling

> Hardly the fir-boles, now discharged its ire
> Full where some pine-tree's solitary spire
> Crashed down, defiant to the last.
> ("Lairesse," 181–86)

Two more passages may fairly represent the high descriptive style Browning assumes for the occasion. We see the satyr's wood at noon:

> E'en of peaks
> Which still presume there, *plain each* pale point speaks
> In wan transparency of waste incurred
> By over-daring; *far from me be such!*
> Deep in the hollow, rather, where *combine*
> Tree, shrub and briar to roof with shade and cool
> The remnant of some lily-strangled pool,
> Edged round with *mossy fringing soft and fine.*
> *Smooth lie* the bottom slabs, and overhead
> Watch elder, bramble, rose and service-tree
> And one beneficent rich barberry
> Jeweled all over with *fruit-pendents red.*
> ("Lairesse," 271–82, my italics)

In afternoon, Darius meets the "Macedonian" beneath the sky's "sapphirine":

> Here come they trooping silent: heaven suspends
> Purpose the while they range themselves. I see!
> Bent on a battle, two vast powers agree
> This present and no after-contest ends
> One of the other's grasp at rule in reach
> Over the race of man—host fronting host,
> As statue statue fronts—wrath-molten each,
> Solidified by hate,—earth halved almost,
> To close once more in chaos. Yet two shapes
> Show prominent, each from the universe
> Of minions round about him, that disperse
> Like cloud-obstruction when a bolt escapes.
> ("Lairesse," 320–31)

Even passages lengthy as these are scarcely sufficient to give the effect of nearly two hundred lines in this style. The diction, syntax, and imagery of these lines are in specific instances not altogether different from Browning's characteristic approach to poetry. The compound adjective or noun, for example, occurs in much of Browning's poetry. The Greek hosts are "wrath-molten"; Artemis's bow is "slack-strung," and its horn "ivory-linked." Yet the combination of consciously "poetic" diction, with dense alliteration, rhyme, and frequent syntactic inversion sets this section apart even from early descriptive passages of "Pauline" and *Sordello* and turns this central section of the poem into a parody of false ideals in art. Browning may perhaps even intend an element of self-parody, for words like "sapphirine," "lucid," "climes," occur most frequently in descriptive passages of his early poems.[37]

The first passage of "the Walk" involves heavy alliteration and assonance. In "Thunders on thunders, doubling and redoubling / Doom" we already have alliteration of interdentals /θ/ and /d/ ; and the repetition of these sounds produces a much stronger, more hammering effect than alliteration of sibilants or nasals would. The /d/ is continued along with an internal near-rhyme in "hardly," "discharged," "down," and "defiant," and the grandiloquent effect is further increased by the alliterative /š/ of "sharp," "shone," and "sheard," and by the rhyme and assonance of "fire," "ire," "spire," "pine," "defiant." All within the space of five lines. Of course the poet is describing the storm of Jove's rage at the heroically defiant Prometheus, and we might take these lines not for parody but for serious sublimity. The style here becomes clearly hyperbolic, however, as Browning continues the dense alliteration in the next section, 9, and couples it with deliberately artificial inversions of syntax. Instead of "whom do these eyes discern but thee," Browning gives us "whom discern / These eyes but thee"; instead of "her fingers grasp the slack-strung bow," we have "Ha, the bow / Slack-strung her fingers grasp."

Such syntactic inversions occur still more often in the next section. The high density of subject-verb and adjective-noun reversals gives Browning's description of the satyr's wood a mock-Miltonic quality. In these eleven and a half lines, there are six such reversals (italicized here) including the particularly Miltonic "mossy fringing soft and fine" and "fruit-pendents red." If we translate the first into Browning's typical style, the contrast becomes pointed. The Robert Browning of the historical monologues or of the first part of this poem would most likely give us not "mossy fringing soft and fine" but "soft fine mossy fringe"; compare this reinvented line, for example, with Browning's descriptions of "Earth's common surface, rough, smooth, dry or damp" or with the bishop's wish to bequeath to his sons mistresses with "great smooth marbly limbs." Similar syntactic reversals, heavy alliteration, and recognizably "poetic" diction and sentiments continue through the afternoon and evening sections of "the Walk." In the confrontation of Darius and Alexander, the poet combines the acme of the sublime in imagery—lightning—with dense alliteration and a rhetoric of repetition. The commanders cleave the universe of their "minions" while "host" is "fronting host / As statue statue fronts." The figurative language too lacks precision. We have these minions being both "wrath-molten" and "solidified by hate." Their commanders are like lightning, and they themselves in their division are, it seems, like the cleaving of the earth. Finally, in the evening, these "Human heroes" platitudinously "tread the world's dark way / No longer." Classical Greece becomes a fading ghost and beauty "drops away."

In this central section of "Gerard de Lairesse," Browning sets out to create an example of what happens to the thought and the language of poetry when "mere" beauty becomes its end and when fancy too easily transforms imaginings into poetry instead of striving to see accurately or to see into the world's material. In "Gerard de Lairesse" Browning takes leave of the familiar dimensions of history, abandons historical detail, eliminates allusions to a wider historical context. History is almost wholly mythologized and language is inflated accordingly. The crucial duality underlying this satire and in Browning's poetry generally is not fancy and imagination, but fancy and fact.

Though in "Gerard de Lairesse" we perhaps see most clearly the connections between this poetics and the language of Browning's poetry, Browning's treatment of these concerns began much earlier than the *Parleyings*. In *Sordello*, for example, Browning has already begun to examine the possibilities for falsity associated with fancy and its language. Sordello himself is represented in the first two books as a poet whose fancies are broken in upon by reality. The description of Sordello's fanciful life is in some ways a milder version of "the Walk" in "Gerard de Lairesse." Browning compares Sordello to the palmer worm stripping the life from trees:

> So fed Sordello, not a shard dissheathed;
> As ever, round each new discovery, wreathed
> Luxuriantly the fancies infantine
> His admiration, bent on making fine
> Its novel friend at any risk, would fling
> In gay profusion forth.
> (*Sord.*, 1.637–42)

In his "making fine" Sordello makes the same mistake as his rival Eglamor. At the beginning of Book 2, Browning gives us a short description of the setting and Eglamor's version of it:

> The woods were long austere with snow: at last
> Pink leaflets budded on the beech, and fast
> Larches, scattered through pine-tree solitudes,

> Brightened, "as in the slumbrous heart o' the woods
> Our buried year, a witch, grew young again
> To placid incantations, and that stain
> About were from her cauldron, green smoke blent
> With those black pines"—so Eglamor gave vent
> To a chance fancy. Whence a just rebuke
> From his companion; brother Naddo shook
> The solemnest of brows: "Beware," he said,
> "Of setting up conceits in nature's stead!"
>
> (*Sord.*, 2.1–12)

Just as Eglamor is answered in *Sordello*, so Browning immediately rebukes himself for the poetry of "the Walk" in "Parleying with Gerard de Lairesse." Hard on the ghost of Greece's heels, the familiar Browning voice interrupts, exclaiming:

> Enough! Stop further fooling, De Lairesse!
> My fault, not yours! Some fitter way express
> Heart's satisfaction that the Past indeed
> Is past, gives way before Life's best and last,
> The all-including Future. What were life
> Did soul stand still therein, forgo her strife
> Through the ambiguous Present to the goal
> Of some all-reconciling Future.
>
> ("Lairesse," 363–70)

Here, once more, we have the voice so often common to Browning and to his speaking men and women. The colloquial tone, the exclamations, frequent caesura, and enjambment give us a sense of speech interrupting itself, or exclamation being compelled into poetry. Browning counsels the painter to retain the flower of the past and, at the same time, to continue the climb to where the present and future's "fruitage ripens in the blaze of day!" He asks:

> O'erlook, despise, forget, throw flower away,
> Intent on progress? No whit more than stop
> Ascent therewith to dally, screen the top
> Sufficiency of yield by interposed
> Twistwork bold foot gets free from.
>
> ("Lairesse," 377–81)

The knotted syntax, the omission of articles, the logical ellipses, and the strong stresses of this passage go toward the creation of a metaphor that in itself is difficult. Browning draws a conscious contrast between this figure (and the words creating it) and the conventional simile of the poet he addresses who would "push back reality" and "recognize no worth / In fact new-born" unless it is pallidly rendered "as the western rack / Of fading cloud bequeaths the lake some gleam / Of its gone glory!" ("Lairesse," 387–89). Here again, Browning gives us examples of two languages—the language of the ambiguous present and the language of poetized "pushed back" reality. We have the false classical high style and the argumentative, colloquial and musically unconventional language necessary to modern verse.

Browning carefully constructs a modern language for the lyric as well. The ambiguous present, we can infer, also has its lyrics. Music is not limited to classical harmonies: and just as false style must be rejected, so too, Browning implies, we must not let death and ignorance make us lose "care / For a creation." To "dead Greek lore" Browning opposes a simple lyric of simple things:

> Dance, yellows and whites and reds,—
> Lead your gay orgy, leaves, stalks, heads
> Astir with the wind in the tulip-beds!
>
> There's sunshine; scarcely a wind at all
> Disturbs starved grass and daisies small
> On a certain mound by a churchyard wall.
>
> Daisies and grass be my heart's bedfellows
> On the mound wind spares and sunshine mellows:
> Dance you, reds and whites and yellows!

In contrast to the classical thunder of "the Walk," we find in this lyric the poignantly familiar and perhaps, as DeVane suggests, a reference to Elizabeth Barrett Browning's grave (*Handbook,* 519). Browning makes a poem of understatement, and its symmetry and restraint bring to mind some of Hardy's lyrics. A modern eye in spring sees death and life side by side, the certain mound along with starved grass and daisies small, and the lyric is a dance among them.

IRONY AND THE SPEAKING STYLE

In the "Parleying with Gerard de Lairesse," we find Browning juxtaposing at least three styles: the style of deliberate poetizing, the colloquial style, and the simpler music of the final lyric. Keeping in mind these different possibilities for the language of poetry, I think we can characterize the colloquial speaking style as normative for Browning in his historical poems. The colloquial is the language fitted to poetry's province—the clayey field, the ambiguous past and the ambiguous present. Variation from the colloquial is often a key to character and to Browning's ironies. Like Gerard de Lairesse, Browning's self-conscious poetizers divorce themselves from the low ground of history. In contrast, the simpler lyric style may serve as a touchstone of truth or sincerity. And the juxtapositions of styles in the speech of a monologuist are an index of a speaker's internal contradictions.

In describing the relationship among Browning's historical concerns, his theory of language, and his style, we must also recognize the diversity of languages Browning's characters and personae speak. Robert Preyer, for example, has distinguished two styles in Browning: the simple style that involves colloquial diction and speech, rhythmic speed, and a "rational consecution" of narrative and syntax; and the difficult style that is marked by temporal and syntactic displacement and is used to describe mysteries that resist logic or the tentative and problematic in human behavior.[38] Even among Browning's radically historical poems, however, there is a much greater stylistic diversity than a dualistic distinction can account for. Browning frequently modifies the metrics, the acoustical effects, and the diction of these poems to portray character in a variety of different ways, as Park Honan's study of Browning's characters clearly shows. In the monologues the language, no less than historical vision, of the speaker often guides our judgment of him. In reading the monologues, then, we acquire some notion that a proper use or view of language arises when one speaks out of an encounter with the truth. In this sense, for Browning, too, sincere language is the language of poetry; but for Browning the glimpse of the truth is likely to be so problematic, so partial, or so difficult in emerging through details and particular limited perspectives that sincere speech remains knotty and familiar and cannot necessarily take the shape of conventional melody.

In the monologues and *The Ring and the Book*, as in "Gerard de Lairesse," Browning characterizes the worst perverters of language as poetizers.[39] In juxtaposing the pitfalls of grandiloquence to other sorts of language, we see what kind of language is, for Browning, proper speech. Recognizing the worst of Browning's poetizers, in turn, provides an additional basis for understanding characters like Cleon and Bishop Blougram.

Browning's ultimate poetizers are the lawyers in *The Ring and the Book*. Not only are they rhetoricians by profession, but both explicitly characterize themselves as poets. As Honan notes, Archangeli, like Mr. Sludge, Prince Hohenstiel-Schwangau, and Tertium Quid, uses rhyme self-consciously. Honan takes this self-conscious rhyming as a consequence of Browning's mimetic ends. Browning, he says, "is too conscious of the lyric nature of the device to use it frequently and freely as a natural means of self-expression."[40] Though Honan's view is compelling, rhyme is not necessarily excluded by mimetic ends; Browning creates, for example, the musical rhymes of "Master Hugues of Saxe-Gotha" (a kind of musical mimesis) and, at the opposite extreme, the understated couplets of "My Last Duchess." Browning's occasional rhymers are self-conscious not simply for mimetic authenticity but because their rhymes, in the context of a blank verse monologue, reveal them as poetizers. Archangeli, as Honan points out, begins,

> What, to-day we're eight?
> Seven and one's eight, I hope, old curly pate!
> —Branches me out his verb-tree on the slate
> (*RB*, 8.2–4)

Coming at the beginning of the monologue, this doggeral seems fairly innocuous. Archangeli himself comes close to labelling it jog-trot rhyme: "It trots / Already through my head, though noon be now, / Does suppertime" (8.14–16). Soon, however, we see Archangeli has too little respect for truth to understand properly the language of law or of poetry. His word play, at first a game, begins to have serious consequences as he makes phrases about Guido's marriage. His "*duxit in uxorem*" becomes "*Toedas jugales iniit, subiit*" and then "*Connubio stabili sibi junxit*" (8.127–30). Archangeli views these phrases as poetic elaboration and is unaware of the irony in saying Guido and Pompilia underwent the "torch" of marriage or were joined in a stable bond.

Archangeli thinks of himself as a frustrated poet: he breaks off this first Latin sentence by declaring, "Virgil is little help to who writes prose" (8.134). He laments, "Unluckily, law quite absorbs a man, / Or else I think I too had poetized" (8.147–48). He is determined "to garnish law with idiom." He justifies Guido as one who by his murder has proved man to be creation's glory, and he then compliments himself, "(Come, that's both solid and poetic!)" (8.531). He gives a brutal description of the murder weapon that culminates in *"Furor ministrat arma,"* and then he decides he is carried away by poetry and must "subdue the bard / And rationalize a little" (8.1170–71). Finally, he plans to polish his speech and gives clear evidence that poetizing is just one more operation respecting neither language nor truth:

> To–morrow stick in this, and throw out that,
> And, having first ecclesiasticized,
> Regularize the whole, next emphasize,
> Then latinize, and lastly Cicero-ize,
> Giving my Fisc his finish.
>
> (8.1729–33)

So Archangeli concludes in a rush of rhetoric and rhyme. He has created, more than his imagery-reckless mind can know, a "monster of defense."

If Archangeli is a doggerel "poetizer," Bottinius, the prosecutor, has higher aspirations. The Fisc attempts the epic; he aims higher than Archangeli and, in Browning's characterization and in his own words, he is the would-be soaring poet. The poet-persona says of Bottinius in the first book:

> Give you, if we dare wing to such a height,
> The absolute glory in some full-grown speech
> On the other side, some finished butterfly,
> Some breathing diamond–flake with leaf-gold fans.
>
> (1.1158–61)

The Fisc is facile, "composite." He has "language—ah, the gift of eloquence!" It is his "Language that goes, goes easy as a glove, / O'er good and evil, smoothens both to one" (1.1171–73). The Fisc himself characterizes his defense of Pompilia as a great theme, an "epic plunge." In contrast to the poet's invocation to his long poem in twelve books, the Fisc's speech is a parody or negative image of *The Ring and the Book*. The Fisc sacrifices truth to the sacredness of argument. "Anything, anything," he says, "to let the wheels of argument run glibly to their goal" (9.486–89). Like Gerard de Lairesse's, the Fisc's criterion for language and for art is smoothness: and as Lairesse in *The Art of Painting* admires Poussin, so the Fisc admires Ciro Ferri, the follower of Poussin whom he judges to have surpassed both "the Florentine" and the "Urbanite." The Fisc begins his speech with an extended similitude from painting and concludes this exordium by describing the ideal painter who, like himself, turns away from fact. This artist turns inward "Quite away from aught vulgar and extern," and the result is a painting finished, its base in fact so thoroughly transformed as to be indistinct:

> Fed by digestion, not raw food itself,
> No gobbets but smooth comfortable chyme
> Secreted from each snapped-up crudity,—
> Less distinct, part by part, but in the whole
> Truer to the subject,—the main central truth
> And soul o' the picture, would my Judges spy,—
> Not those mere fragmentary studied facts
> Which answer to the outward frame and flesh—
> (9.95–103)

Bottinius then would make the wheels of argument run smooth; he dares the epic but so confuses the metaphorical wings lifting him that he cannot distinguish the count from Caponsacchi. He likens one or both of them to Holofernes, and he casts Pompilia, unlikely as it may seem, as Judith. Himself he compares to Icarus:

> If I entangle me
> With my similitudes,—if wax wings melt,
> And earthward down I drop, not mine the fault:
> Blame your beneficence, O Court, O Sun,
> Whereof the beamy smile affects my flight!
> (9.573–77)

The Fisc's confusing similitudes, however, are not so easily excused. His epic daring and his pursuit of the glib culminate in a likening of Caponsacchi to Judas, which is the equally offensive flip-side of Archangelis's comparison of Guido to Christ. The pursuit of smoothness at the expense of fact and the pursuit of extended figures that substitute convention for thought make for an art both aesthetically and morally deficient.

Though Archangeli and Bottinius are poetizers, their speech is both glib and rough, ornately figured and straightforward. They create smooth talk for the court and unwittingly reveal their real selves to us. In these extreme examples, language itself is at issue, but this general attitude toward language provides one key to other Browning poems. "The Bishop Orders His Tomb" could be called, among other things, a study in the regularity of platitude. The bishop's thoughts are marked by frequent ellipses and line-internal juncture; and the picture of a man caught in a highly ambiguous present and speaking as he thinks is established quickly by lines such as, "Nephews—sons mine . . . ah God, I know not! Well—" ("The Bishop," 3). The strong stresses, juncture, and the deliberate colloquialness of lines like this one stand in contrast to the bishop's more regularly metrical lines. Where meter is simply conventional it matches conventional sentiment. After a difficult and rough beginning, the bishop falls back on the attitude made easy, probably, by years of playing the cleric's part:

And as she died so must we die ourselves,
And thence ye may perceive the world's a dream.
("The Bishop," 8–9)

The bishop curses Gandolf, then describes his tomb, and finally smooths over death again. Compare his declaration, "And I shall fill my slab of basalt there, / And 'neath my tabernacle take my rest," with the excited strongly stressed line describing the marble as "fresh-poured red wine of a mighty pulse" ("The Bishop," 26–27, 30). Death soon comes to the bishop's mind again, this time in the biblical style the bishop has smoothed the wrinkles from: "Swift as a weaver's shuttle fleet our years: / Man goeth to the grave, and where is he?" ("The Bishop," 51–52). The bishop, however, ignores his own question, and the next time he thinks forward to death, his language is easy as ever (until he gets to the incense which even in thought excites his senses):

> And then how I shall lie through centuries,
> And hear the blessed mutter of the mass,
> And see God made and eaten all day long,
> And feel the steady candle-flame, and taste
> Good strong thick stupefying incense-smoke!
> ("The Bishop," 80–84)

The most striking juxtaposition of the metrically regular platitude with the mix of the bishop's real concerns comes near the end. It is the bishop's last attempt to gloss over the roughness of death:

> No Tully, said I, Ulpian at the best!
> Evil and brief hath been my pilgrimage.
> All *lapis*, all, sons! Else I give the Pope
> My villas! Will ye ever eat my heart?
> ("The Bishop," 100–104)

The bishop's speech becomes more and more disjointed and excited until the metrically regular look at death becomes so frightening that he imagines the stones sweating "as if the corpse they keep were oozing through" ("The Bishop," 117). For the bishop, as for the lawyers of *The Ring and the Book*, the language that goes too easily may be deceptive.

Conventionally melodious or even eloquent verse, however, need not always indicate duplicity or insincerity on the part of Browning's speakers. Indeed, Browning varies his style for both mimetic and ironic ends, and, in consequence, local effects must be seen in context. Though metrical regularity emphasizes the conventionality of platitudes in "The Bishop Orders His Tomb," in "Fra Lippo Lippi" the simplest metrical line ("Where sportive ladies leave their doors ajar") foregrounds Lippi's excitement.[41]

For all his distrust of poetizing and of accepting harmony at face value, and for all his awareness of the possibilities for lying through metaphors and analogies, Browning does not discard the lyric impulse. He finds a place in *The Ring and the Book* both for "soaring" poetry and for a travesty of it. The serious attempts at elevated style, however, are usually earned, and in *The Ring and the Book* they are relatively rare. After the alloy, the hammer and file, the struggle with his matter, Browning is left with a ring "justifiably golden" to which he no doubt feels he can "justifiably" add a flower, his invocation of "Lyric Love." Here is soaring, certainly; but like the Pope's judgment of Pompilia, and unlike Bottinius's idealized picture, it comes only after the consideration of fragmentary fact. The Pope's most elevated passages are also, perhaps better, earned. The Pope speaks a more formal language than the lawyers, as is suited to his position and character, and his most elevated language is balanced by a discussion of the way words "more than any deed, characterize / Man as made subject to a curse" (10.349–50). Among men, the Pope says, words must inevitably falsify things, but we must at least go on with language while remaining conscious of difficulties. "Be man's method for man's life at least!" the Pope says. Two of the most elevated passages in the Pope's speech are the description of Pompilia's meeting with Caponsacchi (10.654–70) and the judgment of Pompilia. In the first passage, alliteration and anaphora combine to convey the Pope's imagination of "passion in the place." In the second (10.998–1088) the elevation is highly rhetorical. The Pope at his most eloquent delivers a resounding periodic sentence, balanced in syntax and alliteration, and concluding in a metaphorical likening of Pompilia to a flower. But even here, the Pope's flight is earthbound as his flower grows among briars on the ground his blood "manures":

> It was not given Pompilia to know much,
> Speak much, to write a book, to move mankind,

Be memorized by who records my time.
Yet if in purity and patience, if
In faith held fast despite the plucking fiend,
Safe like the signet stone with the new name
That saints are known by,—if in right returned
For wrong, most pardon for worst injury,
If there be any virtue, any praise,—
Then will this woman-child have proved—who knows?—
Just the one prize vouchsafed unworthy me,
Seven years a gardener of the untoward ground,
I till,—this earth, my sweat and blood manure
All the long day that barrenly grows dusk:
At least one blossom makes me proud at eve
Born 'mid the briars of my enclosure! Still
(Oh, here as elsewhere, nothingness of man!)
Those be the plants, imbedded yonder South
To mellow in the morning, those made fat
By the master's eye, that yield such timid leaf,
Uncertain bud, as product of his pains!
While—see how this mere chance-sown, cleft-nursed seed,
That sprang up by the wayside 'neath the foot
Of the enemy, this breaks all into blaze,
Spreads itself, one wide glory of desire
To incorporate the whole great sun it loves
From the inch-height whence it looks and longs! My flower,
My rose, I gather for the breast of God
(10.1014–41)

The Pope's language connects Pompilia to the lyric love of Book 1. The Pope, of course, does not sustain this lofty style. He is soon addressing those "ambiguous" creatures, the Comparini.

Perhaps a more characteristic moment of intensity in *The Ring and the Book* is Pompilia's description of the April day when she is called to escape Arezzo. Pompilia experiences actual inspiration, yet her words might be better characterized as a lyric speaking than a lyric soaring:

> Up I sprang alive,
> Light in me, light without me, everywhere
> Change! A broad yellow sunbeam was let fall
> . . . .
> On the house-eaves, a dripping shag of weed
> Shook diamonds on each dull gray lattice-square,
> As first one, then another bird leapt by,
> And light was off, and lo was back again,
> Always with one voice,—where are two such joys?—
> The blessed building-sparrow! I stepped forth,
> Stood on the terrace,—o'er the roofs, such sky!
> My heart sang, "I too am to go away,
> I too have something I must care about.
>
> (7.1212–27)

Pompilia's emotion is conveyed, not through complex periodic sentences, a special diction, or extended metaphor, but in the accumulation of simple syntactic elements (even a fragmentation of syntax), alliteration, and specific concrete detail. Her language is matter-of-fact, "I too am to go away."

Simple intensity, of course, is Pompilia's nature, but even among Browning's more learned characters the truest moments can be moments of clear speech. For the most part distrusting rhetorical eloquence and elevated poetic diction, Browning cultivates the range of the speaking voice. Browning walks deliberately on what Eliot calls a plateau or "tableland." But, in Browning's province, this land itself is carefully varied. Browning can be knotty, discursive, prolix, or simply clear, and in his best work even discursiveness serves a purpose. Browning's monologues often extend the possible range of poetic diction and style in their careful modulations of speech.

"The Epistle Containing the Strange Medical Experience of Karshish," is representative of the way Browning makes the middle speaking style work, for "Karshish" falls between the more extreme colloquialness of "Fra Lippo Lippi" and the discursiveness of "Bishop Blougram's Apology." We sense in Karshish some of the explosive vitality Browning seems to admire in Lippi or even in the Bishop of St. Praxed's, but Karshish's enthusiasm is tempered by the fact that he is, after all, writing a letter and by his role as a physician. To be more precise, Karshish is both a physician in the modern sense and a magical healer as well. He combines a penchant for the naturalistic explanation with a sensitivity to the supernatural.

Browning makes this dichotomy clear by subtly varying diction and rhythm. Karshish begins his letter with a rhythmically and syntactically complicated greeting. In a strongly stressed parenthesis he sets forth the problem in "God's handiwork" that is the epistle's central concern:

> (This man's-flesh he hath admirably made
> Blown like a bubble, kneaded like a paste,
> To coop up and keep down on earth a space
> That puff of vapour from his mouth, man's soul)
> ("Karshish," 3–6)

The extra stresses here, the alliterative and colloquial "coop up and keep down" give us a sense of Karshish speaking his mind directly (as who does not in an aside?). The series of simple sentences and end-stopped lines beginning the next paragraph has a similar effect. By the middle of this paragraph (line 42) we begin to hear Karshish's other voice in the physician's diction; he brings in formal locutions ("I was nearly bold to say") along with technical terms. Fully half the lines begin with a reversed foot or two strong stresses. Karshish takes Lazarus as a case to describe; he remarks his symptoms, "mania-subinduced / By epilepsy," and goes on to detail his behavior until he comes to the very consciousness of life beyond death that Lazarus seems to have (line 178). Here Karshish's diction becomes simpler, virtually monosyllabic—words like "preposterously," "praetermission," "exasperation," disappear and the metrical pattern becomes easier to follow. Karshish says Lazarus holds a thread of life and feels,

> The spiritual life around the earthly life:
> The law of that is known to him as this,
> His heart and brain move there, his feet stay here
> . . . .
> And oft the man's soul springs into his face
> As if he saw again and heard again
> His sage that bade him 'Rise' and he did rise.
> 						("Karshish," 184–86, 191–93)

Soon Lazarus sinks back to ashes, and Karshish's vocabulary becomes more Latinate ("sedulous recurrence," "whereby," "studiously," "professedly," "especial," "prone submission"). In these lines (197–208), too, a number of elisions must be made to accommodate the polysyllabic words to a blank verse metrical pattern. This subtle alternation of complex and simple diction creates for us the divisions in Karshish's own mind. Meter heightens these contrasts.

Karshish's technical language might easily be described by the carping critic whom J. H. Stirling creates in his 1868 review of Browning. Though he praises Browning, Stirling to some degree concurs with his invented critic who complains that Browning is prosaic: "A weak, soft, plaintive, pleading thing, it is mostly—a breath conversationally low, he thinks; a small thin stream that runs by, almost uninfluenced by rhythm, almost unchecked by rhyme; broken only at times against single words like stones in mid-current, or losing itself and disappearing under the angle of an inversion."[42] As a physician Karshish does breathe this "low" air, and the rhythm of his speech is conversational in its groupings of strong stresses, or weak syllables, initial inversions or polysyllabic words. As a man responding to and describing an encounter with a miracle, Karshish uses simpler words, and meter again makes his excitement real to us. His final words point the contrast sharply:

> Jerusalem's repose shall make amends
> For time this letter wastes, thy time and mine;
> Till when, once more thy pardon and farewell!

> The very God! think, Abib; dost thou think?
> So, the All-Great, where the All-Loving too—
> So, through the thunder comes a human voice
> Saying, "O heart I made, a heart beats here!
> Face, my hands fashioned, see it in myself.
> Thou hast no power nor mayst conceive of mine,
> But love I gave thee, with myself to love,
> And thou must love me who have died for thee!"
> The madman saith He said so: it is strange.
> ("Karshish," 301–12)

In "Karshish," Browning carefully modulates speech. We sense the central meaning of Karshish's meeting with Lazarus struggling to emerge from his language. Karshish's simple language is not glib like the bishop's, nor is his technical discourse a deliberate falsification. Rather these variations in voice represent the range of attitudes of a man who comes to truth through difficulty. A poem like "Karshish" is not a distillation of this central experience, but an indirect approach to it through the inclusion of its surrounding circumstances. Through Karshish's difficulties we see his experience obliquely, by refraction. Thus Karshish's language of science, though it does not express the deepest emotions and spiritual realities, is essential to the poem. In one sense Karshish's medical facts have a counterpoetic weight; but Browning integrates Karshish's professional voice into the poem as the necessary balance without which the simpler language would lose its particular impact. The language of poetry is not divorced from the language of science, or from the matter of fact, but in this case includes it.

In general then, Browning varies his language to two ends. First, a character's speech serves the mimetic end of characterization—the Pope's usual language is more formal than Pompilia's; Lippi's speech is more metrically irregular and extreme than Karshish's epistle. This kind of variation falls within the limits that evolve from Browning's view of language, a view more congenial to the lower ranges of poetic style than to explorations of the sublime. Secondly, within individual poems we must consider stylistic variations in context. A comparatively simple realization of meter in "Karshish" expresses the physician's attempt to put into words the experience his scientific proclivities incline him to explain away, while the simpler lines of "The Bishop Orders His Tomb" stand out as platitudes the bishop merely mouths without pondering.

Keeping in mind the qualities of language Browning distrusts and the varying impact of any single stylistic feature, I turn next to poems more problematic than "Karshish." I have already suggested "Cleon" and "Bishop Blougram's Apology" present difficulties of establishing where our perspective comes to match the poet's or the speaker's perspective. A close look at the language of these two characters may bring us closer to a clear interpretation of Browning's historical ironies. At the same time, it indicates that where the placement of historical irony is unclear, stylistic variation alone provides no certain resolution of a poem's difficulties.

In "Cleon" style provides a better index of character than it does in "Bishop Blougram's Apology." "Cleon" is the counterpart in the second volume of *Men and Women* to "Karshish" in the first, and the contrast between the two speakers is immediately apparent. Karshish calls himself "the picker-up of learning's crumbs / The not-incurious in God's handiwork." Poet that he is, Cleon commences:

> Cleon the poet (from the sprinkled isles,
> Lily on lily, that o'erlace the sea,
> And laugh their pride when the light wave lisps
>   "Greece")—
> To Protus in his Tyranny: much health!
>
> ("Cleon," 1–4)

Cleon's next paragraph sets forth his happy situation on his sprinkled isle:

258   *HISTORY AND THE PRISM OF ART*

> They give thy letter to me, even now:
> I read and seem as if I heard thee speak.
> The master of thy galley still unlades
> Gift after gift; they block my court at last
> And pile themselves along its portico
> Royal with sunset, like a thought of thee:
> And one white she-slave from the group dispersed
> Of black and white slaves (like the chequer-work
> Pavement, at once my nation's work and gift,
> Now covered with this settle-down of doves),
> One lyric woman, in her crocus vest
> Woven of sea-wools, with her two white hands
> Commends to me the strainer and the cup
> Thy lip hath bettered ere it blesses mine.
> ("Cleon," 5–18)

Cleon's "lyric woman" comes to us as a lyric vision. Cleon shows himself poet from the start. The passage is, for Browning, rather simple metrically, and the diction is a combination of one- and two-syllable words and simple compounds. The lyrical style here, too, comes from dense alliteration and consonance of liquids and glides /w/ : "lily on lily," "light wave laughs," "lyric woman," "woven of sea-wools." With these also comes the assonance of "court" and "portico," "cover," "doves," and "cup." The last line of the passage provides a harmonious chiasmus of sound:

> Thy lip hath bettered 'ere it blesses mine.
> 1   2   3   3 2   1

The acoustic density of Cleon's beginning shows him in the role of poet, but by the end of his monologue his lyric assurance has crumbled and the laughing pride of Greece is gone. The poem limps to a close, as Cleon says of Paul:

> He writeth, doth he? well, and he may write.
> Oh, the Jew findeth scholars! certain slaves
> Who touched on this same isle, preached him and
>   Christ;
> And (as I gathered from a bystander)
> Their doctrine could be held by no sane man.
> ("Cleon," 349–53)

The contrast of styles points clearly to the pain of Cleon's situation; he is bound to the accomplishments of his culture and, despite their beauties, is limited by them. Cleon is surely not a "poetizer" of the Bottinius variety, and his lyric beginning is not mocked as the lawyer's epic pretensions are. Yet Cleon's last words are a necessary counterweight to his initial vision; and revealing, as they do, his inner condition, they ring less lovely than his greeting but more true.

In moving from his beginning to this conclusion, Cleon's monologue works somewhat the way the "Epistle of Karshish" does. Cleon speaks his own kind of discursive language, and he creates extended figures in complicated terms. He makes a case for late Greek culture as the composite of all past achievements by likening his faculty for touching past glories to the air filling a sphere, "which not so palpably nor obviously, / Though no less universally, can touch / The whole circumference" ("Cleon," 103–6). In comparison to Cleon in his mode of self-congratulation or explanation, his later description of the paradox of pleasure and age has a particular urgency. He feels horror quickening as he anticipates death:

> When all my works wherein I prove my worth,
> Being present still to mock me in men's mouths,
> Alive still, in the praise of such as thou,
> I, I the feeling, thinking, acting man,
> The man who loved his life so over-much,
> Sleep in my urn.
> ("Cleon," 317–22)

Browning's stylistic variation makes us understand that for Cleon the most important truth is not the "lyric woman" but the vision that counters her, the "I, I . . . sleep in my urn."

Like Cleon in these passages, Bishop Blougram too speaks in a varied voice. His speech is more colloquial and chatty than Cleon's—he is less concerned with speaking in a dignified way. Whereas Cleon is a poet, Blougram is consciously a rhetorician. He proposes, for example, "A simile!" ("Blougram," 99), and he is willing to argue in any fashion through syllogisms, analogies, or arguments ad hominem. Like Bottinius, Blougram sometimes lets his analogies get away from him and consequently makes arguments that seem preposterous even at first glance (see his comparison of himself to a beast, line 349, or his clothes metaphor in which he defends living in and *for* this world, line 780). For all this, and for all his prolix argumentativeness, Blougram does have a sense for language. Not only do his own words sometimes seem to express true conviction, but he is aware of the possibility that words may obscure faith. He accuses Gigadibs of being the real beast, one whose faith is convenient and conventional. Gigadibs, Blougram says, would exult

> if I could put you back
> Six hundred years, blot out cosmogony,
> Geology, ethnology, what not,
> (Greek endings, each the little passing-bell
> That signifies some faith's about to die),
> And set you square with Genesis again,—
> ("Blougram," 678–83)

The bishop can and does handle "Greek endings" and complicated arguments. He will use almost any rhetorical trick to make his point; and yet the comparative simplicity of his statements on faith and doubt gives an authentic air to his affirming the necessity of doubt. His diction and the similes he chooses are direct, forceful, and colloquial ("And that's what all the blessed evil's for"). He only begins to return to his more difficult vocabulary and the dubious simile when he begins to turn once more to what he supposes are Gigadibs's objections (see lines 651–75). Though it is difficult to tell how far Browning treats Blougram ironically, the variations in language within the monologue and in comparison with other poems indicate that we should perhaps give Blougram credit for being a faithful doubter. He is by no means completely overcome with—or unaware of—his casuistry.

In "Bishop Blougram," as in the epistle and *The Ring and the Book,* Browning carefully controls the level of language and modulates his characters' words against the norm of the speaking style. As is clear in "Gerard de Lairesse" and in his treatment of self-conscious poetizers, Browning's harsh or knotty style is a deliberate effort to connect poetry to "veritable earth." For Browning, poetry has become a struggle with resistant matter, and especially with the rags and scraps of history. Browning's poetry of "clayey soil" looks forward in its metaphorical provenance to the rock-drill metaphor of Pound's *Cantos* and to the "fertile (?) mud" and artesian well rock sample of William Carlos Williams's *Paterson,* Book 3.[43] More significantly, Browning redefines the poetic and the prosaic, and by including the prosaic in his own poetry he opens the way for later, more radical, poetic experiments. "Looking low ere looking high," Browning creates the special music of resilient and flexible speech. Browning's creation of new possibilities for language, no less than his complex ironies, his innovative narrative structures, and his personae who interpret facts, opens the way for the innovations of modernist poetics.

CHAPTER SEVEN
CONCLUSION

> These old credulities, to nature dear,
> Shall they no longer bloom upon the stock
> Of History, stript naked as a rock
> 'Mid a dry desert?
>
> —Wordsworth, "At Rome.—Regrets in Allusion to Neibuhr, and Other Modern Historians"

> He who smites the rock and spreads the water
> Bidding drink and live a crowd beneath him,
> Even he, the minute makes immortal,
> Proves, perchance, but mortal in the minute.
>
> —Browning, "One Word More"

WORDSWORTH'S *MEMORIALS OF A TOUR IN ITALY, 1837*, a series of poems contemporaneous with Browning's *Sordello*, questioned the necessity, the usefulness, and the poetic possibilities of modern history. Wordsworth reluctantly judged that in the age of modern historiography with its insistence on the matter of fact the truth must steer a "humbler course perplexed and slow." Though he consoled himself with the idea that belief remained "the soul of fact," Wordsworth clearly felt that the new practice of history was poetry's necessary obstacle, if not its natural antithesis. As the preeminent historical poet in the next generation, Browning at once embraced the naked facts of history and faced the Wordsworthian dilemma—how to retain the poet's power, even the poet's prophetic power, while remaining faithful to what Wordsworth admitted were the historian's "sound and grave realities." Wordsworth postulated a harmony in his "Plea for the Historian" between Clio and her sister Muses, animated by the Muses' parents, Mnemosyne and Jove. But in practice the attempt to bring Clio and her sisters into harmony raised more questions than Wordsworth's formulation could answer.

Unlike Wordsworth, Browning embraced historical subjects, historical details, enthusiastically rather than reluctantly. Yet, as I have suggested, his contextualist view of history led him to understand history as obstacle and poetry as the art of struggle with obstacles of fact and of form. At its best Browning's poetry is always a fresh experiment—an experiment with narrative, with point of view, or with language. In its irony, its style, its attempt to embrace the "rags and scraps" of history, Browning's poetry has had a significant impact on his successors, both British and American.

I would not suggest that Browning's importance is limited to his historical poetry or that Browning's understanding of his art was unambiguously contextualist or thoroughly ironic. To the contrary, Browning's language more than his historical understanding was significant for the poetry of Hardy and Hopkins (though one can argue that Browning's historical poems influenced Hardy's satires). It is, again, Browning's language rather than his understanding of history that influenced Sassoon in his more colloquial moments and, more recently, the style of Ted Hughes. From this perspective one might argue that Browning's style in itself furthered a strain in English verse that was earlier exemplified in the linguistic energy of Chaucer and Donne. Browning's influence has not been limited to his historical poems. Neither was his historical poetry consistently contextualist in its presentation of history and in its conceptualization of the poet's relationship to his subject. One can easily enough identify the Browning who, Hardy said, had the historical optimism of a greengrocer. One finds Browning reaching after easy certainties in "Rabbi Ben Ezra" or the "Epilogue" to *Asolando.* And, as I have suggested, one can find history conceptualized as heroic adventure in such brief narratives as "How They Brought the Good News from Ghent to Aix." This heroic emphasis also penetrates the actions of Caponsacchi in *The Ring and the Book* and the song of David in "Saul." These poems suggest that Browning admired action at least as much as he doubted one's ability always to recognize the consequences of and limitations upon action. Nonetheless Browning embedded Caponsacchi in a larger and more ambiguous than heroic world, and he suggested, especially in his poet-personae, that a poet's prophecy is necessarily hedged with failure. Wordsworth pictured the poet who came after Niebuhr as one left with rocks in a dry desert; Browning presented Moses as the type for the poet, as one who brings water from the rock. Still, Browning cautioned that even prophecy has its limits: He "the minute makes immortal, / Proves, perchance, but mortal in the minute."[1] Browning's complex attitude toward poetry as prophecy is but one of the ambiguities and tensions inherent in his understanding of history, and it is Browning's difficult encounter with history that opened the way for his modern successors.

Browning's contextualism, I have argued, is developed out of a sense that history is opaque, difficult, resistant to explanation and to poetic language. In history the poet finds a complex web of interconnections; historical individuals—poets included—are necessarily situated in this web of circumstance, a web so complex that the only perfect historian is God. The poet like the historian must attempt the difficult task of connecting the finite to the infinite, the temporally conditioned to permanent values, the spectacle of continual flux to a providential order. As he examines history in these terms Browning creates poet-personae who are both powerful and limited. They resuscitate the matter of history and at the same time call attention to the necessary obliqueness of their enterprise through parenthetical commentary, self-consciousness, or even self-mockery. For the contextualist poet the best presentation of history is not a straightforward narrative; the interconnections of the historical web require that many threads be followed, if possible at once. History in Browning's view is not a steady march toward a clearly understood end; rather, Browning's texts show us a progressive revelation arising in various circumstances, but governed by no clearly envisioned telos. The satisfactions that Browning's longer historical poems can offer, consequently, are the satisfactions of analysis and completeness rather than of peripety and denouement. This attempted simultaneity in narrative structures is matched in the multiplication of historical perspectives and in the ironies arising from the juxtaposition of these perspectives. Hayden White has argued that the contextualist way of conceptualizing the historical field is expressed in the dominant figure of irony. Browning's ironies, both local and general, are an expression of the contextualist view that historical individuals are, in varying degrees, limited by their circumstances. Irony affords the poet both a local strategy for analyzing his subjects' limitations and a more general leverage against history. Similarly, by emphasizing walking poetry and by avoiding the, to him, false sublime, Browning seeks to transform the limitations of history into art. Embracing the obstacles in an opaque history and the obstacles in language to an art perfectly expressive of truth, Browning attempts to bridge the gap between aspiration and finitude. The light from the past that comes to the poet is already filtered through the opacity of time; the poet's language, in Browning's metaphor, is a further refraction, a prism of art.

This analysis of Browning's historical poetry has suggested the intimate connections between his contextualist conceptualization of history and his poetic forms. The congruences among Browning's historical understanding and his personae, his narrative strategies, his language, and his historical ironies arise from a predominantly contextualist understanding of history. Implicit in my analysis of Browning's texts is an argument that historical poetry, if we take it seriously, must be subject to the same kind of analysis of rhetorical, figurative, and linguistic strategies to which histories have increasingly been subjected.[2] This examination of Browning's poetry at once suggests an approach to other historical poetry and provides two significant ways of reevaluating Browning's importance for modern poetry. First, I will suggest, Browning's historical poetry established an aesthetic of inclusiveness for modern historical poetry. This aesthetic went well beyond Browning's formal innovations in the historical monologues. Second, an understanding of the connections between Browning's historical view and his poetic forms allows us to specify how modern poems including history both resemble and differ from Browning's. A brief examination of the historical interests of Ezra Pound, William Carlos Williams, and Charles Olson will suggest the varied ways Browning's legacy for the long historical poem has been reconceived.

Aside from the importance of his innovations in poetic diction, Browning's most obvious influence on modern poetry has been his development of the dramatic monologue. Numerous critics from Robert Langbaum to Betty Flowers to Carol Christ have discussed the dramatic monologue's importance in the nineteenth and twentieth centuries, citing Browning's influence on William Morris, Eliot, Pound, and others. Browning's monologues clearly established a formal precedent for Robert Frost's and Randall Jarrell's monologuists and for the monologues of Allen Tate and Robert Lowell.[3] More recently, Richard Howard, Pamela White Hadas, and Fred Chappell have used the monologue to explore historical or quasi-historical subjects. Howard is Browning's closest follower, treating in monologues or, lately, in dialogues, historical characters from Gladstone, to Rodin, to Browning himself. Hadas uses the monologue to give voice to a variety of historical women in Jewish and Christian history and from the American past. Chappell's most recent volume of poetry, *Castle Tzingal,* a series of monologues with an unspecifiable medieval setting, owes its literary ancestry to Browning, Pound, and Kafka.[4] The examples might easily be multiplied, so important has the monologue become in the twentieth century. As Christ has persuasively argued, the dramatic monologue has served as an answer to the burden of romanticism, helping nineteenth- and twentieth-century poets "maintain a precarious balance between the burden of personality that their poetry so often concerned and the escape from mere subjectivity through personality made art."[5]

As my examples indicate, the historical monologue has been especially important for American poets, though modern British poets have also used the form.[6] At least as important to American poetics, though less often noticed, is the precedent of Browning's long poems including history. In fact I would argue that Browning's most important descendents in the historical poem of "epic" proportions are American poets. Browning's standard of inclusiveness and his experiments with narrative structure, personae, and language are significant precursors of the long historical poems of Pound, Williams, and Olson.[7] For these poets, as for Browning and Carlyle, "true History" is the "only possible Epic." The twentieth-century poet, no less than the Victorian, inhabits a world in which history is often perceived as chaos and the effectiveness of language as an ordering force is uncertain. Like Browning, Pound, Williams, and Olson were driven to ask how the poet can know history or make poems out of it.

The connections among these modern historical poems are not reducible to any simple literary genealogy, though as I have argued elsewhere, Pound obviously learned much from Browning's poetry[8] and had, in his turn, a significant effect on Williams's and Olson's understanding of the long poem. My purpose in concluding, therefore, is not primarily to trace Browning's influence, but to suggest the variety of ways, following Browning, that historical concerns have shaped the modern long poem.

In the nineteenth century as well as in our own, historical questions have had consequences for poetic form. As Wordsworth's own practice in *The Prelude* indicates, the impulse of the "Chronicler" to set events in a sequential order is no guarantee of their orderly significance. Time, especially historical time, is more complicated than it might at first appear. As history is admitted into the romantic and the post-romantic poem, the chronicler's "realities" cannot be rescued whole from the ravages of time; the realities in poetic fictions are made through struggle with the difficult opaque past. Chronicle gives way to narrative experiment. The poet, like Browning, or Olson or Lowell, must ask what can be rescued from the teeth of time and how one can be sure that the recovery is not itself a "dazzling flattery."

In the struggle for poetic and historical truth, the position of the poet as historian also becomes problematic. Caught between modesty and assertion, the poet seeks to accomplish the impossibly modest Rankean feat of telling it as it really was and to accomplish at the same time the Aristotelian goal of being more "philosophic" than the historian (or, in Shelley's words, the goal of seeking universals rather than mere particulars). As we have seen, Browning's poet-speakers are both powerful and limited. *Sordello*'s narrator glides like a god in and out of the troubadour's world; the narrator of *The Ring and the Book* finally maintains his authority by presenting historical materials and by directly defending his obliquity. Pound's presence in his poems is of course still more complex than Browning's, and his many voices mingle to instruct, to comment, to combine the dissimilar, or to startle us. According to the poem's fiction, we give up, for the most part, a single coherent intelligence through which everything is seen.

For later poets, too, the poet's place in a poem including history has remained problematic. If we move forward, for example, to Olson's manifesto on projective verse, we see that he wished to go beyond Pound, even as Pound early in his career built upon and, in Olson's view, went beyond Browning. Despite his praise for his predecessors, Olson wished to remake poetry both in method and in substance. He praised Eliot's "notable line," which like Pound's took its dramatic "speech-force" from Browning, but he argued that Eliot fails as a "dramatist."[9] As for Pound,

Olson complained in the Mayan letters (1951) to Robert Creeley that Pound had too much of "the 19th century stance."[10] Olson would "assume history is prime, even now," but, he told Creeley, "the substance has changed." Consequently, the poet as historian must avoid Pound's method of "EGO AS BEAK." According to Olson, Pound's method gives us space "& its live air," but it is "beautiful because it destroys historical time."[11] Going away from the Poundian ego, however, Olson cannot escape the poet-historian's paradoxical situation. As Robert von Hallberg has argued, though Olson wished to reduce "all voices to the significance of their statements," Maximus (Olson) gradually becomes the central point of reference in the Maximus poems: "Olson sits at the center of his own elegiac poem, his world."[12]

In our century as in the last, the poet's standpoint is inseparable from an understanding of historical order. In Pound's work radical chaos is countered by a reaching for a radical coherence; order is provided by Pound's view of economic laws, by his metaphorical syntheses, and by his dependence on a utopian order breaking into chaos. The Malatesta cantos or the Fifth Decad of *The Cantos,* as they concentrate on particular historical epochs, however, come close to the contextualist's method of historical colligation. Though their presentation offers more surface difficulties than Browning's poems do, they have some of Browning's emphasis on connecting, not chronologically but "simultaneously," the varied materials of an epoch. Despite a shared emphasis on simultaneity, Browning and Pound differ in their understandings of personal vision and the end of history. And here, I would suggest, Browning is closer to a poet like William Carlos Williams than he is to Pound. Browning's delight in the "resuscitation" of history is primary in poems such as *Sordello, The Ring and the Book,* and many of the dramatic monologues, and his didactic interests, though present, remain secondary. For Browning, in this sense, "means to the end" are "themselves in part the end" (*RB,* 1.698). The end of history—the didactic end of historical writing, or the apocalyptic or progressive end of history itself—is not Browning's immediate and primary concern. His poetic project, to be sure, relies on a progressive teleology; and yet his poems are not often designed to demonstrate the direction or even the inevitability of progress. The perfection of the cultures Browning explores will not be accomplished by vision breaking into and transforming the world. On the contrary the world's imperfections may find themselves still to be perfected in Browning's heretically imperfect heaven.

Browning's cheerful and experimental inclusiveness looks forward to Williams's experimental historical poem of America in which connections among particulars are taken to be sufficient in themselves. Allowing order and disorder their places, Williams described *Paterson* as a "failing experiment, toward assertion with broken means but an assertion, always, of a new and total culture, the lifting of an environment to expression."[13] Commenting on Williams's historical experiment Richard Eberhart has equated, quite literally, Williams's historical and poetic ends by suggesting "a tragedy has an end, but history does not."[14] Eberhart's formula is too simple with regard to history, but it points to the fact that in *Paterson* historical telos is less significant than Williams's delight in historical juxtapositions.

Still, the end of history, and thus the shape of writings including history, was an important problem for Williams, as it was for Browning earlier, and as it has been still more recently for Robert Lowell. With a less relenting view of historical ends and of historical poetry, Lowell begins the title poem of his volume *History* by pointing to the difference between life and art, history and written history:

> History has to live with what was here,
> clutching and close to fumbling all we had—
> it is so dull and gruesome how we die,
> unlike writing, life never finishes.[15]

Historical order, finally, becomes a question of poetic closure and of personal composure. Lowell's assertion itself could provide the basis for a bleak commentary on *The Cantos*.

Yet for Lowell and more especially for Pound, Williams, and Olson, as for Browning earlier, historical ordering was too dearly bought if it became an ordering of exclusion—excluding dissonant facts, ideas, or language. In Williams's well-known formulation:

> Dissonance
> (if you are interested)
> leads to discovery.[16]

As we have seen, Browning's distrust of the false sublime—and his own reinterpretation of received tradition—led him to a kind of dissonant language that critics labeled prosaic. Although Wordsworth's understanding of poetic language drove a wedge between prose and the prosaic, after Browning and notably after Pound's poetic experiments the category of the *prosaic* was transformed into the category of *prose*. The antithesis of the poetic and the prosaic was, in various ways, subsumed by a perceived complementarity of poetry and prose. The minglings of poetry and prose in *The Cantos*, *Paterson*, and *Maximus*, despite their different ends, stand as redefinitions of poetry and music. The admiration for music is not lacking in these poems, but the understanding of music in language changes as each of these poets claims in some way to make language new.

The notion that language is renewed by inclusion is not in itself particularly new. Nor is the redefinition of music in poetry. Following T. S. Eliot more or less accurately, Hugh Kenner has, for example, located Chaucer, Landor, Browning, Pound, and even Ben Jonson in a tradition of poetry that refuses to evoke "swarms of inarticulate feelings."[17] An easier distinction than Kenner's grouping, a distinction as old as that between the language of Wyatt and Surrey, acknowledges a felt difference between the speaking and the singing style. With regard to modern poetry, however, the appropriate distinction is not precisely that between speech and song; rather, a better distinction can be drawn between poems that insist on radical inclusiveness of language (those of Browning, Pound, Olson, and Williams) and poems that strive for a new decorum for speech and song (those of Yeats, Lowell, and, to some extent, Eliot). To put it another way, we can see the encounter with the prosaic as the logical outcome of poetry that suspects the evocative power of too easy music, and that has also begun by suspecting the lyre can seriously mislead the pen.

At the same time, such long poems as *Sordello, The Ring and the Book, The Cantos,* or *Paterson* have gone to some length to make the lyre—and the lyric—able to sustain the weight of inclusiveness. As traditional narrative becomes fragmented and as the poet takes a paradoxical but important place in the poem, Pound's definition of the epic is confronted by the lyric and found inadequate. Pound could as well have said, not that the "epic is a poem including history," but that the lyric is a poem including history. In the face of the explicitly epic dimensions of *The Cantos,* one might argue further that the epic has become a poem including the lyric. The definitions and the practice of epic and lyric, the overlapping of narrative, dramatic, and lyric forms, and the combination of harmony and dissonance suggest the intimate links between historical conceptualization and poetic form.

To look at poetic language, at the problem of prose, and at the equivocal position of the poet-persona in modern poems including history establishes their common tradition but minimizes their important differences. A systematic treatment of these poems is beyond my present scope. Briefly, however, I would account for the differences in these historical poems by noticing that each poet chooses a different dominant figurative strategy.[18] Though all of them use various forms of figurative language, each poet relies heavily on one figure as a vehicle for representing history. Browning creates order out of a historical situation by connecting its details and by pointing to its ironies. Pound, in contrast, reaches for an order existent, except in isolated exempla, outside of history, and his syntheses and metaphors reach toward that end. For Pound the historical given is more deeply chaotic than it is for Browning; and Pound reaches for greater certainty than Browning by seeking for causal laws and for historical exempla of proper order. In *The Cantos* perspectivism and irony give way to a belief, like the anarchist's, in a utopia that might be achieved at any time. Pound seeks historical correlatives of his vision and equates the exempla of history and his own vision through ideogram, or metaphor. The bent of both Williams and Olson is clearly different from both of these approaches to history. Despite their substantial differences, there is in Williams's and in Olson's work the tendency to see history in macrocosmic / microcosmic terms. Paterson and Gloucester *stand for* America in varied and significant ways. Whatever their differences Olson and Williams force us to ponder historical wholes through extrapolation from the parts or portions they describe. Williams begins *Paterson* by asserting the identity of the man and the city. His purpose, he declares, is "by multiplication a reduction to one." In a less literal way, Olson suggests man as the microcosm and as the measure of Gloucester, of America, of the poem:

> The old charts
> are not so wrong
> which added Adam
> to the world's directions
>
> which showed any of us
> the center of a circle
> our fingers
> and our toes describe.[19]

Whereas Olson expands the man to measure geography and finally sees history *as* geography, Williams paradoxically reduces by multiplication American history to one city. In Olson's view Williams's effort failed even as it succeeded: by thus limiting his microcosm ("by making his substance historical of one city") and identifying it with Dr. Paterson, Williams lets "time roll him under."[20] Olson widened his own scope temporally and geographically; he attempted to explain history by moving from the microcosm to macrocosm. Though they acknowledge Pound's pioneering method of including history in the poem, Williams's and Olson's methods are equally far from Pound's metaphors and from Browning's ironies. All four poets, however, reach for figurative means of order in the face of very real and possible failure to encompass historical complexity.

For these modern poets following Browning, then, history becomes an unavoidable obstacle, a source of dissonance requiring struggle. Despite their differences, we need not take any one of these poetic strategies or any one of these views of historical ends as fundamentally antihistorical, whatever the arguments about spatial form or the modern mythical method might imply. It is true that Olson came to criticize "culture" and "history" as a kind of fall from the "mythological." Yet his poems do not aspire to a naive status as myth but to a "dialectical unity" that Olson defines as mythological.[21] Such dialectical unity presupposes the inclusion of much historical matter. Olson's projective verse, his understanding of the poem as field, presents special problems for the inclusion of history; yet, as Olson well knew, the "field" has its own archaeology.[22] Williams was never so taken with the idea of myth as Olson was. Book 5 of *Paterson* does move away from the local historical particularity of the first four books, yet even this second conclusion illustrates the difficulty of ending a historical long poem with a poet-historian at its center. Book 5 is only possible as it builds upon an established identity of history with his / story, macrocosm and microcosm. More than Williams, Pound seeks the conformation of the historical world to his own vision, and it is Pound's struggle with history, more than Browning's, that was the direct precursor of Williams's and Olson's work. Yet even Pound's stance is not antihistorical, though the world's failure to conform to Pound's vision evokes an elegiac nostalgia for mythic forces remaking the world. For Pound the chaos of history calls again and again for historical and poetic order. The envisioned end or goal of history is deferred (to the past or to the future) as the poet's end is not. Whatever their historical questions, for Pound, Olson, and Williams, as for Browning before them, the poetic enterprise was defined in an encounter with history.

Behind Pound's poetry of struggle was Browning's attempt to find the poet-personae, the narrative structure, and the language appropriate to poems including history. Browning's encounter with history was no less a struggle than Pound's, Williams's, or Olson's, yet his contextualist relativism combined with an underlying teleology left him often with an ironic equipoise, a balancing of historical necessity against historical knowledge. The twentieth-century reader of Browning's poems may feel almost more at ease with Browning's historical ironies—in which we see through and beyond a character's historical situation—than with Pound's historical vision, or Williams's locale, or Olson's microcosm.[23] But no more than Browning's Victorian readers can we be entirely at ease with Browning's works. The difficulties of Browning's historical view are reflected in those poems that even now can baffle historical or critical judgment.

The end of Browning's struggling grammarian is a case in point. "A Grammarian's Funeral" occurs we are told "shortly after the revival of learning in Europe." The scholar's pall-bearer assures us of his master's faith, learning, and loftiness, and of his essential superiority to the multitudes below him. Whether we should accede wholeheartedly to the disciple's view is open to question, for the funeral mixes the ridiculous equally with the sublime, and the verse form itself is far from a stately and dignified measure. The disciple announces the arrival at the burial place and passes his judgment on his master:

> Well, here's the platform, here's the proper place:
>   Hail to your purlieus,
> All ye highfliers of the feathered race,
>   Swallows and curlews!
> Here's the top-peak; the multitude below
>   Live, for they can, there:
> This man decided not to Live but Know—
>   Bury this man there?
> Here—here's the place, where meteors shoot, clouds form,
>   Lightnings are loosened,
> Stars come and go! Let joy break with the storm,
>   Peace let the dew send!
> Lofty designs must close in like effects:
>   Loftily lying,
> Leave him—still loftier than the world suspects,
>   Living and dying.
>   ("A Grammarian's Funeral," 133–48)

In the context of Browning's distrust of the sublime, this burial on a mountaintop "crowded with culture" (another loaded word, compare Cleon's "culture," for example[24]) excites as much suspicion as agreement. Browning ironically leaves us to answer as we can the disciple's rhetorical question: did his master "not magnify the mind, show clear / Just what it all meant?" The very words of the disciple's last judgment contribute to the poem's essential irony. Is there a pun in the grammarian's "lofty designs" and lofty "lying"? Is he truly "loftier than the world suspects," or is his thrice repeated loftiness as "dead from the waist [waste] down" as his grammar? The scholar is refracted through the disciple's eyes and through the poet's quite different historical perspective. The grammarian's end is but the beginning of his history: the potential irony of his living and dying is an interpretive possibility for the grammarian's Renaissance disciples, for the poet, and for us.[25]

Browning's importance for modern poets and the continuing attraction of such poems as "A Grammarian's Funeral," "Andrea del Sarto," *Sordello,* or *The Ring and the Book* suggest that Browning's historical imagination remains closely connected with our own. The premises from which many of Browning's modern readers construct their own historical prejudices and even their antihistorical biases are grounded in the same potentially ironic situation as Browning's. To read Browning's poetry requires a complex judgment about the distance between his historical understanding and our own. Browning's poetry glories in this struggle with history as it challenges his readers to examine the mutual dependence of historical understanding and the interpretation of poems.

ABBREVIATIONS

ES	"Essay on Shelley"
GK	*Guide to Kulchur*
Handbook	*A Browning Handbook*
L and A	*Browning's Roman Murder Story*
P	*Personae*
PE	*The Poetry of Experience: The Dramatic Monologue in Modern Literary Tradition*
RB	*The Ring and the Book*
RB and EBB	*The Letters of Robert Browning and Elizabeth Barrett Barrett, 1845–1846*
RB and JW	*Robert Browning and Julia Wedgwood: A Broken Friendship as Revealed by Their Letters*
Sord.	*Sordello*

NOTES

Chapter One

1. John Ruskin, *Modern Painters*, 4, *The Works of John Ruskin*, Library Edition (New York: Longmans, Green, 1904), 6:446.

2. John Maynard suggests that Browning came to "use the perspectives and conceptions of historical thinking as a fundamental, perhaps even the fundamental principle in many of his best poems," *Browning's Youth* (Cambridge: Harvard University Press, 1977), 346. See also Roger Sharrock, "Browning and History," in *Robert Browning: Writers and Their Background*, ed. Isobel Armstrong (Athens, Ohio: Ohio University Press, 1975), 77–103.

3. For such a Marxist reading, see Patrick Brantlinger, *The Spirit of Reform: British Literature and Politics, 1832–1867* (Cambridge: Harvard University Press, 1977); a view of history as nightmare may underlie both Morse Peckham's "Historiography and *The Ring and the Book*," *Victorian Poetry* 6 (1968): 242–57, and Robert Langbaum's "Browning and the Question of Myth," in *The Modern Spirit: Essays on the Continuity of Nineteenth- and Twentieth-Century Literature* (New York: Oxford University Press, 1970), 76–100.

4. See Henry James, "The Novel in *The Ring and the Book*," in *Notes on Novelists* (New York: Biblo and Tannen, 1969), 385–411; J. Hillis Miller, *The Disappearance of God: Five Nineteenth-Century Writers* (Cambridge: Harvard Uni-

versity Press, 1969). Morse Peckham discusses the opaqueness of the past as "otherness" and suggests that the "otherness of the past" was important to histories, to historical fictions, and even to historical architecture in the nineteenth century. Peckham, "Afterword: Reflections on Historical Modes in the Nineteenth Century," *Victorian Poetry, Stratford-upon-Avon Studies* 15 (London: Edward Arnold, 1972), 277–300.

5. On Ruskin and history, see Elizabeth K. Helsinger, *Ruskin and the Art of the Beholder* (Cambridge: Harvard University Press, 1982), 140–67.

6. See Wallace Ferguson, *The Renaissance in Historical Thought* (New York: Houghton Mifflin, 1948); Frank M. Turner, *The Greek Heritage in Victorian Britain* (New Haven: Yale University Press, 1981); and Elinor S. Shaffer, *'Kubla Khan' and "The Fall of Jerusalem": The Mythological School in Biblical Criticism and Secular Literature, 1770–1880* (London: Cambridge University Press, 1975).

7. Turn of the century examples in this vein are Walter Bagehot, "Wordsworth, Tennyson, and Browning; or Pure, Ornate, and Grotesque Art in English Poetry," in *Literary Studies,* ed. Richard Holt Hutton, 2 vols., 4th ed. (London: Longmans, Green, 1891), 2:338–90; George Santayana, "The Poetry of Barbarism, 1900," in *Selected Critical Writings,* ed. Norman Henfrey (London: Cambridge University Press, 1968), 1:84–116. G. K. Chesterton argues that Browning's grotesque is the consequence of his energy and of the intrinsically miraculous character of the object itself, in *Robert Browning* (New York: Macmillan, 1906), 151. For further discussion of Browning as unpoetic see chapter 6. A useful summary of criticism is found in *Browning: The Critical Heritage,* ed. Boyd Litzinger and Donald Smalley (London: Routledge and Kegan Paul, 1970).

8. E. S. Shaffer notes how many of Browning's poems are pointed to his time, and she argues that Browning's "perceptual skepticism" was closely bound up with higher critical apologetics and "made the preservation of his faith possible" (p. 210).

9. José Ortega y Gasset, "A Chapter from the History of Ideas—Wilhelm Dilthey and the Idea of Life," *Concord and Liberty*, trans. Helene Weyl (New York: Norton, 1946), 144.

10. On the problematic of existence see Thomas Carlyle, "Biography," *Critical and Miscellaneous Essays*, 3, *Complete Works*, Centenary Edition, 28 vols. (London: Chapman and Hall, 1899), 44–45; on perfection in history see "On History Again," *Critical and Miscellaneous Essays*, 3:168.

11. Robert Browning, "Cleon," lines 120–21, *The Complete Works of Robert Browning*, ed. Charlotte Porter and Helen A. Clarke, Florentine Edition, 14 vols. (New York: Thomas Y. Crowell, 1900). All further references, unless otherwise specified, are to this edition and are indicated parenthetically in the text by line number or by book and line numbers for longer works.

12. I am using "historicism" in the general sense of Ernest Troeltsch and Friedrich Meinecke, a sense that emphasizes historical individuality and cultural relativity, rather than in the restricted sense, closer to Peckham's, of Karl Popper's *The Poverty of Historicism*. For a useful summary of the vagaries of definition, see William Iggers, *The Dictionary of the History of Ideas*, s.v. "historicism." Also useful are G. P. Gooch, *History and Historians of the Nineteenth Century* (London: Longmans, Green, 1913); and Fritz Stern's anthology, *The Varieties of History from Voltaire to the Present* (New York: Meridian Books, World Publishing, 1956).

13. James Loucks and Richard Altick, *Browning's Roman Murder Story* (Chicago: University of Chicago Press, 1968), 13–37. As this chapter indicates, I agree with Loucks and Altick about the importance of Carlyle; I would only suggest that Rankean historiography is not wholly antithetical to Carlyle's historical view. Hereafter cited parenthetically in the text as L and A.

14. James Anthony Froude, "The Science of History," *Short Studies on Great Subjects*, ed. David Ogg (Ithaca: Cornell University Press, 1963), 34.

15. Mircea Eliade, *Cosmos and History: The Myth of the*

Eternal Return, trans. Willard R. Trask (New York: Harper and Row, 1959), 153.

16. Langbaum, "Browning and Myth." Douglas Bush calls Browning's method "antique realism" in *Mythology and the Romantic Tradition in English Poetry* (Cambridge: Harvard University Press, 1969), 358–85.

17. Langbaum's own interests in Browning's historical poems belie his narrow emphasis on myth as circular pattern. See especially *The Poetry of Experience: The Dramatic Monologue in Modern Literary Tradition* (London: Chatto and Windus, 1957). Hereafter cited parenthetically in the text as *PE*.

18. In English poetics the association between primitive language and poetic language, from Adam Smith through Macaulay and beyond, suggests the basis for modern discussions of the "mythopoeic" (a word, according to the *OED*, first used in 1846). Yet another version of the myth-history, poetry-history, primitive-modern dichotomy is explicated by Claude Levi-Strauss in the "Ouverture" to *The Raw and the Cooked*. Though he admits that history "can never divest itself of myth" in *Myth and Meaning* ([New York: Schocken, 1979], 43), he maintains that myth provides a "closed system" and history is an "open system." As Jack Goody has pointed out, this gap is significant enough to found a number of additional dichotomies: myth is opposed to history; neolithic society to modern; mythical thought to scientific thought; imagination, intuition, and perception to abstract thought. See Goody, *The Domestication of the Savage Mind* (Cambridge: Cambridge University Press, 1977), 7; Claude Levi-Strauss, *The Raw and the Cooked: Introduction to a Science of Mythology*, trans. John and Doreen Weightman (New York: Harper and Row, 1969), 13. Hayden White quotes Levi-Strauss to argue that the "conflation" of history and myth disturbs literary theorists who presuppose a radical division between fact and fancy; see "Historical Text as Literary Artifact," in *The Writing of History: Literary Form and Historical Understanding*, ed. Robert H. Canary and Henry Kozicki (Madison: University of Wisconsin Press, 1978), 45. Peter Munz argues for the interdependence of myths and histories, for the process of

"true myth issuing in significant history" and of "true history issuing in significant myth," in "History and Myth," *Philosophical Quarterly* 6 (1956): 1–16.

19. Elizabeth Barrett to Browning, 20 March 1845, *Letters of Robert Browning and Elizabeth Barrett Barrett, 1845–46*, ed. Elvan Kintner, 2 vols. (Cambridge: Belknap Press, Harvard University Press, 1969), 1:24. Hereafter cited as *RB and EBB*.

20. William O. Raymond, "Browning and the Higher Criticism," *The Infinite Moment and Other Essays in Robert Browning*, 2d. ed. (Toronto: University of Toronto Press, 1965), 30.

21. Raymond quotes Mrs. Orr's recollection of Browning's telling her in 1869: "I know all that may be said against it [the Christian scheme of salvation], on the ground of history, of reason, of even moral sense. I grant that it may be a fiction. But I am none the less convinced that the life and death of Christ, as Christians apprehend them, supply something which humanity requires, and that it is true for them" ("Browning and the Higher Criticism," 39).

22. Shaffer, 220, 224.

23. Numerous recent critical essays have described the common ground of fictions and histories, though most have focused on novels rather than poems. See especially Peter Gay, *Style in History* (New York: Basic Books, 1974); David Levin, *In Defense of Historical Literature: Essays on American History, Autobiography, Drama, and Fiction* (New York: Hill and Wang, 1967); György Lukács, *The Historical Novel*, trans. Hannah Mitchell and Stanley Mitchell (London: Merlin Press, 1962); J. Hillis Miller, "Narrative and History," *ELH* 41 (1974): 455–73; Hayden White, "Historical Text as Literary Artifact"; and White, "Historicism, History, and the Imagination," *Tropics of Discourse: Essays in Cultural Criticism* (Baltimore: Johns Hopkins University Press, 1978), 118.

24. Aristotle, *Poetics*, trans. Ingram Bywater, in *The Basic Works of Aristotle*, ed. Richard McKeon (New York: Random House, 1941), 1464.

25. Carlyle, "Corn-Law Rhymes," *Essays*, 3:152.

26. See "Corn-Law Rhymes" and also "The Diamond Necklace," *Essays*, 3:330.

27. From another perspective, however, one might say that the chaos of history was not quite so chaotic for Browning as for Carlyle; Browning's view of history was less apocalyptic than Carlyle's, and thus for him history was more immediately admissible to poetry.

28. Browning to Ruskin, 10 December 1855, quoted in *The Works of John Ruskin, Letters, 1827–69*, 36:xxiv–xxxv.

29. For an elaboration of Scott's historical view, see Avrom Fleishman, *The English Historical Novel: Walter Scott to Virginia Woolf* (Baltimore: Johns Hopkins University Press, 1971), 39.

30. See for example Park Honan's fine work on *Browning's Characters: A Study in Poetic Technique* (New Haven: Yale University Press, 1961); Thomas J. Collins, "Browning's Essay on Shelley," *Victorian Poetry* 1 (1963): 1–6; Clyde de L. Ryals, *Becoming Browning: The Poems and Plays of Robert Browning, 1833–1846* (Columbus: Ohio State University Press, 1983).

31. Herbert F. Tucker, Jr. *Browning's Beginnings: The Art of Disclosure* (Minneapolis: University of Minnesota Press, 1980), 209–222.

32. Luria's nobility is often attributed to the influence of Elizabeth Barrett, and the play's failure with some justice is attributed to Browning's preoccupation with his courtship; I suggest here, too, that the original conception of the play was in itself problematic. See William Clyde DeVane, *A Browning Handbook*, 2d. ed. (New York: Appleton-Century-Crofts, 1955), 186–87. Hereafter cited parenthetically as *Handbook*.

Chapter Two

1. Hayden White, *Metahistory: The Historical Imagination in Nineteenth-Century Europe* (Baltimore: Johns Hopkins University Press, 1973), 18. On colligation White also cites W. H. Walsh's *Introduction to the Philosophy of History*, 3d. ed.

(London: Hutchinson University Library, 1967); and Isaiah Berlin's "The Concept of Scientific History," in *Philosophical Analysis of History*, ed. William Dray (New York: Harper and Row, 1966).

2. See White, who comments on Croce's view of Burckhardt: "'Like all pessimists,' Croce wrote, 'he [Burckhardt] had in him a streak of unsatisfied hedonism'.... And it was this that made him want to flee the world rather than face it and work to save those parts of it which he valued most highly. This is perhaps why both his books and his life were conceived as 'works of art' in defense of 'works of art'" (*Metahistory*, 263).

3. Jerome McGann, *Don Juan in Context* (Chicago: University of Chicago Press, 1976), 101, 114, 154, 160.

4. Raymond Williams, *Culture and Society, 1780–1950* (New York: Harper and Row, 1966), xvi.

5. Carlyle, "On History," *Essays*, 2:86–87.

6. Browning might well have taken issue with Carlyle's assertion that most biography should be summary because most men are sheeplike. See Carlyle, "Boswell's Life of Johnson," *Essays*, 3:86.

7. As we shall see, among the exceptions to this generalization is Browning's poem "Gold Hair: A Story of Pornic."

8. Brantlinger, 161. Brantlinger also criticizes Browning for lacking Ruskin's social concerns, for failing to understand social processes, for lacking real democratic sympathies, and for historical inaccuracies—particularly in his presentation of the Pope in *The Ring and the Book*. Browning's skepticism about language and about social institutions, Brantlinger argues, undermines a positive view of reform.

9. *RB and EBB*, 1:27, 26 February 1845.

10. Maynard, 33.

11. Shaffer, 219.

12. Ibid., 221.

13. Browning's metaphors for his art in *The Ring and the Book* strikingly resemble the imagery in the last four

stanzas, 52–55, of Shelley's "Adonais." In *The Ring and the Book* we find the Pope's convex glass, or mirror, in which men reflect (and reduce) the infinite; in Book 1, moreover, we find the many-colored facets of the "revolving year" whirling into a unity of white, the fire lurking inside; and finally, we see the web as a metaphor for art. In "Adonais" Shelley creates his "dome of many coloured glass" that stains the "white radiance of Eternity"; a light, Shelley says, has "passed from the revolving year"; and he concludes, "that sustaining Love / Which through the web of being blindly wove / Burns bright or dim" (Shelley, *Poetical Works*, ed. Thomas Hutchinson, rev. G. M. Matthews [London: Oxford University Press, 1970], 443). See also Mircea Eliade, "The 'God who Binds' and the Symbolism of Knots," *Images and Symbols: Studies in Religious Symbolism*, trans. Philip Mairet (London: Harvill Press, 1961), 92–124.

14. Terry Eagleton, *Criticism and Ideology: A Study in Marxist Literary Theory* (London: NLB, Atlantic Highlands Humanities Press, 1976), 114, 119.

15. For a summary of critical positions see P. J. Keating, "Robert Browning: A Reader's Guide," in *Browning*, ed. Isobel Armstrong, 299–342. One might also see the web according to White's scheme as being between organicist and mechanist models of history (the mechanist form of historical conceptualization being generally associated with radical ideology).

16. Wilhelm Dilthey, *Gesammelte Schriften*, 17 vols. (1914–74), vols. 1–12 (Stuttgart: B. G. Tuebner, and Gottingen: Vandenhoeck and Ruprecht), vols. 13–17 (Gottingen: Vandenhoeck and Ruprecht), 1:37, 87; quoted in Rudolh A. Makkreel, *Dilthey: Philosopher of the Human Studies* (Princeton: Princeton University Press, 1975), 63.

17. Dilthey, *Gesammelte Schriften*, 5:172, quoted and translated in Makkreel, 135.

18. Dilthey, *Pattern and Meaning in History: Thoughts on History and Society*, ed. and trans. H. P. Rickman (New York: Harper and Brothers, 1962), 163.

19. Dilthey, *Pattern and Meaning*, 139.

20. Ibid.

21. Lukács, 83.

22. Ibid. Interestingly Browning himself was an admirer of both Scott and Balzac: he gave Pen an edition of Scott's Waverley novels in 1862 and he proudly possessed a complete edition of Balzac. See A. L. N. Munby, ed., *Sales Catalogues of Libraries of Eminent Persons*, vol. 6, *Poets and Men of Letters*, ed. John Woolford (London: Mansell, 1972), 156. On Balzac, Browning wrote to Elizabeth Barrett, "I entirely agree with you in your estimate of French and English Romance-writers. I bade the completest adieu to the latter on my first introduction to Balzac, whom I greatly admire for his faculty, whatever he may choose to do with it," 27 April 1846, *RB and EBB*, 2:658.

23. Browning, *Poetical Works, 1833–64*, ed. Ian Jack (London: Oxford University Press, 1970), 38.

24. A. K. Cook, *A Commentary Upon Browning's "The Ring and the Book"* (London: Humphrey Milford, Oxford University Press, 1920). Though Browning appeals to verification in *Sordello*, he eschewed notes, telling Martineau he had to choose between the poet and the historian. See DeVane, *Handbook*, 74. On Browning and fact see the *Victorian Newsletter* controversy that includes Donald Smalley, "Browning's View of Fact in *The Ring and the Book*," *Victorian Newsletter* 16 (Fall 1959): 1–9; Robert Langbaum, "The Importance of Fact in *The Ring and the Book*," *VN* 17 (Spring 1960): 11–17; Paul Cundiff, "Robert Browning: Indisputably Fact," *VN* 17 (Spring 1960): 7–11; and Cundiff, *Browning's Ring Metaphor and Truth* (Metuchen, N.J.: Scarecrow Press, 1972).

25. Michael E. Darling, "Notes on Browning's 'Gold Hair' and 'Apparent Failure,'" *Studies in Browning and His Circle* 7 (1979):71.

26. See John Maynard, "Browning's 'Sicilian Pastoral,'" *Harvard Library Bulletin* 20 (1972): 436–43; David Shaw, *The Dialectical Temper: The Rhetorical Art of Robert Browning* (Ithaca: Cornell University Press, 1968), 116–19; and Eleanor Cook, *Browning's Lyrics: An Exploration* (Toronto: University of Toronto Press, 1974), 176.

27. Marilyn Sirugo, "The Site of 'Love Among the Ruins,'" *Studies in Browning and His Circle* 4 (1976): 41–48.

28. Edmund Spenser, "The Ruines of Time," *Poetical Works*, ed. J. C. Smith and Edward de Selincourt (London: Oxford University Press, 1970), 471.

29. See, for example, Browning's letter to John H. Ingram, 11 February 1876, in which the poet recalls: "As to our great admiration for Poe's power, that anybody who cared to question my wife or myself on the subject would be certain to hear" (*Letters of Robert Browning Collected by Thomas J. Wise*, ed. Thurman L. Hood [New Haven: Yale University Press, 1933], 170). The *Sotheby Sale Catalogue* listed in Browning's library an 1880 edition of Poe's *Letters and Opinions*, ed. by J. H. Ingram; see *Sales Catalogues*.

30. Maynard, "'Sicilian Pastoral,'" 439.

31. William Clyde DeVane, "Browning and the Spirit of Greece," in *Nineteenth-Century Studies*, ed. Herbert Davis, William Clyde DeVane, and R. C. Bald (Ithaca: Cornell University Press, 1940), 179–98; Tucker, *Browning's Beginnings*, 209–22.

CHAPTER THREE

1. Robert Browning to Julia Wedgwood, 19 November 1868, *Robert Browning and Julia Wedgwood: A Broken Friendship as Revealed by their Letters*, ed. Richard Curle (New York: Frederick A. Stokes, 1937), 144.

2. A number of studies have examined Browning's connections to English poetic tradition, notably those by Thomas Collins, Philip Drew, and Frederick Pottle. I further discuss this relationship, with particular emphasis on Browning's style, in chapter 5.

3. Among Browning's seventeenth-century editions were *Il Nepotisme di Roma, or the History of the Pope's Nephews* (1669); Hobbes's *Tracts* (1681); the *Eikon Basilike* (1649); and Nonnus Panapolitanus's *Conversia Graeci Evangelii secundum Joannem, in Latinum sermonem ad verbum translate* (1620; inscribed RB, 2 May 1843). See *Sales Catalogues*, vol. 6, entries 880, 623, 798, 743, 565, 964.

4. Irvine and Honan describe how Robert Browning

Sr. was forced to move to Paris after losing a breach of promise suit to Mrs. Von Muller, in *The Ring, the Book, the Poet* (London: Bodley Head, 1975), 283. Browning Sr. describes "walking among the books" in a letter to Robert Browning, n.d., catalogue no. 230, Fitzwilliam Museum, Cambridge. Although these letters are undated they were certainly written between 20 July 1852, when Browning Sr. moved to Paris and his death in 1866. It is probable, moreover, that many date from the 1850s. The locations of these letters and of other papers of Browning Sr. are listed by John Maynard in an appendix to *Browning's Youth*.

5. Browning Sr. to Robert Browning, n.d., no. 230, Fitzwilliam Museum.

6. Both the Pope and Robert Browning Sr. cite Luitprand as a generally trustworthy chronicler; see Browning Sr., letter to Robert Browning, n.d., no. 229, Fitzwilliam Museum.

7. Ibid.

8. On the "Nomenclator," see Browning Sr. to Sarianna Browning, 17 September 1858, no. 224a, Fitzwilliam Museum.

9. Browning Sr. to Browning, n.d., no. 230, Fitzwilliam Museum. Browning Sr. may have felt it necessary to specify that "no novels" should be written on Marozia as a response to the vogue of the historical novel; equally, he may be responding to a family interest in historical fictions. In addition to his son's poems and plays on historical subjects, his brother William Shergold Browning wrote historical novels and an essay on writing historical fiction as well as a *History of the Huguenots*. See Maynard, *Browning's Youth*, 88.

10. Robert Browning Sr., ms. notebook, Harry Ransom Humanities Research Center, University of Texas, Austin, Texas. Browning Sr.'s object in the notebook is to develop an entertaining but accurate account of the controversies and military campaigns in the reign of Edward I. He gives, for example, a fast-paced account of Wallace's battle with Percy near Glasgow. Browning's plans for his history clearly went beyond military history and extended to social history and to questions of church and state. Browning Sr.'s

sources range from the Domesday Booke to local histories and records, to the 1860 English edition of Ranke's *History of the Popes of Rome*. For a complete listing of Ranke's works and the dates of their first publication in English, see *Encyclopaedia Britannica*, 15th ed., 15:508.

11. Browning's friend William Wetmore Story wrote in 1850 of attending Ranke's lectures at the University of Berlin. Story to James Russell Lowell, 30 January 1850, *Browning to his American Friends*, ed. Gertrude Reece Hudson (New York: Barnes and Noble, 1965), 252.

12. William Wordsworth, *Poetical Works*, ed. Edward de Selincourt and Helen Darbishire, 2d ed. (Oxford: Clarendon Press, Oxford University Press, 1963), 211, lines 325–30.

13. Charles Richard Sanders, "The Carlyle-Browning Correspondence and Relationship: I and II," *Bulletin of the John Rylands Library* 57 (1975): 213–46, 430–62.

14. On *Cromwell*, see Sanders, 227; see also *New Letters of Thomas Carlyle*, ed. Alexander Carlyle (New York: John Lane, 1904), 1:246–47. On giving up poetry, see Browning to Elizabeth Barrett, 17 February 1845, *RB and EBB*, 1:24; on Browning's negotiations for the Cromwell letter, see Browning to Elizabeth Barrett, 11 February 1845, *RB and EBB*, 1:16; on *Frederick*, see Carlyle to Browning, 4 December 1835, *Letters of Thomas Carlyle to John Stuart Mill, John Sterling, and Robert Browning*, ed. Alexander Carlyle (London: T. Fisher Unwin, 1923), 294–96.

15. Sanders, 450.

16. Sanders quotes this passage from *RB and EBB*, 17 May 1846, 2:160.

17. See Browning to Bessie Raynor Belloc, 18 March 1881, *New Letters*, 262–63.

18. Elizabeth Barrett and R. H. Horne, unsigned essay, *A New Spirit of the Age* (New York, 1844), 333–48, in *Thomas Carlyle: The Critical Heritage*, ed. Jules Paul Seigel (London: Routledge and Kegan Paul, 1971), 244.

19. See Sanders, 234.

20. Sanders, 235.

21. See George Levine, *The Boundaries of Fiction: Carlyle, Macaulay, Newman* (Princeton: Princeton University Press, 1968), and various studies of the novel beginning with Ian Watt's *The Rise of the Novel,* for examination of the view that realism and the realistic novel are the major achievement of nineteenth-century literature. The relation of "fact" and "fiction" is especially crucial and problematic in the Victorian historical novel. See especially Lukács, *Historical Novel,* and Avrom Fleishman, *The English Historical Novel.*

22. See Morse Peckham, "Historiography."

23. Carlyle, "On History," *Essays,* 2:87.

24. For a similar view of Browning's relativism—and its limits—see Loucks and Altick and also Kay Austen, "Browning Climbs the Beanstalk: The Alienated Poet in *The Ring and the Book,*" *Studies in Browning and his Circle* 5 (1977): 26. I differ somewhat from Kay Austen's suggestion that Browning's question, "How else know we save by worth of word" is "veiled irony" directed at the deficiencies of Browning's public; although this may be true, Browning shows that even the prophetic poet needs the help of words, of live facts "deadened down."

25. Hill Shine points out the significance of this passage in *Carlyle's Fusion of Poetry, History, and Religion by 1834* (Port Washington, N.Y.: Kennikat Press, 1967; rpt. Chapel Hill, 1938), 80.

26. Carlyle to Mill, 28 October 1833, *Letters to Mill,* 79–80.

27. Levine, 40. As Levine notes, Carlyle came gradually to reject all fiction as lying.

28. Levine, 40–41. Coincidentally, it was Henry James himself who described "The Novel in *The Ring and the Book.*"

29. Ranke comments on this relationship between particulars and values in the Preface to the first edition of *Histories of the Latin and Germanic Nations.* Here he makes his famous declaration that history does not aspire to instruct but to "show how, essentially, things happened" (*wie es eigentlich gewesen*). And Ranke goes on to ask whether his

particulars will not seem "hard, fragmentary, colorless, tiring." He says that, despite his failures, "a lofty ideal does exist": "One tries, one strives, but in the end one has not reached the goal. . . . The main thing is always what we deal with: as Jakobi says, our subject is mankind as it is, explicable or inexplicable, the life of the individual, of the generations, of the peoples, and at times the hand of God over them" (trans. Wilma A. Iggers, in Ranke, *The Theory and Practice of History,* ed. George G. Iggers and Konrad von Moltke [Indianapolis: Bobbs-Merrill, 1973], 138).

30. Leonard Krieger, *Ranke: The Meaning of History* (Chicago: University of Chicago Press, 1977), 15.

31. Ranke, in Stern, *Varieties of History,* 59.

32. Krieger, 348.

33. Friedrich Meinecke, in Stern, 270. See also his *Historism: The Rise of a New Historical Outlook,* trans. J. E. Anderson (London: Routledge and Kegan Paul, 1972).

34. This is not to imply that Carlyle's and Ranke's historical views coincided in all particulars or even in all essentials. Rather, I would simply point to the common problem of subjectivity in history that both of them found implicit in the romantic emphasis on the individual.

35. See Robert Browning to Alfred Domett, 22 May 1842, in *Robert Browning and Alfred Domett,* ed. Frederic G. Kenyon (New York: E. P. Dutton, 1906), 37.

36. Alfred Domett, marginal comment in Robert Browning's *Sordello,* 1st ed. (London: Edward Moxon, 1840), 196; Ashley 247, British Library, London.

37. The narrator of *Sordello,* for example, comments somewhat scornfully about his details, "Yourselves may spell it yet in chronicles" (1.189).

38. Kay Austen argues persuasively that Books 1 and 12 can be seen as Browning's self-defense against unsympathetic critics, though she goes too far in suggesting that for Browning, Caponsacchi, and the Augustinian Don Celestine "alienation" amounts to renunciation of the world, pp. 28–29.

39. Leonard Krieger quotes Ranke as saying of the *English History* that in it he had tried "to extinguish my own

self, as it were, to let things speak and the mighty forces which have arisen in the course of the centuries." Ranke made this statement to Hans Herzfeld who quotes it in his "Vorwort" to Ranke, *Uber die Epochen der neueren Geschichte,* ed. Hans Herzfeld (Schloss Laupheim, n.d.), 19; quoted in Krieger, 5.

40. The resolution of the subject/object dichotomy is of course quite different for Carlyle and for Ranke. Carlyle, for example, would overcome subjective limitations by creating what Philip Rosenberg describes as a "polycentric perspective" in his histories. See *The Seventh Hero: Thomas Carlyle and the Theory of Radical Activism* (Cambridge: Harvard University Press, 1974), 32. Moreover, as Rosenberg points out, Carlyle would view history from the perspective of the "two eternities" (Rosenberg, 32); or as Elizabeth Barrett says of Carlyle, "Life suggests to him the cradle, the grave, and eternity, and scarce a step between" (Barrett and Horne, *Spirit of the Age,* 243). For the historian Carlyle can promise no success in attaining eternal perspective; historical documents, consequently, become runic. As he glimpses their meaning, the historian glimpses history in its true and apocalyptic nature. For Ranke the resolution of subjective and objective is more mundane. For him, the historian's subjectivity is more important in the history of his own nation, objectivity is easier to attain in writing the history of foreign nations; a combination of perspectives becomes possible in universal history (Krieger, 348). For Carlyle the perspective of eternity and for Ranke universal history are compelling ideals, not easily to be compassed by any individual historian.

41. In *Truth and Method,* Hans Georg Gadamer characterizes such dichotomies most broadly as a tension between idealism and empiricism that he associates with the rise of historicism especially in the mid-nineteenth century. See also Gadamer's view that Ranke would "go behind" the documents in an attitude of "aesthetic self-forgetfulness." See *Truth and Method,* trans. Garett Barden and John Cumming (New York: Seabury Press, 1975), 196.

42. Thomas J. Collins, "Browning's Essay on Shelley: In Context," *Victorian Poetry* 2 (1964): 120. See also Collins,

Robert Browning's Moral-Aesthetic Theory, 1833–55 (Lincoln: University of Nebraska Press, 1967).

43. Philip Drew, "Browning's Essay on Shelley," *Victorian Poetry* 1 (1963):3.

44. Robert Browning, "An Essay on Shelley," in *Complete Works*, 281–300. All further references to the essay are indicated parenthetically by page number (*ES*, 281–300).

45. See M. H. Abrams, *The Mirror and the Lamp: Romantic Theory and the Critical Tradition* (New York: W. W. Norton, 1958), 242.

46. Arthur Henry Hallam, "On Some Characteristics of Modern Poetry, and on the Lyrical Poems of Alfred Tennyson," in *The Writings of Arthur Henry Hallam*, ed. T. H. Vail Motter, Modern Language Association of America, General Series, no. 15 (N.Y.: MLA, 1943), 190; and William Wordsworth, Preface to *Poems* (1815), in *Literary Criticism of William Wordsworth*, ed. Paul M. Zall (Lincoln: University of Nebraska Press, 1966).

47. In 1833, the same year Fox reviewed "Pauline," he published Robinson's essay on Goethe in which, following Schiller and the Schlegels, Robinson distinguishes lyric from epic, subjective from objective, and real from ideal poetry. W. J. Fox himself, reviewing Tennyson's poems in 1833, divides poetry into two classes by distinguishing poetry of observation from poetry of reflection: "The classic portrayed human character by its exterior demonstrations and influences on the material objects of sense, the modern delineates the whole external world from its reflected imagery in the mirror of human thought and feeling." Here Fox creates his own version of Schiller's distinction in his essay "On Naive and Sentimental Poetry." See Francis E. Mineka, *The Dissidence of Dissent: The Monthly Repository, 1806–38* (Chapel Hill: University of North Carolina Press, 1944), 307. William Irvine and Park Honan also indicate the *Monthly Repository* as a possible antecedent to the "Essay on Shelley."

48. John Stuart Mill, "What Is Poetry," 106, and "Two Kinds of Poetry," 128, in *Essays on Literature and Society*, ed. J. B. Schneewind (New York: Collier Books, 1965).

49. Wordsworth, Preface (1815), 150–51. Patricia Ball discusses the Milton/Shakespeare duality among the romantics and Victorians and describes the self-conscious poet in terms of a chameleon/egotist duality in *The Central Self: A Study in Romantic and Victorian Imagination* (London: Athalone Press, University of London, 1968).

50. Abrams, *Mirror*, 241.

51. Abrams, *Natural Supernaturalism: Tradition and Revolution in Romantic Literature* (New York: W. W. Norton, 1971), 182–87.

52. Carlyle, of course, develops a cyclical model of history in which societies or nations are best represented by the phoenix burning and rising from its ashes. As Carlyle's figure indicates, however, his cycle is an apocalyptic one of revolution in contrast to Browning's more evolutionary model.

53. Interestingly, Browning may here be borrowing a metaphor from Shelley to suggest a combination of qualities. Browning characterizes Shelley as a subjective poet carrying pictures "on the retina of his own eyes." Yet Shelley himself introduces *The Cenci*, an objective production in Browning's view, by claiming: "I lay aside the presumptive attitude of an instructor, and am content to paint, with such colors as my own heart furnishes, that which has been" (*Poetical Works*, 276). Using the same metaphor, Browning declares that the subjective poet "does not paint pictures and hang them on the walls"; neither, by his own account, does Shelley, unless those pictures be colored from his own heart.

54. See Richard D. Altick, "Browning's 'Transcendentalism,'" *JEGP* 58 (1959):24–28, on the pejorative use of "transcendentalism" by Browning's critics and by Carlyle. My view that Browning rejected a 'transcendental' definition of poetry is essentially in agreement with Altick's, though perhaps I see less change of direction in Browning's work than Altick does.

55. Austen, 29.

56. See the editions of "Pauline" in the Oxford, *Poetical Works*, line 1019.

57. Abrams, *Mirror*, 283.

58. The terms "persona" and "poet-speaker" are used here as appropriate to the roles of these three first-person poets who figure in "Pauline," *Sordello*, and *The Ring and the Book*. Because these speakers are, in varying degrees, autobiographically close to Browning, it is more fruitful for comparison to discuss them as characters in poems than as representatives of the "real" Robert Browning.

59. For a different interpretation see C. Willard Smith, *Browning's Star-Imagery: The Study of a Detail in Poetic Design* (Princeton: Princeton University Press, 1941; rpt. ed. New York: Octagon Books, 1965).

60. Browning uses this image twice in Book 6, at lines 11–16, and 365–70.

61. John's disciple bears the same name Xanthus as the disciple Browning invents for the apostle in "A Death in the Desert." Shaffer points out that this emphasis on the human and fallible side of prophecy was common in higher critical apologetics.

62. Cook's *Commentary* is particularly useful for tracing biblical allusions in *The Ring and the Book*.

63. A version of the optical metaphor is also important in *Paracelsus*. Paracelsus sees man as the point of convergence for "all those scattered rays" of creation (5.691); as man progresses through error toward truth a "reflux of light" shows him where he has been. As he approaches God, "anticipations, symbols, types / Of a dim splendour" rise in him (5.775–76).

64. The connection of these images is put forward by Smith in *Browning's Star-Imagery*, 212–13.

65. David W. Shaw points to the importance of incarnation in *Sordello* and quotes the narrator's statement that Sordello needs to experience such a power or its representative, "This human clear, as that divine concealed" (*Sord.* 6.602). *The Dialectical Temper*, 37. See also William Whitla, *The Central Truth: The Incarnation in Robert Browning's Poetry* (Toronto: University of Toronto Press, 1963).

66. Collins, "Browning's Essay on Shelley."

67. Loucks and Altick, *Browning's Roman Murder Story,*

334, point out the importance of the absolute truth for the Pope and for John. In their search for truth "the conflicts of detail which so concern the liberal-minded are of no importance . . . the Pope, like St. John before him, therefore is not a narrator but an interpreter, not a historian but a philosopher and prophet." Loucks and Altick correctly assess the truth of the Pope and of John as a critique of the "historical truth" of Higher Criticism. But, as John would suggest, the Pope, like all men who have not had John's special revelation, is limited by his very humanity; he knows through the facts of this world and in this respect is as much like the poet-historian as the poet-prophet. History and interpretation, moreover, need not be antithetical.

68. For a more detailed discussion of the implied author and historical judgment in dramatic monologues, see chapter 5.

69. John Maynard, in "Broad Canvas, Narrow Perspective: The Problem of the English Historical Novel in the Nineteenth Century," puts the analogous problem of the historical novel succinctly: the problem lies "precisely in the articulation of the relation between individual experience and historical overview. Specifically, the problem amounts to a tendency to avoid or evade a direct confrontation of the two, a desire to talk about history on the one hand and about the individual on the other without fully realizing the consequence of seeing individual life in a historical perspective" (in *The Worlds of Victorian Fiction*, ed. Jerome Buckley, *Harvard English Studies*, no. 6 [Cambridge: Harvard University Press, 1975], 261).

70. A good example of this approach is Thomas Collins's *Robert Browning's Moral-Aesthetic Theory*.

71. A better way of viewing the subjective/objective dichotomy is William O. Raymond's argument that "Pauline" and *Sordello* subordinate "historical environment and circumstance" to the "inner world of man's spiritual being," though this is a more accurate account of "Pauline" than of *Sordello*. The latter is in many respects about the connections between "historical environment" and "spiritual being." See Raymond, "Paracelsus," in *The Infinite Moment*, 150.

72. See Maynard, *Browning's Youth,* 216; Frederick Albert Pottle, *Shelley and Browning: A Myth and Some Facts* (Chicago: Pembroke Press, 1923; rpt. ed. Hamden, Conn.: Archon Books, 1965); Philip Drew, *The Poetry of Robert Browning* (London: Methuen, 1970), 40; and Masao Miyoshi who argues for "Pauline" as a dramatic poem in "Mill and 'Pauline': The Myth and Some Facts," *Victorian Studies* 9 (1965): 155–63.

73. J. W. Harper also notes a similarity between "Pauline" and "Porphyria's Lover" in "'Eternity our due,'" 63.

74. Robert Preyer points to a similar ambivalence in perspective in "A Reading of the Early Narratives," *ELH* 26 (1959): 531–48: "The poem wavers back and forth: one moment on fire with vatic ambitions, the next moment longing for release from these alienating dreams."

75. Daniel Stempel, "Browning's *Sordello* and the Art of Makers-See," *PMLA* 80 (1965):554–61.

76. Ibid., 558.

77. We should be cautious, I think, in judging the historical background of *Sordello* trivial on the basis of Browning's 1863 letter in which he calls it "decoration"; quite conceivably, this epithet simply reflects Browning's realization that the historical background in *Sordello* was less perfectly integrated than in various later monologues. The ideal Sordello, after all, would have been man and bard at once, capable like Dante of coalescing insight and outsight, spiritual and political realities, glass and fire.

78. Robert R. Columbus and Claudette Kemper, "*Sordello* and the Speaker: A Problem in Identity," *Victorian Poetry* 2 (1964):263. Mark D. Hawthorne suggests Browning's parentheses serve to indicate digressions ("Browning's *Sordello:* Structure Through Repetition," *Victorian Poetry* 16 [1978]:204–16).

79. Kay Austen is equally interested in this passage.

80. See, for example, the parenthetical poet-commentator in "Old Pictures in Florence" (in which Browning provides a variety of parenthetical footnotes), and, for the character exposing his own motives, "Bishop Blougram's Apology."

81. Ball, 214.

82. Ronald Bush, *The Genesis of Ezra Pound's 'Cantos'* (Princeton: Princeton University Press, 1976), 83.

83. Columbus and Kemper defend *Sordello* as a "study of consciousness," as an examination of Sordello and of the speaker who "seeks an understanding of the phantom whom he has himself created from hints, facts of a vague history drawn from the dim past," p. 251. They persuasively contend *Sordello* is not an "eclipsed historical study."

84. William Clyde DeVane, "The Virgin and the Dragon," in *The Browning Critics*, 181–96.

85. John Killham, "Browning's Modernity: *The Ring and the Book* and Relativism," in *Major Victorian Poets*, 170.

86. Isobel Armstrong, "*The Ring and the Book:* The Uses of Prolixity," in *Major Victorian Poets*, 177–97.

87. J. Hillis Miller, *The Disappearance of God*, 151.

Chapter Four

1. Thomas Carlyle, "On History," *Essays*, 2:88–89.

2. See Paul Ricoeur who observes that "every narrative combines two dimensions in various proportions, one chronological and the other nonchronological. The first may be called the episodic dimension, which characterizes the story as made out of events. The second is the configurational dimension, according to which the plot construes significant wholes out of scattered events" ("Narrative Time," *Critical Inquiry* 7 [1980]: 169–90).

3. Ricoeur, 186. Ricoeur's characterization of "naive forms of narration" seems to me useful as long as "naive" is not considered a judgment of aesthetic value. For an argument on the subject of naive chronicles, see Marilyn Robinson Waldman, "'The Otherwise Unnoteworthy Year 711': A Reply to Hayden White," *Critical Inquiry* 7 (1981):784–92; and Hayden White, "The Narrativization of Real Events," *Critical Inquiry* 7 (1981):793–98.

4. Carlyle, "On History," *Essays*, 2:88.

5. Ibid.

6. J. Hillis Miller's recent fascination with similar threads and labyrinths has led him to some interesting observations on history as problematic enterprise, as the web reweaving itself however often it is 'deconstructed.' See especially, "Narrative and History," *ELH* 41 (1974):455-73.

7. György Lukács observed in connecting historical novels and histories, it is not "philologically demonstrable influence which is important but rather the *common character of the reactions to reality* which in history and literature produce analogous subjects and forms of historical consciousness" (*Historical Novel,* 173).

8. These categories are roughly parallel with Maurice Mandelbaum's division of histories into the sequential, the explanatory, and the interpretive, though my scheme combines "explanatory" and "interpretive" under the contextual rubric. Of my examples below, Mandelbaum would probably consider Sismondi's history sequential, Trotsky's explanatory, and Burckhardt's interpretive. Burckhardt, in fact, provides Mandelbaum with an important instance of interpretive history (*The Anatomy of Historical Knowledge* [Baltimore: Johns Hopkins University Press, 1977], 24-45).

9. Hayden White, *Metahistory,* 18.

10. Ibid., 19.

11. Jacob Burckhardt, *Civilization of the Renaissance in Italy,* trans. S. G. C. Middlemore, 2 vols. (New York: Harper and Row, Harper Colophon Books, 1958), 1:26.

12. Mandelbaum, 40.

13. Karl J. Weintraub, *Visions of Culture* (Chicago: University of Chicago Press, 1966), 140.

14. Jacob Burckhardt, *Force and Freedom: Reflections on History,* trans. and ed. James Hastings Nichols (New York: Pantheon Books, 1943), 306.

15. Michael Mason, "The Importance of *Sordello,*" in *Major Victorian Poets,* 125-51.

16. Burckhardt, *Renaissance,* 1:143.

17. See for comparison Park Honan's discussion of the

dramatic monologue and the moment of crisis in *Browning's Characters* (New Haven: Yale University Press, 1961), 129–48.

18. Hajo Holborn, "Dilthey's Critique of Historical Reason," *Journal of the History of Ideas* 11 (1950):117.

19. Ibid.

20. Dilthey, *Pattern and Meaning*, 132.

21. Elder Olson outlines at least four "different kinds of unifying principle in plots: the consequential, the descriptive, the pattern, and the didactic" (*Tragedy and the Theory of Drama* [Detroit: Wayne State University Press, 1966], 47).

22. On Browning's lyric strength see Eleanor Cook, *Browning's Lyrics;* on the oxymoronic force, the generic tensions of Browning's dramatic lyrics, see Herbert F. Tucker, Jr., "Browning's 'Lyric' Intentions," *Critical Inquiry* 7 (1980):275–96; for a different, and I think too simple, view of 'lyric' as requiring a "sympathy only response," see Victor Vogt, "Narrative and Drama in the Lyric: Robert Frost's Strategic Withdrawal," *Critical Inquiry* 5 (1979):529–51.

23. Ezra Pound, "Three Cantos," *Poetry* 10 (June–August 1917):117.

24. Mason, 136.

25. Mark D. Hawthorne, however, argues that these two sections do not break apart, but are carefully unified ("Browning's *Sordello*," 204–16).

26. Robert Browning, *The Complete Works*, ed. Roma A. King, Jr. (Athens: Ohio University Press, 1970), 2:389, note 322.

27. In reading we find our suspicions are not likely to be excited; for the narrator himself takes responsibility for the Elcorte story (4:545), and Salinguerra seems perfectly satisfied that his wife and child were killed in the Vicenza retreat (4:695–848).

28. Roma King comments that the complex syntax, ellipses, and disregard for chronological time in *Sordello* are an attempt to "give the reader an immediate sense of the developing experience" (*The Focusing Artifice: The Poetry of Robert Browning* [Athens: Ohio University Press, 1968], 25).

29. Elizabeth Barrett to Robert Browning, 21 December 1845, *RB and EBB*, 1:342.

30. Robert Browning, *The Poems*, ed. John Pettigrew and Thomas J. Collins (New Haven: Yale University Press, 1981), 1:106, 1n.

31. Robert Browning, *Sordello*, 1st edition (London: Edward Moxon, 1840).

32. Bruce R. McElderry, Jr., "The Narrative Structure of Browning's *The Ring and the Book*," *Research Studies of the State College of Washington* 11 (1943):204.

33. Isobel Armstrong, "The Ring and the Book," in *Major Victorian Poets*, 179.

34. Boyd Litzinger, "The Structural Logic of *The Ring and the Book*," in *Nineteenth-Century Literary Perspectives: Essays in Honor of Lionel Stevenson*, ed. Clyde de L. Ryals (Durham, N.C.: Duke University Press, 1974), 113.

35. See Tucker for a sensitive comment on the equally strong beginning and closure of the "Soliloquy of the Spanish Cloister." Tucker points out that the monk's very vowels and consonants growl into and out of speech with a chiasmus of "Gr-r-r—there go" and "Ave, virgo! Gr-r-r" ("Browning's Lyric Intentions," 282).

36. In his first words to the watchmen, Lippi urges them to hunt up his cloister and harry out "whatever cat, there, haps on his wrong hole" with the "wee white mouse" "that's crept to keep him company." In his painting Lippi fittingly looks for "a hole," a "corner for escape," finds the escape in a "little lily thing" and scuttles off like a man caught playing "hot cockles" with someone else's wife. Lippi begins his monologue by asserting, "I am poor brother Lippo" and by asking—and answering at some length—"Who am I?" He ends by repeating that he is a "poor monk" and by asserting his own presence in his painting: "up shall come . . . who but Lippo! I!—/ Mazed, motionless and moonstruck—I'm the man!" Lippi's final self-assertion, like his initial surprise, can only be capped by exclamation. "Zooks!" he says (lines 3, 23, 360–65, 392).

37. Clyde de L. Ryals, "'Prince Hohenstiel-Schwangau': Browning's 'Ghostly Dialogue,'" in *Nineteenth-Century Perspectives*, 117–18.

38. In a number of shorter monologues, of course, the silent reactions of the monologuists' interlocutors serve a similar purpose: the two best examples of this process are perhaps "Andrea del Sarto" and "The Bishop Orders His Tomb at St. Praxed's Church."

39. Paul Ricoeur, *Time and Narrative*, trans. Kathleen McLaughlin and David Pellauer (Chicago: University of Chicago Press, 1984), 1:87.

40. Ibid.

41. Joseph Frank, "Spatial Form in Modern Literature," *The Widening Gyre* (New Brunswick, N.J.: Rutgers University Press, 1963); "Spatial Form: An Answer to Critics," *Critical Inquiry* 4 (1977):231–52.

42. W. J. T. Mitchell, "Spatial Form in Literature: Toward a General Theory," *Critical Inquiry* 6 (1980):546.

43. Ibid., 542.

44. See Geoffrey Hartman, *Wordsworth's Poetry, 1787–1814* (New Haven: Yale University Press, 1971), 208–59.

45. Ibid., 212–22.

46. Mitchell, "Diagrammatology," *Critical Inquiry* 7 (1981):628–32.

47. As the triadic and spiral geometries of its readers attest, *The Ring and the Book* is structurally yet more tectonic than *Sordello*. To speak of Browning's architectonics, however, is not to imply that Browning himself used architectural metaphor in the way that Wordsworth did; nor is it to suggest that all "tectonic" structures are the same. Rather, I am using "tectonic" in Mitchell's sense, as the proper antithesis to "linear" form. On the interplay of organic and architectural images in *The Prelude*, see Mitchell, "Diagrammatology."

48. Frank, "Answer to Critics," 235, 241; *Widening Gyre*, 16, 13–14. Much like Browning, Frank attempts to trap time in spatial metaphors; thus for Frank, to grasp past and present simultaneously is "pure time," and pure time "is not time at all—it is perception in a moment of time, that is to say, space" (*Widening Gyre*, 24). Browning, too, metaphorically makes space of time. He describes *earthly* time as a series of spheres. The time in which one lives is a sphere "girt with circumstance" (*Sord.*, 6. 476–77), or with "condi-

tions." Too much aspiration carries one beyond the sphere of time into eternity and unfits him for life, so that like Sordello, he dies. Specifically, Sordello fails "by craving to expand the power he had / And not new power to be expanded" (6.490–91). Sordello in fact would go "quite out of time and this world" into a realm of eternity above the sphere where we know and act. For all his spiritual aspiration, Sordello constricts rather than expands himself. The narrator looking back on Sordello's time conceives a wider sphere of circumstances than the troubadour himself; and the poet-speaker also expands his own sphere to take in another age. Just as Browning's narrator stays within the spheres of time, so for Browning "spatial" time is not, as it is for Frank, an abolition of history and an assertion of the "cosmic, cyclical and infinite" (*Widening Gyre*, 60).

49. Frank, "Answer to Critics," 239.

50. Ibid., 237. Perhaps Paul Ricoeur's comment in "Narrative Time" on "anti-narrativist epistemologists and structuralist literary critics" applies even more directly to Frank's views on historical idolatry. Such theoreticians, Ricoeur remarks, seem even to be moved by a strange resentment toward time, the kind of resentment that Nietzsche expressed in his Zarathustra," 172.

51. Nathan Scott, "Mimesis and Time in Modern Literature," *The Broken Center: Studies in the Theological Horizon of Modern Literature* (New Haven: Yale University Press, 1966), 25–76.

52. Frank Kermode, "Critical Response," *Critical Inquiry* 4 (1978):583.

53. Ricoeur, "Narrative Time," 179–80. Ricoeur's dialectic of "configuration and succession" perhaps parallels John Dewey's description of "compression" in the arts as the establishment of pattern in succession. See *Art as Experience* (New York: Minton, Balch, 1934), 182.

54. Ricoeur, "Narrative Time," 186. Ricoeur goes on to argue that history, equally, reaches this "deep level of repetition." Like *Sordello*, *The Prelude* is a poem in which the hero becomes who he is. *The Prelude*, however, emphasizes the *becoming* and coming back of the poet to himself, while Sordello is concerned in a more static sense with who the troubadour *is*.

Chapter Five

1. J. Hillis Miller, *The Disappearance of God*, 108.
2. D. C. Muecke, *Irony and the Ironic* (London: Methuen, 1970), 73.
3. Ryals, *Becoming Browning*, 247–56.
4. Ibid.
5. Ibid., 5.
6. Anne K. Mellor, *English Romantic Irony* (Cambridge: Harvard University Press, 1980), 24.
7. D. C. Muecke, *The Compass of Irony* (London: Methuen, 1969), 126–27.
8. Ibid., 121, 220.
9. Wayne Booth, *The Rhetoric of Fiction* (Chicago: University of Chicago Press, 1961), 151.
10. Ralph Rader, "The Dramatic Monologue and Related Lyric Forms," *Critical Inquiry* 3 (1976):150.
11. Langbaum limits *ethos* to characterization through a dramatic or "Aristotelian complete action" (*PE*, 157); I think, however, that an action in which a character changes moral direction is not necessarily the only form in which *ethos* or "moral characterization," and hence judgment, enters a poem. Aristotle himself distinguishes character (*ethos*) from plot or a complete action and insists upon the primacy of plot for tragic drama. As commentator O. B. Hardison puts it, "Agent (*pratton*) should be carefully distinguished from character (*ethos*), for agents—people who perform actions—are necessary to a drama; but character in the technical Aristotelian sense is something that is added later and, in fact, is not even essential to successful tragedy, as we learn in Chapter VI (1.59) [of the *Poetics*]" (*Aristotle's Poetics: A Translation and Commentary for Students of Literature* [Englewood Cliffs, N.J.: Prentice-Hall, 1968], 82). See also Elder Olson who distinguishes poems according to their "objects of imitation" and points out that various lyrics may or may not involve "moral character" in "A Conspectus of Poetry, Part II," *Critical Inquiry* 4 (1977):390.
12. Aristotle, *The Basic Works*, ed. Richard McKeon (New York: Random House, 1941), *Nichomachean Ethics*, trans. W. D. Ross, 2.1, lines 3–5; 2.5, pp. 952–57.

13. Philip Drew, *The Poetry of Robert Browning*, 28.

14. Friedrich Meinecke, in Stern, *Varieties of History*, 270.

15. Ernst Troeltsch, *Historismus*, 211, as quoted by Meinecke in Stern, 283.

16. Meinecke, in Stern, p. 283.

17. John Ruskin, *Modern Painters, Works*, 6:446.

18. Wordsworth, in the 1802 Preface, finds "a thousand obstacles" between the biographer or historian and the "image of things," *Literary Criticism*, 50–51. Shelley, too, sees poetry as dealing with the "unchangeable forms of human nature" and not the connections of "time, place, circumstance, cause and effect" (*A Defense of Poetry*, ed. John E. Jordan [New York: Bobbs-Merrill, 1965], 36).

19. Shelley, *Defense*, 36.

20. For a similar point see William Cadbury, "Lyric and Antilyric Forms," 54.

21. Park Honan in *Browning's Characters*, 132, discusses these divisions in terms of historical crises. He says crises may establish character in two ways: (1) the speaker may react to a crisis in a way the reader does not expect; or (2) the crisis may cause the speaker's personality to split into two or more opposing elements, as in "Fra Lippo Lippi." Honan perceptively points to the juxtaposition of perspectives as an important feature in the monologues, though as Honan himself recognizes, "historical crisis" must be taken rather broadly if it is to include the variety of internal and external clashes in Browning's monologues.

22. Rader, 133, and Laurence Perrine, "Browning's Shrewd Duke," *PMLA* 74 (March 1959):157–59; Philip Drew also takes issue with Langbaum's view of sympathy in *The Poetry of Browning*, 24–34.

23. Rader, 133. Victor Vogt argues that we get a "more powerful sense of the duke's character in the very act of judging him" ("Narrative and Drama in the Lyric," 547n).

24. Herbert Tucker argues that the duchess's reactions, her joy, are disproportionate and that the duchess's reactions fascinate and baffle the duke who is drawn to her

portrait in an attempt to figure the duchess out ("Browning's Lyric Intentions," 294). Despite this distinction, I believe both Tucker and I would agree in rejecting William Cadbury's opinion that in "My Last Duchess" one "must supply, from outside knowledge, awareness of the poet displaying his narrator, and to make the effort is to disrupt our reading of the poem" (Cadbury, 51).

25. Tucker, "Browning's Lyric Intentions," 291.

26. Rader, 151, 138.

27. Tucker, "Browning's Lyric Intentions," 294.

28. Louis S. Friedland, "Ferrara and 'My Last Duchess,'" *Studies in Philology* 33 (1936): 656–84; and Perrine, 158.

29. Tucker, "Browning's Lyric Intentions," 295.

30. In one sense of course both Empedocles and Cleon are alike—in being driven to despair by their age. For further analysis of "Empedocles" and "Cleon," see A. W. Crawford, "Browning's 'Cleon,'" *JEGP* 26 (1927):485–90; and William Clyde DeVane, "Browning and the Spirit of Greece," 194–96.

31. Matthew Arnold, "Empedocles on Etna," *Poetry and Criticism of Matthew Arnold*, ed. A. Dwight Culler (Boston: Houghton Mifflin, 1969), 72.

32. Tucker, *Browning's Beginnings*, 215.

33. For a balanced interpretation of the speaker's "distance" in "Galuppi," see Eleanor Cook, 173–80; I agree with DeVane's notion that Browning's sympathies incline toward the speaker of "Galuppi," but I do not find the speaker unsophisticated (*Handbook*, 221); Edgar F. Harden offers an ironic reading of the poem in "A New Reading of Browning's 'A Tocatta of Galuppi's,'" *Victorian Poetry* 11 (1973):330–36.

34. Wayne Booth, *A Rhetoric of Irony* (Chicago: University of Chicago Press, 1974), 36–37.

35. Shaw, *Dialectical Temper*, 173.

36. Booth, *Irony*, 148.

37. Honan, 134.

38. The argument over Blougram, of course, became heated when F. E. L. Priestley challenged G. K. Chesterton's negative view of the bishop. Recent interesting interpretations include R. G. Collins's argument that Gigadibs is not in fact converted by the bishop but is inspired to "go off and seek his fortune and forget philosophical nonsense" ("Browning's Practical Prelate: The Lesson of 'Bishop Blougram's Apology,'" *Victorian Poetry* 13 [1975]:1–20). As will become clear, I am more inclined toward Collins's view than toward the view of Robert G. Laird in "'He Did Not Sit Five Minutes'" ("The Conversion of Gigadibs," *University of Toronto Quarterly* 45 [1976]:295–313). Laird argues that Gigadibs is based on R. H. Horne, though Julia Markus makes a perhaps more persuasive case for Gigadibs as Francis Mahony, or "Father Prout." See "Bishop Blougram and the Literary Men," *Victorian Studies* 21 (1978):171–95.

39. Laird mentions the possible connection of Blougram with Pope Sylvester (A.D. 314–35) who took the decision of the Council of Nicea that "the benefits of the sacraments . . . were transmitted independently of the state of grace of the priest offering them," p. 307.

40. Susan Hardy Aiken, "Bishop Blougram and Carlyle," *Victorian Poetry* 16 (1978):323–40.

41. Cf. Fra Lippo Lippi who is at work on a painting of "Jerome knocking at his poor old breast / With his great round stone to subdue the flesh."

42. Bishop Blougram avoids on Christian ground the elaborate and treacherous argument from analogy, though he can't resist an only slightly less dangerous comparison between pure faith and the "disemprisoned heart" withering up in the desert sun. Though the latter analogy could support an argument for the "case-hardened life," it does at least have some scriptural precedent and it is presented with what many readers have felt is a genuine conviction.

Chapter Six

1. Algernon Charles Swinburne, "The Chaotic School," in *New Writings by Swinburne*, ed. Cecil Y. Lang

(Syracuse: Syracuse University Press, 1964), 41. Swinburne contrasts Browning with Shelley, Keats, and Landor, who are "melodious, spontaneous, perfect at their best."

2. Tilottama Rajan, "Romanticism and the Death of Lyric Consciousness," in *Lyric Poetry: Beyond New Criticism*, ed. Chaviva Hosek and Patricia Parker (Ithaca: Cornell University Press, 1985), 194–207.

3. Santayana explicitly relates the rise of the "poetry of barbarism" to the modern experience of historical discontinuity. Santayana says we live in a period that "tends to read its own character in the past, and to regard all other periods as no less fragmentary and effervescent than itself." In earlier times, he maintains, "Human nature and the life of the world were real and stable objects . . . the actors changed, but not the characters or the play" ("The Poetry of Barbarism," 1:86).

4. Walter Bagehot complained that Browning neglects beauty and pleasure and is "the most of a realist we know" in "Wordsworth, Tennyson, and Browning," 2:338–90. See also Carol Christ, *The Finer Optic: The Aesthetics of Particularity in Victorian Poetry* (New Haven: Yale University Press, 1975), 65–104.

5. George Saintsbury, *A History of English Prosody*, 3 vols. (London: Macmillan, 1906–1910) 3:216.

6. *Dublin Review* 8 (May 1840):551–53; quoted in *Browning: The Critical Heritage*, 64. *The Wellesley Index to Victorian Periodicals* identifies the reviewer as George Irvine (Toronto: University of Toronto Press, 1972) 2: entry 180.

7. Wordsworth, Preface to *Lyrical Ballads*, 50.

8. Ibid., 52.

9. Shelley, *A Defense of Poetry*, 35–37.

10. William Hazlitt, "On the Prose Style of Poets," *The Plain Speaker*, in *The Collected Works of William Hazlitt*, ed. A. R. Waller and Arnold Glover (London: J. M. Dent, 1903) 7:10.

11. Carlyle to Browning, 21 June 1841, *New Letters of Thomas Carlyle*, ed. Alexander Carlyle (1904; rpt. Hildesheim, Germany: Georg Olms, 1969), 1:234.

12. Carlyle to Browning, 25 April 1856, in *Browning: The Critical Heritage*, 198–200.

13. Carlyle, "The Hero as Poet," *On Heroes, Hero-Worship and the Heroic in History,* 5:83.

14. Browning, "Deaf and Dumb," *Browning: Poetical Works, 1833–64,* 938. The prism of art also appears in the Prometheus episode of "Gerard de Lairesse."

15. Abrams, *Mirror,* 298–335.

16. Wordsworth, Preface, 47n.

17. Ibid., 46.

18. To define "prosaic," "prosaist," and "prosaism" in the sense of unpoetic, the *Oxford English Dictionary* cites only two examples before 1800. The words seem to have gained currency between 1800 and 1850, as indicated by examples from Wordsworth, Coleridge, Carlyle, Hunt, Isaac D'Israeli, and Lewes.

19. Saintsbury, 218–20.

20. Hazlitt, 10–11. Wordsworth no doubt would argue that Hazlitt is mistaken in his notion of poetry in that poetry must be made with equal care and has the same vital juices as prose. Despite such divergences, for Hazlitt, prose is made by blows out of unpromising materials that surely resemble Wordsworth's "obstacles" or Shelley's "stories of facts"; poetry involves a congeniality of matter and language. For Hazlitt poetry must, indeed, come as easily as the leaves to the tree, while prose, and even the poetry of prose, emerges from the encounter of mind with resistant matter. Coleridge does not address this question directly in his comments on Wordsworth's Preface and poetry, but he perhaps would resolve such dilemmas by viewing "legitimate" poetry as an indivisible congruence of subject, diction, and meter. Coleridge has a strong sense of the poem as both spontaneous lyric and made thing, and at the same time he finds a complementarity of matter and manner necessary. He says that meter, "having been connected with *poetry* most often and by a peculiar fitness, whatever else is combined with meter has nevertheless some property in common with poetry, as an intermedium of affinity, a sort (if I may dare borrow a well-known phrase from technical chemistry) of *mordant* between it and the super-added meter." Subject matter, diction, and meter coalesce as the

poet brings "the whole soul of man into activity." And although at times the language of poetry is identical to the language of prose, Coleridge cites Daniel's *Civil Wars* as an example of syntax and diction that can justly be called prosaic in the negative sense of the term (*Biographia Literaria,* ed. John Shawcross, 2 vols. [Oxford: Oxford University Press, 1973], 2:55).

21. Both Leigh Hunt and Carlyle, for example, strive to see the naturalness of Browning's dissonance, and they do concede that his work is natural; but it is a reluctant concession to the poet's originality. See Hunt's 1835 review in *The London Journal,* quoted in *Browning: The Critical Heritage,* 43.

22. George Eliot, "Belles Lettres," review of *Men and Women,* by Robert Browning, *Westminster Review,* n.s., 9 (January 1856):290, 295–96. Eliot dwells less on Browning's prosaicness than other reviewers do. J. H. Stirling, for example, says at least half-seriously that in Browning's work "tune there is none—we have line upon line, instead, that is flatly prose. No: music it cannot be called" ("The Poetical Works of Robert Browning," *North British Review* 49 [1868]:192).

23. Hazlitt, 9, 10.

24. Browning to John Ruskin, 10 December 1855, quoted in *Works of John Ruskin, Letters, 1827–69,* 36:xxxiv–xxxv.

25. Robert Langbaum points to this poem as Browning's essay on symbolism, his description of the modern mythological method that works through psychology and realism, in "Browning and the Question of Myth." Interestingly, John Keats also contrasts soaring and walking poetry. He writes to Reynolds: "I have of late been moulting: not for fresh feathers and wings: they are gone, and in their stead I hope to have a pair of patient sublunary legs. I have altered, not from a Chrysalis into a butterfly, but the Contrary, having two little loopholes, whence I may look out into the stage of the world" (Letter to J. H. Reynolds, 11 July 1819, *The Letters of John Keats, 1814–1821,* ed. Hyder Edward Rollins, 2 vols. [Cambridge: Harvard University Press, 1958], 2:128).

26. George Henry Lewes, "Robert Browning and the Poetry of the Age," *British Quarterly Review* 6 (1847):496.

27. Elizabeth Barrett to Browning, 20 March 1845, *RB and EBB*, 1:43.

28. Browning to Julia Wedgwood, 19 November 1868, *RB and JW*, 145.

29. These poems are discussed in greater detail by Philip Drew in an excellent treatment of "Browning and the Rejection of the Romantic Tradition," *The Poetry of Browning: A Critical Introduction* (London: Methuen, 1970), 61–69.

30. Clarice Short, "Childe Roland, Pedestrian," *Victorian Poetry* 6 (1968):175–77; for the influence of Gerard de Lairesse, see DeVane, *Handbook*.

31. When the blinded Gloucester is reunited with Lear, he offers to kiss his hand; Lear replies, "Let me wipe it first; it smells of mortality" (4. 6. 125).

32. David V. Erdman, "Browning's Industrial Nightmare," *Philological Quarterly* 36 (1957):417–35; on Roland and Browning's reaction to medievalism, see Beverly Taylor, "Browning and Victorian Medievalism," *Browning Institute Studies* 8 (1980):57–72.

33. Clyde de L. Ryals, *Browning's Later Poetry, 1871–1889* (Ithaca: Cornell University Press, 1975), 219. Drew makes a convincing case for "Gerard de Lairesse" as an argument with Matthew Arnold and other Victorian Hellenists, 55–59.

34. Gerard de Lairesse, *The Art of Painting in All Its Branches*, trans. John Frederick Fritsch (London, 1778), 45. William Clyde DeVane refers to Lairesse's work in *Browning's Parleyings: The Autobiography of a Mind* (New Haven: Yale University Press, 1927), 213–51.

35. Browning to Julia Wedgwood, 19 November 1868, *RB and JW*, 144.

36. Review of *Parleyings*, by Robert Browning, *Athenaeum*, 19 February 1887, quoted in *Browning: The Critical Heritage*, 496.

37. See Leslie N. Broughton and Benjamin F. Stelter, *A*

Concordance to the Poems of Robert Browning (New York: G. E. Stechert, 1924).

38. Robert Preyer, "Two Styles in the Verse of Robert Browning," *ELH* 32 (1965):62–84.

39. Constance Hassett also addresses this issue in *The Elusive Self in the Poetry of Robert Browning* (Athens: Ohio University Press, 1982).

40. Park Honan cites Mr. Sludge's similar comments: "Bless us, I'm turning poet!" (1184); and "There's verse again, but I'm inspired somehow" (1285), 264.

41. For the concept of foregrounding see Jan Mukarovský, "Standard Language and Poetic Language," trans. Paul L. Garvin, in *Linguistics and Literary Style*, ed. Donald C. Freeman (New York: Holt, Rinehart, and Winston, 1970), 40–56.

42. Stirling, 191–92.

43. See for comparison Pound's statement in the Ur-Cantos that Valla, an exemplar of good language, had "more earth and sounder rhetoric" than Ficino ("Three Cantos," *Poetry* 10 [June–August 1917]:249). See also William Carlos Williams, *Paterson* (New York: New Directions, 1963), Book 3, section 3, pp. 166–67.

Chapter Seven

1. For a commentary on Browning and Moses and a complementary view of Browning and the poet-prophet, see Linda H. Peterson, "Biblical Typology and the Self-Portrait of the Poet in Robert Browning," in *Approaches to Victorian Autobiography*, ed. George P. Landow (Athens: Ohio University Press, 1979), 235–68.

2. See for further references, White, *Metahistory* and *Tropics of Discourse*.

3. Betty S. Flowers, *Browning and the Modern Tradition* (London: Macmillan, 1976); Carol T. Christ, *Victorian and Modern Poetics* (Chicago: University of Chicago Press, 1984).

4. Richard Howard's significant historical poetry includes *Untitled Subjects* (1969), *Findings* (1971), *Two-Part Inventions* (1974), *Fellow Feelings* (1976), *Misgivings* (1979), *Lining Up* (1984), all published by Atheneum; Pamela White Hadas, *Beside Herself: Pocahontas to Patty Hearst* (New York: Alfred A. Knopf, 1983); and Fred Chappell, *Castle Tzingal* (Baton Rouge: Louisiana State University Press, 1984).

5. Christ, *Victorian and Modern Poetics*, 52.

6. Of course both Yeats and Eliot developed their own forms of the monologue, though both worked more from the tradition of Tennyson than from that of Browning and neither chose the radically inclusive approach of Pound.

7. Whitman also provided a notion of inclusiveness and attempted to define an American subject and language.

8. Mary Ellis Gibson, "Robert Browning and Ezra Pound: Pourquoi nier son père?" *Browning Society Notes* (1980):1–10.

9. Charles Olson, "Projective Verse," in *Selected Writings of Charles Olson,* ed. Robert Creeley (New York: New Directions, 1966), 26.

10. Ibid., 83.

11. Ibid., 82–85.

12. Robert von Hallberg, *Charles Olson: The Scholar's Art* (Cambridge: Harvard University Press, 1978), 168–69.

13. William Carlos Williams to Henry Wells, 12 April 1950, *Selected Letters,* ed. John C. Thirlwall (New York: McDowell, Obolensky, 1957), 286. In speaking of "culture" in his *Autobiography,* Williams connects it to the resources of the artist and implicitly sets himself in a tradition of poets who defined their art in opposition to (sexual and other) frustration: "But a culture allows us to beat our enemy, the husband—as Homer, the Troubadours, Shelley, Browning (not Shakespeare) never tired of telling us, and Pound in youth never tired of repeating" (*Autobiography* [New York: Random House, 1951], 376).

14. Richard Eberhart, "A Vision of Life and Man that Drives the Poet On," in *The Merrill Studies in "Paterson",* ed.

John Engels (Columbus, Ohio: Charles E. Merrill, 1971), 18.

15. Robert Lowell, *History* (New York: Farrar, Straus, and Giroux, 1973), 24.

16. Williams, *Paterson*, 207.

17. Kenner, *The Poetry of Ezra Pound* (Norfolk, Conn.: New Directions; rpt. New York, 1968), 19–21.

18. These differing figurative strategies resemble closely the divisions outlined in Hayden White's theory of tropes. See *Metahistory*, 31–38.

19. Charles Olson, *The Maximus Poems* (New York: Jargon, Corinth Books, 1960), 60.

20. Olson, *Selected Writings*, 82–83.

21. von Hallberg, 47–50.

22. Olson connects archaeology, geography, and aesthetics, notably in the Mayan letters.

23. Similarly Richard Howard's monologues or Lowell's early and late poems achieve an ironic balance that speaks more directly than Pound's visions to many readers' senses of history.

24. I agree here with Richard Altick who notes the similar uses of "culture" in "Cleon" and "A Grammarian's Funeral"; see "'A Grammarian's Funeral': Browning's Praise of Folly," *SEL* 3 (1963): 449–60. For a different interpretation of "Cleon" and Browning's grammarian see Martin J. Svaglic, "Browning's Grammarian: Apparent Failure or Real?" *Victorian Poetry* 5 (1967):95–103.

25. The argument about Browning's grammarian is continued by Robert L. Kelly, "Dactyls and Cerlews: Satire in 'A Grammarian's Funeral,'" *Victorian Poetry* 5 (1967):105–12.

BIBLIOGRAPHY

Abrams, M. H. *Natural Supernaturalism: Tradition and Revolution in Romantic Literature.* New York: W. W. Norton, 1971.

———. *The Mirror and the Lamp: Romantic Theory and the Critical Tradition.* New York: W. W. Norton, 1958.

Aiken, Susan Hardy. "Bishop Blougram and Carlyle." *Victorian Poetry* 16 (1978):323–40.

Altick, Richard. "'A Grammarian's Funeral': Browning's Praise of Folly." *SEL* 3(1963):449–60.

———. "Browning's 'Transcendentalism.'" *JEGP* 58 (1959): 24–28.

Aristotle. *Poetics.* Translated by Ingram Bywater. In *The Basic Works of Aristotle.* Edited by Richard McKeon. New York: Random House, 1941.

Armstrong, Isobel. "*The Ring and the Book:* The Uses of Prolixity." In *Major Victorian Poets: Reconsidered.* Edited by Isobel Armstrong. London: Routledge and Kegan Paul, 1969.

———. ed. *Robert Browning: Writers and Their Background.* Athens: Ohio University Press, 1975.

Arnold, Matthew. *Poetry and Criticism of Matthew Arnold.* Edited by A. Dwight Culler. Boston: Houghton, Mifflin, 1969.

Austen, Kay. "Browning Climbs the Beanstalk: The Alienated Poet in *The Ring and the Book.*" *Studies in Browning and His Circle* 5 (1977):26.

Bagehot, Walter. "Wordsworth, Tennyson, and Browning; or Pure, Ornate, and Grotesque Art in English Poetry." In *Literary Studies*. Edited by Richard Holt Hutton, 4th ed., vol. 2. London: Longmans Green, 1891.

Ball, Patricia. *The Central Self: A Study in Romantic and Victorian Imagination*. London: Athalone Press, University of London, 1968.

Berlin, Isaiah. "The Concept of Scientific History." In *Philosophical Analysis of History*. Edited by William Dray. New York: Harper and Row, 1966.

Booth, Wayne. *A Rhetoric of Irony*. Chicago: University of Chicago Press, 1974.

―――. *The Rhetoric of Fiction*. Chicago: University of Chicago Press, 1961.

Brantlinger, Patrick. *The Spirit of Reform: British Literature and Politics, 1832–1867*. Cambridge: Harvard University Press, 1977.

Broughton, Leslie N. and Benjamin F. Stelter. *A Concordance to the Poems of Robert Browning*. New York: G. E. Stechert, 1924.

Browning, Robert. *Browning to His American Friends*. Edited by Gertrude Reece Hudson. New York: Barnes and Noble, 1965.

―――. *The Complete Works of Robert Browning*. Edited by Charlotte Porter and Helen A. Clarke. 14 vols. Florentine Edition. New York: Thomas Y. Cromwell, 1900.

―――. *The Complete Works*. Edited by Roma A. King, Jr. Athens: Ohio University Press, 1969.

―――. *Letters of Robert Browning Collected by T. J. Wise*. Edited by Thurman L. Hood. New Haven: Yale University Press, 1933.

―――. *Poetical Works*. 1833–64. Edited by Ian Jack. London: Oxford University Press, 1970.

―――. *The Poems*. Edited by John Pettigrew and Thomas J. Collins. New Haven: Yale University Press, 1981.

―――. *Sordello*. 1st. ed. London: Edward Moxon, 1840.

Browning, Robert and Elizabeth Barrett. *Letters of Robert Browning and Elizabeth Barrett Barrett, 1845–1846*. Edited by Elvan Kintner. 2 vols. Cambridge: Belknap Press, Harvard University Press, 1969.

Browning, Robert and Julia Wedgwood. *Robert Browning and Julia Wedgwood: A Broken Friendship as Revealed by Their Letters.* Edited by Richard Curle. New York: Frederick A. Stokes, 1937.

Browning, Robert, Sr. Letters. Fitzwilliam Museum, Cambridge, England.

――――. Manuscript Notebook. Harry Ransom Humanities Research Center, University of Texas at Austin, Austin, Texas.

Burckhardt, Jacob. *Civilization of the Renaissance in Italy.* Translated by S. G. C. Middlemore. 2 vols. New York: Harper and Row, Harper Colophon Books, 1958.

――――. *Force and Freedom: Reflections on History.* Translated and edited by James Hastings Nichols. New York: Pantheon Books, 1943.

Bush, Douglas. *Mythology and the Romantic Tradition in English Poetry.* Cambridge: Harvard University Press, 1969.

Bush, Ronald. *The Genesis of Ezra Pound's "Cantos".* Princeton: Princeton University Press, 1976.

Carlyle, Thomas. *Complete Works.* 28 vols. Centenary Edition. London: Chapman and Hall, 1899.

――――. *Letters of Thomas Carlyle to John Stuart Mill, John Sterling, and Robert Browning.* Edited by Alexander Carlyle. London: T. Fisher Unwin, 1923.

――――. *New Letters of Thomas Carlyle.* 1904 Reprint. Hildesheim, Germany: Georg Olms, 1969.

Chappell, Fred. *Castle Tzingal.* Baton Rouge: Louisiana State University Press, 1984.

Chesterson, G. K. *Robert Browning.* New York: Macmillan, 1906.

Christ, Carol T. *The Finer Optic: The Aesthetics of Particularity in Victorian Poetry.* New Haven: Yale University Press, 1975.

――――. *Victorian and Modern Poetics.* Chicago: University of Chicago Press, 1984.

Coleridge, Samuel Taylor. *Biographia Literaria*. Edited by John Shawcross. Oxford: Oxford University Press, 1973.

Collins, R. G. "Browning's Practical Prelate: The Lesson of 'Bishop Blougram's Apology.'" *Victorian Poetry* 13 (1975):1–20.

Collins, Thomas J. "Browning's Essay on Shelley: In Context." *Victorian Poetry* 2 (1964):119–24.

———. *Robert Browning's Moral-Aesthetic Theory: 1833–55*. Lincoln: University of Nebraska Press, 1967.

Columbus, Robert R. and Claudette Kemper. "*Sordello* and the Speaker: A Problem in Identity." *Victorian Poetry* 2 (1965):251–67.

Cook, A. K. *A Commentary Upon Browning's "The Ring and the Book."* London: Humphrey Milford, Oxford University Press, 1920.

Cook, Eleanor. *Browning's Lyrics: An Exploration*. Toronto: University of Toronto Press, 1974.

Crawford, A. W. "Browning's 'Cleon'." *JEGP* 26 (1927):485–90.

Creeley, Robert, ed. *Selected Writings of Charles Olson*. New York: New Directions, 1966.

Cundiff, Paul. *Browning's Ring Metaphor and Truth*. Metuchen, N.J.: Scarecrow Press, 1972.

Dale, Peter. *The Victorian Critic and the Idea of History*. Cambridge: Harvard University Press, 1977.

Darling, Michael E. "Notes on Browning's 'Gold Hair' and 'Apparent Failure.'" *Studies in Browning and His Circle* 7 (1979):71.

DeVane, William Clyde. *A Browning Handbook*. 2d. ed. New York: Appleton-Century-Crofts, 1955.

———. "Browning and the Spirit of Greece." In *Nineteenth Century Studies*. Edited by Herbert Davis, William Clyde DeVane, and R. C. Bald. Ithaca: Cornell University Press, 1940.

———. *Browning's Parleyings: The Autobiography of a Mind*. New Haven: Yale University Press, 1927.

———. "The Virgin and the Dragon." In *The Browning Critics.* Edited by Boyd Litzinger and Kenneth Leslie Knickerbocker. Lexington: University of Kentucky Press, 1965.

Dewey, John. *Art as Experience.* New York: Minton, Balch, 1934.

Dilthey, Wilhelm. *Pattern and Meaning in History: Thoughts on History and Society.* Edited and translated by H. P. Rickman. New York: Harper and Brothers, 1962.

Domett, Alfred. Marginalia in Robert Browning's *Sordello.* (London, 1840). Ashley 247. British Library, London.

Dray, William, ed. *Philosophical Analysis of History.* New York: Harper and Row, 1966.

Drew, Philip. "Browning's Essay on Shelley." *Victorian Poetry* 1 (1963):1–6.

———. *The Poetry of Robert Browning.* London: Methuen, 1970.

Eagleton, Terry. *Criticism and Ideology: A Study in Marxist Literary Theory.* London: NLB, Atlantic Highlands Humanities Press, 1976.

Eberhart, Richard. "A Vision of Life and Man that Drives the Poet On." In *The Merrill Studies in "Paterson."* Edited by John Engels. Columbus, Ohio: Charles E. Merrill, 1971.

Eliade, Mircea. *Cosmos and History: The Myth of the Eternal Return.* Translated by Willard R. Trask. New York: Harper and Row, 1959.

———. "The 'God Who Binds' and the Symbolism of Knots." In *Images and Symbols: Studies in Religious Symbolism.* Translated by Philip Mairet. London: Harvill Press, 1961.

Eliot, George. "The Poetical Works of Robert Browning." *North British Review* 49 (1868):192.

———. Review of *Men and Women*, by Robert Browning. Westminster Review n. s. 9 (January 1856):290, 295–96.

Engels, John, ed. *The Merrill Studies in "Paterson."* Columbus, Ohio: Charles E. Merrill, 1971.

Erdman, David V. "Browning's Industrial Nightmare." *Philological Quarterly* 36 (1957):417–35.

Ferguson, Wallace. *The Renaissance in Historical Thought.* New York: Houghton Mifflin, 1948.

Fleishman, Avrom. *The English Historical Novel: Walter Scott to Virginia Woolf.* Baltimore: Johns Hopkins University Press, 1971.

Flowers, Betty S. *Browning and the Modern Tradition.* London: Macmillan, 1976.

Frank, Joseph. "Spatial Form in Modern Literature." In *The Widening Gyre.* New Brunswick, N.J.: Rutgers University Press, 1963.

———. "Spatial Form: An Answer to Critics." *Critical Inquiry* 4 (1977):231–52.

Freeman, Donald C., ed. *Linguistics and Literary Style.* New York: Holt, Rinehart, and Winston, 1970.

Friedland, Louis S. "Ferrara and 'My Last Duchess.'" *Studies in Philology.* 33 (1936):656–84.

Froude, James Anthony. "The Science of History." In *Short Studies on Great Subjects.* Edited by David Ogg. Ithaca: Cornell University Press, 1963.

Gadamer, Hans Georg. *Truth and Method.* Translated by Garret Barden and John Cumming. New York: Seabury Press, 1975.

Gay, Peter. *Style in History.* New York: Basic Books, 1974.

Gibson, Mary Ellis. "Robert Browning and Ezra Pound: 'Pourquoi nier son père?'" *Browning Society Notes* (1980):1–10.

Gooch, G. P. *History and Historians of the Nineteenth Century.* London: Longmans Green, 1913.

Goody, Jack. *The Domestication of the Savage Mind.* Cambridge: Cambridge University Press, 1977.

Hadas, Pamela White. *Beside Herself: Pocahontas to Patty Hearst.* New York: Alfred A. Knopf, 1983.

Hallam, Arthur Henry. "On Some Characteristics of Modern Poetry, and on the Lyrical Poems of Alfred Tennyson." In *The Writings of Arthur Henry Hallam.* Edited by T. H. Vail Motter. New York: MLA, 1943.

Harden, Edgar F. "A New Reading of Browning's 'A Tocatta of Galuppi's.'" *Victorian Poetry* 11 (1973):330–36.

Hardison, O. B. *Aristotle's Poetics: A Translation and Commentary for Students of Literature.* Englewood Cliffs, N.J.: Prentice-Hall, 1968.

Hartman, Geoffrey. *Wordsworth's Poetry, 1787–1814.* New Haven: Yale University Press, 1971.

Hassett, Constance. *The Elusive Self in the Poetry of Robert Browning.* Athens: Ohio University Press, 1982.

Hawthorne, Mark D. "Browning's *Sordello:* Structure Through Repetition." *Victorian Poetry* 16 (1978):204–16.

Hazlitt, William. *The Collected Works of William Hazlitt.* Edited by A. R. Waller and Arnold Glover. Vol. 7. "On the Prose Style of Poets." *The Plain Speaker.* London: J. M. Dent, 1903.

Helsinger, Elizabeth K. *Ruskin and the Art of the Beholder.* Cambridge: Harvard University Press, 1982.

Holborn, Hajo. "Dilthey's Critique of Historical Reason." *Journal of the History of Ideas* 11 (1950):117.

Honan, Park. *Browning's Characters: A Study in Poetic Technique.* New Haven: Yale University Press, 1961.

Honan, Park and William Irvine. *The Ring, the Book, the Poet.* London: Bodley Head, 1975.

Howard, Richard. *Fellow Feelings.* New York: Atheneum, 1976.

———. *Findings.* New York: Atheneum, 1971.

———. *Lining Up.* New York: Atheneum, 1984.

———. *Misgivings.* New York: Atheneum, 1979.

———. *Two Part Inventions.* New York: Atheneum, 1974.

———. *Untitled Subjects.* New York: Atheneum, 1969.

James, Henry. "The Novel in *The Ring and the Book.*" In *Notes on Novelists.* New York: Biblo and Tannen, 1969.

Keating, P. J. "Robert Browning: A Reader's Guide." In *Robert Browning: Writers and Their Background.* Edited by Isobel Armstrong. Athens: Ohio University Press, 1975.

Keats, John. *The Letters of John Keats, 1814–1821*. Edited by Hyder Edward Rollins. 2 vols. Cambridge: Harvard University Press, 1958.

Kelly, Robert L. "Dactyls and Cerlews: Satire in 'A Grammarian's Funeral'." *Victorian Poetry* 5 (1967):105–12.

Kenner, Hugh. *The Poetry of Ezra Pound*. Norfolk, Conn.: New Directions, 1951. Reprint ed., New York: Kraus Reprint Co., 1968.

Kenyon, Frederic G., ed. *Robert Browning and Alfred Domett*. New York: E. P. Dutton, 1906.

Kermode, Frank. "Critical Response." *Critical Inquiry* 4 (1978):579–88.

Killham, John. "Browning's Modernity: *The Ring and the Book* and Relativism." In *Major Victorian Poets: Reconsidered*. Edited by Isobel Armstrong. London: Routledge and Kegan Paul, 1969.

King, Roma A., Jr. *The Focusing Artifice: The Poetry of Robert Browning*. Athens: Ohio University Press, 1968.

Krieger, Leonard. *Ranke: The Meaning of History*. Chicago: University of Chicago Press, 1977.

Laird, Robert G. "'He Did Not Sit Five Minutes': The Conversion of Gigadibs." *University of Toronto Quarterly* 45 (1976):295–313.

Lairesse, Gerard de. *The Art of Painting in All Its Branches*. Translated by John Frederick Fritsch. London, 1778.

Landow, George, ed. *Approaches to Victorian Autobiography*. Athens: Ohio University Press, 1979.

Langbaum, Robert. "Browning and the Question of Myth." In *The Modern Spirit: Essays on the Continuity of Nineteenth- and Twentieth-Century Literature*. New York: Oxford University Press, 1970.

———. "The Importance of Fact in *The Ring and the Book*." *Victorian Newsletter* 17 (Spring 1960):7–11.

———. *The Poetry of Experience: The Dramatic Monologue in Modern Literary Tradition*. London: Chatto and Windus, 1957.

Levin, David. *In Defense of Historical Literature: Essays on American History, Autobiography, Drama, and Fiction*. New York: Hill and Wang, 1967.

Levine, George. *The Boundaries of Fiction: Carlyle, Macaulay, Newman*. Princeton: Princeton University Press, 1968.

Levi-Strauss, Claude. *Myth and Meaning*. New York: Schocken, 1979.

―――. *The Raw and the Cooked: Introduction to a Science of Mythology*. Translated by John Weightman and Doreen Weightman. New York: Harper and Row, 1969.

Lewes, George Henry. "Robert Browning and the Poetry of the Age." *British Quarterly Review* 6 (1847):480–509.

Litzinger, Boyd. "The Structural Logic of *The Ring and the Book*." In *Nineteenth-Century Literary Perspectives: Essays in Honor of Lionel Stevenson*. Edited by Clyde de L. Ryals. Durham, N.C.: Duke University Press, 1974.

Litzinger, Boyd and Donald Smalley, eds. *Browning: The Critical Heritage*. London: Routledge and Kegan Paul, 1970.

Loucks, James and Richard Altick. *Browning's Roman Murder Story*. Chicago: University of Chicago Press, 1968.

Lowell, Robert. *History*. New York: Farrar, Straus, and Giroux, 1973.

Lukács, Gÿorgy. *The Historical Novel*. Translated by Hannah Mitchell and Stanley Mitchell. London: Merlin Press, 1962.

Makkreel, Rudolf A. *Dilthey: Philosopher of the Human Studies*. Princeton: Princeton University Press, 1975.

Mandelbaum, Maurice. *The Anatomy of Historical Knowledge*. Baltimore: Johns Hopkins University Press, 1977.

Markus, Julia. "Bishop Blougram and the Literary Men." *Victorian Studies* 21 (1978):171–95.

Maynard, John. "Broad Canvas, Narrow Perspective: The Problem of the English Historical Novel in the Nineteenth Century." In *The Worlds of Victorian Fiction*. Edited by Jerome Buckley. Harvard English Studies, no. 6. Cambridge: Harvard University Press, 1975.

―――. "Browning's 'Sicilian Pastoral.'" *Harvard Library Bulletin* 20 (1972):436–43.

―――. *Browning's Youth*. Cambridge: Harvard University Press, 1977.

McElderry, Bruce R., Jr. "The Narrative Structure of Browning's *The Ring and the Book*." *Research Studies of the State College of Washington* 11 (1943):193-233.

McGann, Jerome. *Don Juan in Context*. Chicago: University of Chicago Press, 1976.

Meinecke, Friedrich. *Historism: The Rise of a New Historical Outlook*. Translated by J. E. Anderson. London: Routledge and Kegan Paul, 1972.

Mellor, Anne K. *English Romantic Irony*. Cambridge: Harvard University Press, 1980.

Mill, John Stuart. "Two Kinds of Poetry." In *Essays on Literature and Society*. Edited by J. B. Schneewind. New York: Collier Books, 1965.

———. "What is Poetry." In *Essays on Literature and Society*. Edited by J. B. Schneewind. New York: Collier Books, 1965.

Miller, J. Hillis. "Narrative and History." *ELH* 41 (1974):455-73.

———. *The Disappearance of God: Five Nineteenth-Century Writers*. Cambridge: Harvard University Press, 1969.

Mineka, Francis E. *The Dissidence of Dissent: The Monthly Repository, 1806-38*. Chapel Hill: University of North Carolina Press, 1944.

Mitchell, W. J. T. "Diagrammatology." *Critical Inquiry* 7 (1981):622-33.

———. "Spatial Form in Literature: Toward a General Theory." *Critical Inquiry* 6 (1980):539-67.

Miyoshi, Masao. "Mill and 'Pauline': The Myth and Some Facts." *Victorian Studies* 9 (1965):155-63.

Muecke, D. C. *The Compass of Irony*. London: Methuen, 1969.

———. *Irony and the Ironic*. London: Methuen, 1970.

Mukarovský, Jan. "Standard Language and the Poetic Language." Translated by Paul L. Garvin. In *Linguistics and Literary Style*. Edited by Donald C. Freeman. New York: Holt, Rinehart, and Winston, 1970.

Munz, Peter. "History and Myth." *Philosophical Quarterly* 6 (1956):1-16.

Olson, Charles. "Projective Verse." In *Selected Writings of Charles Olson*. Edited by Robert Creeley. New York: New Directions, 1966.

———. *The Maximus Poems*. New York: Jargon, Corinth Books, 1960.

Olson, Elder. "A Conspectus of Poetry, Part II." *Critical Inquiry* 4 (1977): 373–96.

———. *Tragedy and the Theory of Drama*. Detroit: Wayne State University Press, 1966.

Ortega y Gasset, José. *Concord and Liberty*. Translated by Helene Weyl. New York: Norton, 1946.

Peckham, Morse. "Afterword: Reflections on Historical Modes in the Nineteenth Century." *Victorian Poetry, Stratford-upon-Avon Studies*, no. 15. London: Edward Arnold, 1972.

———. "Historiography and *The Ring and the Book*." *Victorian Poetry* 6 (1968):242–57.

Perrine, Laurence. "Browning's Shrewd Duke." *PMLA* 74 (1959):157–59.

Peterson, Linda H. "Biblical Typology and the Self Portrait of the Poet in Robert Browning." In *Approaches to Victorian Autobiography*. Edited by George P. Landow. Athens: Ohio University Press, 1979.

Pottle, Frederick Albert. *Shelley and Browning: A Myth and Some Facts*. Chicago: Pembroke Press, 1923. Reprint. Hamden, Conn.: Archon Books, 1965.

Pound, Ezra. "Three Cantos." *Poetry* 10 (June–August 1917):113–21, 180–88, 248–54.

Preyer, Robert. "A Reading of the Early Narratives." *ELH* 26 (1959):531–48.

———. "Two Styles in the Verse of Robert Browning." *ELH* 32 (1965):62–84.

Rader, Ralph. "The Dramatic Monologue and Related Lyric Forms." *Critical Inquiry* 3 (1976):131–51.

Rajan, Tilottama. "Romanticism and the Death of Lyric Consciousness." In *Lyric Poetry: Beyond New Criticism*. Edited by Chaviva Hosek and Patricia Parker. Ithaca: Cornell University Press, 1985.

Ranke, Leopold von. *History of the Popes, Their Church and State*. Translated by E. Fowler. Revised ed. New York: P. F. Collier, 1901.

———. *The Theory and Practice of History*. Edited by George C. Iggers and Konrad von Moltke. Translated by Wilma A. Iggers. Indianapolis: Bobbs-Merrill, 1973.

Raymond, William O. "Browning and the Higher Criticism." In *The Infinite Moment and Other Essays in Robert Browning*. 2d. ed. Toronto: University of Toronto Press, 1965.

Ricoeur, Paul. "Narrative Time." *Critical Inquiry* 7 (1980):169–90.

———. *Time and Narrative*. Translated by Kathleen McLaughlin and David Pellauer. Chicago: University of Chicago Press, 1984.

Rosenberg, Philip. *The Seventh Hero: Thomas Carlyle and the Theory of Radical Activism*. Cambridge: Harvard University Press, 1974.

Ruskin, John. *The Works of John Ruskin*. Vol. 6, *Modern Painters*. Library Edition. New York: Longmans, Green, 1904.

Ryals, Clyde de L. *Becoming Browning: The Poems and Plays of Robert Browning, 1833–1846*. Columbus: Ohio State University Press, 1983.

———. *Browning's Later Poetry, 1871–1889*. Ithaca: Cornell University Press, 1975.

———. "'Prince Hohenstiel-Schwangau': Browning's 'Ghostly Dialogue.'" In *Nineteenth-Century Perspectives: Essays in Honor of Lionel Stevenson*, edited by Clyde de L. Ryals. Durham, N.C.: Duke University Press, 1974.

Saintsbury, George. *A History of English Prosody*. Vol. 3. London: Macmillan, 1906–1910.

Sanders, Charles Richard. "The Carlyle-Browning Correspondence and Relationship: I and II." *Bulletin of the John Rylands Library* 57 (1975):213–46.

Santayana, George. "The Poetry of Barbarism, 1900." *Selected Critical Writings*. Edited by Norman Henfrey. Vol. 1. London: Cambridge University Press, 1968.

Scott, Nathan, "Mimesis and Time in Modern Literature." In *The Broken Center: Studies in the Theological Horizon of Modern Literature*. New Haven: Yale University Press, 1966.

Seigel, Jules Paul, ed. *Thomas Carlyle: The Critical Heritage*. London: Routledge and Kegan Paul, 1971.

Shaffer, Elinor S. *'Kubla Khan' and "The Fall of Jerusalem": The Mythological School in Biblical Criticism and Secular Literature, 1770–1880*. London: Cambridge University Press, 1975.

Sharrock, Roger. "Browning and History." In *Robert Browning: Writers and Their Background*. Edited by Isobel Armstrong. Athens: Ohio University Press, 1975.

Shaw, David. *The Dialectical Temper: The Rhetorical Art of Robert Browning*. Ithaca: Cornell University Press, 1968.

Shelley, Percy Bysshe. *A Defense of Poetry*. Edited by John E. Jordan. New York: Bobbs-Merrill, 1965.

———. *Poetical Works*. Edited by Thomas Hutchinson, revised by G. M. Matthews. London: Oxford University Press, 1970.

Shine, Hill. *Carlyle's Fusion of Poetry, History, and Religion by 1834*. Port Washington, N.Y.: Kennikat Press, 1967.

Short, Clarice. "Childe Roland, Pedestrian." *Victorian Poetry* 6 (1968):175–77.

Sirugo, Marilyn. "The Site of 'Love Among the Ruins.'" *Studies in Browning and His Circle* 4 (1976):41–48.

Smalley, Donald. "Browning's View of Fact in *The Ring and the Book*." *Victorian Newsletter* 16 (Fall 1959):1–9.

Smith, C. Willard. *Browning's Star-Imagery: The Study of a Detail in Poetic Design*. Princeton: Princeton University Press, 1941. Reprint. New York: Octagon Book, 1965.

Spenser, Edmund. *Poetical Works*. Edited by J. C. Smith and Edward de Selincourt. London: Oxford University Press, 1970.

Stempel, Daniel. "Browning's *Sordello* and the Art of Makers-See." *PMLA* 80 (1965):554–61.

Stern, Fritz. *The Varieties of History from Voltaire to the Present.* New York: Meridian Books, World Publishing, 1956.

Svaglic, Martin J. "Browning's Grammarian: Apparent Failure or Real?" *Victorian Poetry* 5 (1967):95–103.

Swinburne, Algernon Charles. "The Chaotic School." In *New Writings by Swinburne.* Edited by Cecil Y. Lang. Syracuse: Syracuse University Press, 1964.

Taylor, Beverly. "Browning and Victorian Medievalism." *Browning Institute Studies* 8 (1980):57–72.

Tucker, Herbert F., Jr. *Browning's Beginnings: The Art of Disclosure.* Minneapolis: University of Minnesota Press, 1980.

―――. "Browning's Lyric Intentions." *Critical Inquiry* 7 (1980):275–96.

Turner, Frank M. *The Greek Heritage in Victorian Britain.* New Haven: Yale University Press, 1981.

Vogt, Victor. "Narrative and Drama in the Lyric: Robert Frost's Strategic Withdrawal." *Critical Inquiry* 5 (1979):529–51.

von Hallberg, Robert. *Charles Olson: The Scholar's Art.* Cambridge: Harvard University Press, 1978.

Waldman, Marilyn Robinson. "'The Otherwise Unnoteworthy Year 711': A Reply to Hayden White." *Critical Inquiry* 7 (1981):784–92.

Walsh, W. H. *Introduction to the Philosophy of History.* 3d. ed. London: Hutchinson University Library, 1967.

Weintraub, Karl J. *Visions of Culture.* Chicago: University of Chicago Press, 1966.

White, Hayden. "Historical Text as Literary Artifact." In *The Writing of History: Literary Form and Historical Understanding.* Edited by Robert H. Canary and Henry Kozicki. Madison: University of Wisconsin Press, 1978.

―――. "Historicism, History, and the Imagination." In *Tropics of Discourse: Essays in Cultural Criticism.* Baltimore: Johns Hopkins University Press, 1978.

―――. *Metahistory: The Historical Imagination in Nineteenth-Century Europe.* Baltimore: Johns Hopkins University Press, 1973.

_____. "The Narrativization of Real Events." *Critical Inquiry* 7 (1981):793–98.

Whitla, William. *The Central Truth: The Incarnation in Robert Browning's Poetry.* Toronto: University of Toronto Press, 1963.

Williams, Raymond. *Culture and Society, 1780–1950.* New York: Harper and Row, 1966.

Williams, William Carlos. *Autobiography.* New York: Random House, 1951.

_____. *Paterson.* New York: New Directions, 1963.

_____. *Selected Letters.* Edited by John C. Thirlwall. New York: McDowell, Obolensky, 1957.

Woolford, John, ed. *Poets and Men of Letters.* Sales Catalogues of Libraries of Eminent Persons. Vol. 6. London: Mansell, 1972.

Wordsworth, William. *Literary Criticism of William Wordsworth.* Edited by Paul M. Zall. Lincoln: University of Nebraska Press, 1966.

_____. *Poetical Works.* Edited by Helen Darbishire and Edward de Selincourt, 2d. ed. Oxford: Clarendon Press, Oxford University Press, 1963.

INDEX

Abrams, M. H., 75
aestheticism, 26–27, 51–52
Aiken, Susan Hardy, 207–8
Altick, Richard, 7, 92, 118, 135–36
"Andrea del Sarto," 1, 3, 9, 22, 27, 33, 46, 51, 141, 149, 178, 196, 197, 205–6, 211, 278; closure in, 139, 140; perspectives in, 193–94
Armstrong, Isobel, 107, 135
Arnold, Matthew, 3, 43, 189
Austen, Kay, 79

Bagehot, Walter, 216
Ball, Patricia, 104
Balzac, Honoré de, 44, 289n.22
Barrett, Elizabeth, 10, 19, 61, 62, 105, 129, 229, 243
"Bishop Blougram's Apology," 5, 27, 138, 139, 140–41, 147, 148, 165, 202, 253, 257, 259–61, 310n.38, 310.42; irony in, 204–13
"The Bishop Orders His Tomb," 9, 27, 45, 175, 177, 180, 204–13, 249–50, 254, 257; perspectives in, 181–84
Bloom, Harold, 54
A Blot in the 'Scutcheon, 17, 20
Booth, Wayne, 199–200, 202
Brantlinger, Patrick, 30
Browning, Robert: aesthetic and style, 220–25, 233, 239–43; appeals to verification, 44–46, 176, 289n.24; Christianity in poetry of, 31–34; critics' views of, 16–17; on the false sublime, 227–44; historical understanding, 22–23; influence on modern poetry, 263–78; ironic mode, 163–68; myth, view of, 9–11; narrative experiments, 121–38; notion of poetry, 11–12; plays of, 17–22; poetic language of, 215–18; poetry of history, 1–11; poetry of obstacles, 13, 218–25; on poet's role, 2, 55–56, 57, 80–85; style of, 215–18, 244, 266; view of history, 1, 2, 26, 30, 217–18, 265, 286n.27
Browning, Robert, Sr., 56, 57, 290n.4, 291nn.9, 10; historical researches, 57–58; view of tenth-century Italian history, 58–59
Burckhardt, Jacob, 14, 26, 27, 28, 112, 116, 120–21, 162, 287n.2; *Civilization of the Renaissance in Italy*, 28, 116, 117; contextualist history of, 116–19; *Force and Freedom*, 118, 162–63; interpretive history of, 116–17

335

Burke, Edmund, 224, 225, 229
Burke, Kenneth, 163
Bush, Ronald, 194–95
Byron, Lord, 112; Browning's debts to, 18; *Childe Harold*, 152; *Don Juan*, 27–28

"Caliban Upon Setebos," 140
Calvinism, 32, 33–34; dichotomy of, 32, 34
Carlyle, Thomas, 5, 6, 12, 14, 31, 56, 57, 61–63, 64, 67–68, 71, 72, 74, 89, 110, 111, 116, 151, 205, 219, 221, 222, 268; Browning's debts to, 18, 29–30; cultural history, 29; cyclical history, 29, 297n.52; *Frederick*, 61; *The French Revolution*, 57, 68; on the historical seer, 65–66; historicism of, 29–30; on the "inward condition of life," 29; lectures "On Heroes," 61; *Life of Cromwell*, 61; notion of poetry, 12; *On Heroes and Hero-Worship*, 57, 68; "On History," 29, 65, 67, 110, 114; *Past and Present*, 29, 57, 61, 62, 68, 115; *Sartor Resartus*, 27, 62, 68; sequential narrative, 114–15; on subjectivity of historical individuals, 64–65
"Childe Roland to the Dark Tower Came," 2, 9, 230–33
Christ, Carol, 267
Christmas-Eve and Easter-Day, 10, 34–35
circularity, 8, 123–25, 127–32. See also myth and history
"Cleon," 3, 25, 26–27, 47, 54, 81, 199, 257–59, 278; aestheticism in, 51–52; Cleon, 51–52, 147, 192, 196, 197, 208, 211, 213; irony in, 201–4; mosaic metaphor in, 52–53; perspectives in, 189–91; view of history in, 52–53; view of perfect historian, 5–6
closure of monologues, 139–41
Coleridge, Samuel Taylor, 74, 179; notion of poetry, 312n.20

colligation among particulars, 25, 26, 28, 112, 116, 270
Collingwood, R. G., 40
Collins, Thomas, 91–92
Colombe's Birthday, 17
Columbus, Robert, 101
consequential narrative, 13, 28
contextualist historical poetry, 30; aesthetic of inclusiveness, 218, 266; Christianity in, 31–34; connections, tracing of, 24; emphasis on particulars, 12; emphasis on pattern, 13, 144–45, 150, 265; heroism in, 30–31; historical irony in, 257, 266, 276–77; historical milieu in, 174–79; historical moments in, 117–18, 119–21; inner tensions of, 30–31; patterned simultaneity, 13, 111, 123–25, 127–32, 137–38; play of perspectives in, 4, 52, 160–61, 162, 168–74, 179–99; spatial form in, 150–58; technical devices of, 101, 113, 123, 149–59, 265; vehicles for representing history, 274
Cook, A. K., 87
Cook, Eleanor, 47
critical history, 6, 7, 8, 56, 59–60, 63

"Deaf and Dumb," 221–22
"A Death in the Desert," 10, 34, 36–37, 80, 84–85, 86, 89, 90–91, 92, 120, 141, 142, 150, 172, 192, 196, 230, 298nn.61, 67; optical metaphor in, 90–91; poet's role in, 84–85
DeVane, William Clyde, 52, 243
Dilthey, Wilhelm, 40, 41, 120–21, 158; web metaphor in, 40, 41–42
discourse, forms of, 11–12. See also fiction and history
Domett, Alfred, 70
Donne, John, 233, 264
Dramatic Lyrics, 17, 20
Dramatic Romances and Lyrics, 17
Dramatis Personae, 1, 45, 139; "Epilogue" to, 10–11, 43
Drew, Philip, 94, 171, 234

Eagleton, Terry, 40–41
Eliade, Mircea, 8
Eliot, George, 40–41, 225–26, 253
Eliot, T. S., 267, 273, 316n.6
"Epilogue": to *Asolando,* 264; to *Dramatis Personae,* 10–11, 43; to *Pacchiarotto,* 230
"An Epistle Concerning the Strange Medical Experience of Karshish," 3, 148, 165, 199, 200–1, 202, 257, 258; ironic speech in, 253–56; visionary experience in, 34; web in, 39–40
Erdman, David, 232
"Essay on Shelley," 56, 69, 72–79, 80, 94, 109
Evangelical Christianity, 18, 27, 32, 34–35
"Evelyn Hope," 51

fiction and history, 11, 285n.23, 293n.21
Fifine at the Fair, 121
Flowers, Betty, 267
Fox, W. J., 18, 74
"Fra Lippo Lippi," 1, 22, 149, 165, 175–76, 177, 179, 228, 253, 254, 256, 308n.21; closure in, 139–40; historical milieu in, 180–81; self-judgment in, 194–96
Frank, Joseph, 151, 155–57, 158
Friedland, Louis S., 188
Froude, James Anthony, 7–8

German historiography, 61, 63
"Gold Hair: A Story of Pornic," 45–46
"A Grammarian's Funeral," 145–46, 277–78

Hallam, Arthur Henry, 74
Hardy, Thomas, 188, 264
Hartman, Geoffrey, 153
Hazlitt, William, 219, 220–21, 223, 224–25, 226–27, 229, 230, 312n.20
heroism, analysis of, 18–20

"Hervé Riel," 46, 112
Higher Criticism, 9–10, 11, 46; progressive revelation, 11, 27
historical novels, 44, 299n.69
historical progress, 8–9, 32–33
historicism, 5–6, 8, 13, 29–30, 282n.4, 283n.12
historiography: German, 61, 63; romantic, 6, 22
history: causation of, 6, 14, 24, 32–34, 173; chaos of, 11–14; circumstances of, 24, 28, 31, 37, 46; complexity of, 7, 112–13; context of, 13, 41, 105, 114–21; determinism, 30–31; individuals and subjectivity, 1, 3, 5, 14, 24, 64–65; irony of, 6, 13, 17, 20, 26, 161; knowledge of, 5, 14, 64, 282n.5; milieu of, 14, 17–18, 30, 45, 174–79; moment of, 6, 21, 23, 34, 114–21; monologues of, 4, 15, 22, 24; narrative of, 17 (*see also* sequential history); order of, 14, 32–33; perspective, 13, 17, 160–214; and politics, 20–21; situations in, 7, 24; as spectacle, 25, 26–27; time of, 8, 10, 25, 33, 43, 47; understanding of, 15, 22–23, 54
Honan, Park, 202, 245
Horne, R. H., 62, 205
"How They Brought the Good News from Ghent to Aix," 46, 264
Huizinga, Johan, 28

"Incident of the French Camp," 46
inclusiveness, aesthetic of, 218, 266, 316nn.6, 7
The Inn Album, 121
interpretation of fact: poet's role in, 55–56; narrative strategies for, 112, 113. *See also* circularity
ironic contrasts, 103–4
ironic drama, history as, 162–68
ironic speech, 199–214, 244–64
irony: in contextualism, 26–27; general, 167–68, 199–200;

irony *(continued)*
  historical, 6, 13, 17, 20, 26, 161; stable, 199; romantic, 165–67

Keats, John, 222, 313n.25
Kemper, Charlotte, 101
Kenner, Hugh, 273
Kermode, Frank, 157, 158
Killham, John, 106
King Victor and King Charles, 18, 20, 21
Krieger, Leonard, 68, 69

Langbaum, Robert, 9, 161, 168–69, 170, 171–72, 174, 182, 184, 192, 267
Levine, George, 68
Lewes, George Henry, 229
Litzinger, Boyd, 136
Loucks, James, 7, 92, 118, 133, 135–36
"Love Among the Ruins," 16, 25, 47–54; concern with time, 47; sources of, 47–50
"A Lover's Quarrel," 51
Lowell, Robert, 267, 269, 271–72, 273
Lukács, Gÿorgy, 44, 114
Luria, 17, 21, 31, 164; analysis of heroism in, 18–19
lyric poetry, 15, 25, 121, 161, 169, 243, 246, 251, 273

McElderry, Bruce, 135
McGann, Jerome, 27–28
Mahony, Rev. Francis, 205
Mandelbaum, Maurice, 116
Mason, Michael, 118, 123
"Master Hugues of Saxe-Gotha," 246; web in, 38–39
Maynard, John, 16, 32, 47, 94, 281n.2
Meinecke, Friedrich, 55, 69, 171–74
Mellor, Anne, 166–67
Men and Women, 1, 47, 51, 52, 225, 227, 257
Meredith, George, 152
metaphors, 31, 117, 287n.13, 297n.53, 302n.6, 305n.47; architectonic, 135–36; "convex glass," 90; mosaic, 53–54; optical, 89–91, 118; pedestrian, 226–29; for poet, 56, 80–92; prism, 222; ring, 71–72; stream, 41, 42, 43, 112; theatrical, 99, 147, 154–55, 165; thread of life, 53; walking, 225–29, 266; web, 24–35, 38–43, 112, 288n.15
Mill, John Stuart, 67, 74
Miller, J. Hillis, 161
Milton, John, 74
Mitchell, W. J. T., 151, 153
monologues: beginning and closure, 131–41, 304nn.35, 36; crisis and character, 308n.21; ironic speech, 199–214, 244–64; language of time, 148–49; perspectives, 168–74, 179–99; political choice in, 20; speaker's relation to time, 149; speech as characterization, 256–57; temporal dialectic, 146–48
"Mr. Sludge, the Medium," 140
Muecke, D. C., 163, 167
"My Last Duchess," 2, 16, 24, 27, 44, 169–70, 171, 180, 181, 218, 246, 308n.24; aristocratic tyranny in, 20; perspectives in, 184–89
myth and history, 8–11, 113–14, 156–58, 284n.18

Napoleon III, 20. *See also* "Prince Hohenstiel-Schwangau"

Old Yellow Book, 59, 72, 86
Olson, Charles, 267, 268, 269–70, 272, 273, 274–75, 275–76, 277
optical metaphors, 89–91, 118
Ortega y Gassett, José, 5

Paracelsus, 31, 44–45, 80, 81, 95
Parleyings with Certain People of Importance in Their Day, 15, 216, 234, 241

"Parleying with Christopher Smart," 217
"Parleying with Francis Furini," 228–29
"Parleying with Gerard de Lairesse," 216, 225, 230, 234–43, 244, 245, 248, 261
Pater, Walter, 3, 14, 40, 119; aestheticism in, 26; "dramatic contrasts," 26; *Renaissance*, 28
pattern, emphasis on, 13, 144–45, 150, 265. *See also* simultaneity
"Pauline," 16, 56, 74, 86, 92, 93, 94–95, 239; poet as prophet in, 80–81
Peckham, Morse, 6, 7, 282n.4
perspectives, play of, 4, 52, 160–62, 168–74, 179–99
Perrine, Laurence, 185
"Pictor Ignotus," 27, 177–78
Pippa Passes, 21, 122, 164
plays, analysis of heroism in, 18–20
Poe, Edgar Allan, 50–51, 290n.29
poet: classification of, 73–74; as historian, 2, 12, 17, 102; as interpreter of history, 55–56, 93; as prophet/seer, 56
poet-personae, 93–109, 298n.58
Pope Innocent III. See *The Ring and the Book*, the Pope
"Porphyria's Lover," 95
Pound, Ezra, 5, 12, 123, 156, 267, 268, 269, 270, 273, 276, 277; *The Cantos*, 14, 154, 155, 261, 270, 272, 273, 274
Preyer, Robert, 244
"Prince Hohenstiel-Schwangau," 64, 120, 138, 141, 142–43, 144, 176, 177, 245
prose and the prosaic, 222–25
"Protus," 52

Rader, Ralph, 169–71, 185, 187
"Rabbi Ben Ezra," 39, 41, 264
Ranke, Leopold von, 6, 65, 67, 71, 75, 89, 119, 120, 173; emphasis on particulars, 68, 293n.29; *English History*, 72; fact and values, 68–69; *The History of the Popes*, 60, 64; individual subjectivity, 64, 68, 69
Red Cotton Night Cap Country, 15
relativism, 25, 66–67, 174
Renaissance, recovery of, 3, 4, 26. *See also* Burckhardt, Jacob; Pater, Walter
Renan, Ernest, 10
republicanism, 20–22
The Return of the Druses, 18–20, 21, 36; analysis of heroism in, 18, 19–20; messianic role of Djabal, 18–20; nature of incarnation in, 36
"Reverie," 230
revelation, 36, 196; problem of, 34–35; progressive, 11, 37
revolution and revolt, 21–22
Ricoeur, Paul, 113, 146–47, 157–58
The Ring and the Book, 3–4, 6, 7, 8, 15, 16, 22, 24, 56, 64, 70, 79, 80, 92, 93, 94, 96–100, 105–9, 111, 112, 113, 116, 117, 118, 132–38, 142, 150, 152, 159, 161, 165, 166, 229, 230, 235, 251, 261, 269, 270, 273, 278; action as puppetry, 97–98; Archangeli, 101–2, 245, 246–47, 249, 250; architectonic metaphors in, 135–36; asides in, 103; Bottinius, 27, 103–4, 247–49, 250, 259, 260; Caponsacchi, 34, 39, 88, 89, 108, 134, 264; comment by juxtaposition in, 102–4; completed pattern of, 137–38; dialogue, use of, 144; Euripides, 3, 99, 144; exploration of motives in, 132–33, 144; Guido, 39, 42–43, 55, 88, 97, 98, 122, 133, 135, 144, 185; Half-Rome, 66–67; historical knowledge, 71; historical evidence, 66; interpretation of fact in, 72; Old Yellow Book, 59, 72, 86, 98; optical metaphors in, 88–91; The Other Half-Rome, 134;

340   INDEX

The Ring and the Book (*continued*)
parallels between poet-speaker and characters, 105–8; poet as historian, 102; poet as prophet, 85–86; poet as relumer, 87–89; poet-persona as tragic dramatist, 98–99; poet's relation to devine truth, 84, 85, 88–89; Pompilia, 34, 39, 42, 109, 133, 135, 252–53, 256; the Pope, 3, 10, 33, 34, 37, 58, 71, 88–89, 99, 103, 106–8, 120, 122, 135, 172, 189, 192–93, 196, 197, 251–52, 256, 299n.67; relativism, 67; ring metaphor in, 71–72; sight as point of view, 89–91; Tertium Quid, 97–98, 134, 245; web in, 39
Robinson, Henry Crabb, 74
Ruskin, John, 1, 3, 4, 45, 112, 175, 227, 228
Ryals, Clyde, 16, 142, 165, 166, 234

Saintsbury, George, 216, 224
Sanders, Charles Richard, 61
"Saul," 34, 264; prophetic vision in, 35–36
Scott, Nathan, 156
Scott, Walter, 14, 44; *The Heart of Midlothian*, 133, 137
sequential history, 114–15, 116–17
Shaffer, Elinor S., 11, 36, 37
Shakespeare, William, 21, 74, 77, 231
Shaw, David, 47, 201
Shelley, Percy Bysshe, 17, 27, 179, 219, 220, 221, 222, 228, 234, 269; "Adonais," 288n.13; *Alastor*, 94; Browning's debts to, 18; *The Cenci*, 74, 77, 297n.53
Shine, Hill, 67
Short, Clarice, 230
simultaneity, 13, 111, 123–25, 127–32, 137–38
"Soliloquy of the Spanish Cloister," 304n.35
Sordello, 3, 15, 16, 17, 19, 20, 28, 31, 45, 56, 60, 71, 72, 80, 85, 86, 92, 93, 94, 95, 96–97, 103, 108–9, 112, 113, 118, 120, 122, 123–32, 137, 141, 142, 143, 149, 150, 152, 155, 156, 159, 161, 165, 166, 176, 177, 215, 217, 218, 229, 233, 239, 241–42, 263, 269, 270, 273, 278, 303n.27, 305n.48, 306n.54; aesthetic impulse in, 27; aristocratic and republican values in, 21; asides in, 101, 102; biblical allusions, 81–82, 83, 84; circular patterning of, 123–25, 127–32; Dante's poetry in, 81–82; development by accretion, 127; historical background, 300n.77; images of poem in, 153–54; narrator as commentator, 100–1; parallels between poet-speaker and characters, 104–5; perception and language in, 111; poet as prophet in, 81–84; poet-persona in, 130–31; poet's task in, 79; repetition in, 125–27, 133; revisions of, 129–31; running heads in, 129–30; subjectivity in, 65–66, 70; technical devices in, 303n.28
A Soul's Tragedy, 17; analysis of heroism in, 20; aristocratic and republican values in, 20–21
spatial form, 150–58
Spenser, Edmund, 48, 49, 74, 152
"The Statue and the Bust," 145, 146
Stempel, Daniel, 76, 100
Stirling, J. H., 255
Story, William Wetmore, 60
Strafford, 16, 17, 122, 164; analysis of heroism in, 18, 19; aristocratic and republican values in, 20, 21
Strauss, David, 10
subjective/objective dichotomy, 63–64, 69, 73–79, 295n.40, 299n.71

Swinburne, Algernon Charles, 214, 215, 232, 234

Tennyson, Alfred Lord, 61; "Tithonus," 169, 170
Thackeray, William Makepeace, 87
theatrical metaphors, 99, 147, 154–55, 165
"A Tocatta of Galuppi's" 197–99
Troeltsch, Ernst, 174
Tucker, Herbert, 17, 52, 53, 187, 188, 190

verification, appeals to, 44–46, 176, 289n.24
Vogt, Victor, 185
von Hallberg, Robert, 270

walking metaphor, 225–29, 266
walking poetry, 313n.25
web metaphor, 40–42; as mode of Browning's historical poetry, 24–25; of history, 24, 38–43, 288n.15
Wedgwood, Julia, 45, 55, 229
Weintraub, Karl, 117, 119
White, Hayden, 25–26, 115, 162, 265
Williams, Raymond, 28
Williams, William, Carlos, 12, 267, 268, 270, 271, 272, 273, 274–75, 277; *Paterson*, 155, 261, 271, 273, 274, 276
Wordsworth, William, 60–61, 74, 179, 221, 222, 224, 226, 264; on critical history, 61; his ideal poet, 219; *Memorials of a Tour in Italy*, 60, 262–63; "Musings Near Aquapendente," 61; preface to *Lyrical Ballads*, 219; *The Prelude*, 152–54, 155, 268, 306n.54; "Tintern Abbey," 199

Yeats, William Butler, 5, 273, 316n.6